A Month-by-Month Guide

NORTHERN CALIFORNIA Gardening

KATHERINE GRACE ENDICOTT

CHRONICLE BOOKS
SAN FRANCISCO

Printed in the United States.

Book and cover design: Julie Noyes Long
Collage illustrations: Melissa Sweet

Library of Congress Cataloging-in-Publication Data

Endicott, Katherine Grace, 1954-
   Northern California gardening : a month-by-month guide / by
Katherine Grace Endicott.
      p.   cm.
   Includes bibliographical references and index.
   ISBN 0-8118-0926-9
   1. Gardening—California, Northern.   I. Title.
SB453.2.C3E54 1996   96-3176
635.9'09794—dc20   CIP

Distributed in Canada by Raincoast Books,
8680 Cambie Street
Vancouver, B.C., V6P 6M9

10 9 8 7 6 5 4 3 2 1

Chronicle Books
275 Fifth Street
San Francisco, CA 94103

Chronicle Books® is registered in the US Patent and Trademark Office.

If you have two loaves of bread, sell one and buy a hyacinth.
—Anonymous Persian Saying

This book is dedicated to those who garden with me:
my daughters, Carolyn and Laurel.

ACKNOWLEDGMENTS

Thanks to all the splendid people and organizations who have helped educate me as well as countless others in the ways of Northern California gardening. Thanks to John R. (Dick) Dunmire who edited three editions of Sunset Western Garden Book *and to Kathleen N. Brenzel who edited the current edition. Thanks to W. George Waters, the editor of* Pacific Horticulture. *Thanks to the staff and volunteers of our botanical institutions who keep me up-to-date: Strybing Arboretum and Botanical Gardens, UC Botanical Garden, UC Davis Arboretum, UC Santa Cruz Arboretum, Filoli, Elizabeth F. Gamble Garden Center, Tilden Native Plant Botanic Garden, Mendocino Coast Botanical Gardens, and Green Gulch Farm. Thanks to the volunteers and the staff who bring us the San Francisco Landscape Garden Show each year. Thanks to the many people I see again and again volunteering their time to educate us in wise gardening practices, among them: Rosalind Creasy, Pam Peirce, Ted Kipping, Joan Hockaday, and Glenn Keator. Thanks to Louise Lacey for publishing the* Growing Native *newsletter, and to the volunteers and staffs of the Native California Plant Societies. Thanks to the organizers at Seeds of Change. Thanks to the propagators at the Saratoga Horticultural Research Foundation who have brought so many fine cultivars to our gardens in Northern California. Thanks to the many people who participate in gardening organizations and plant societies—I would love to list you all but my editors would again remind me that the price of paper has risen recently. And last but not least, thanks to my editors at Chronicle Books who have struggled with me to create a useful guide to gardening in Northern California: Genevieve Morgan, Charlotte Stone, and Christine Carswell. Thanks also to Julie Noyes Long for doing such a superb design job and the instructional illustrations; and to Melissa Sweet for her wonderful collaged illustrations on the section openers and the cover. And thanks to my agent Joy Harris.*

P.S. Thanks to the nurserypeople. Readers would be surprised if they knew how many nurserypeople propagate new varieties in their home gardens and then persuade wholesale nurseries to grow them and get them to market—not for profit but for the love of plants.

Thanks again to everyone. We are all in this together.

CONTENTS

PART ONE: GETTING STARTED

PART TWO: MONTH-BY-MONTH GUIDE

PART THREE: REFERENCE GUIDE

PART ONE: GETTING STARTED

INTRODUCTION

HOW TO USE THIS BOOK

GARDEN BASICS

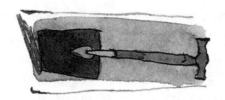

INTRODUCTION TO GARDENING

Gardening is an act of joy; so it would be a shame if anyone turned away from gardening because there was too much to learn. In truth almost all of us learn to garden in the same simple way. Confronted with a piece of earth to care for, one fine day we pick up garden hoses to squirt water on whatever has managed to grow there. Soon, without quite willing it, we find ourselves in a nursery picking out pretty plants with little regard for their eventual size or the suitability of their growing conditions. We put the plants in the ground, and the plants either live or die. It is an excellent beginning.

Gardening is not about improving the house or getting a bit of exercise. That is only what we tell one another when embarrassed by the deeper truth. Gardening is the principal way in which we come to understand that we belong on this earth and are part of it. It is the way in which we care for what is home to our species and to all earthly life forms. It is a great joy, which is why gardeners will spend a perfectly splendid day working outdoors like slave laborers. Few pursuits are so satisfying.

Although we are beginning with a few gardening basics, you do not need to know even those to be a good gardener. In fact, many rules that gardeners firmly believed in have changed so that gardeners are now advised to do the exact opposite. My father loved to grow fruit trees. He taught me to stomp firmly on the ground around a newly planted fruit tree. "Makes the roots feel at home; gets them going," he said. Now gardeners are taught that to stomp on the ground at any time is destructive. Newly planted trees should have their soil gently watered and definitely undisturbed. For your amusement and possible edification, a list of gardening rules that have dramatically changed appears on page 10. There is much useful information available and worth sharing (or what would be the point of this book?) but the best is to find out what works for you in your garden.

Experienced gardeners learn there are many ways to accomplish the same task. Sometimes there seems to be as many gardening systems as there are gardeners. Particularly when you get down to growing specialized plants such as orchids, you will find gardeners deeply committed to one or another of opposing views. Some orchid growers use a specially made soil for growing orchids; others believe it is a serious mistake to use any kind of soil at all—they use only the bark of trees as a growing medium.

To illustrate how the knowledge of gardening is constantly changing, let me tell you a story about one of the most widely planted trees in Northern California—the infamous blue gum (*Eucalyptus globulus*). This story will not only give you an idea of how very wrong horticultural opinions can be, but also how momentous are some of the challenges that face a gardener.

These towering eucalyptus trees have been both the bane and joy of California gardeners for most of this century. Imported originally from Australia and planted by the thousands from 1904 through 1912 in an ill-advised lumber scheme, towering eucalyptus have naturalized in much of California. One can drive for many miles in Northern California without ever losing sight of them. All of this was made possible on bad advice from experts.

Gardeners have learned to curse the messy litter of dried leaves, hard-shelled fruit, and strips of bark that the blue gum sheds. But from a respectful distance the eucalyptus is magical. With the fog dripping off the leaves, a grove of eucalyptus is perfumed with a rich menthol scent. The wind rustles the slender stiff leaves in a symphony of sounds from the softest pianissimo in a breeze to a clattering forte during gales. Best of all, at dusk, the pale leaves of eucalyptus shimmer a reflective silver gray. So in the botanical paradise of our mild climate, we have nurtured our eucalyptus.

The eucalyptus grew and grew for almost seventy years until one day it snowed in coastal Northern California. Of course, it was not supposed to snow, but that day it snowed so hard that snow lay several inches deep along the tree branches. Then there came a series of reverberating cracking noises like shotgun blasts as brittle limbs of the old eucalyptus broke under the unaccustomed weight. We coastal gardeners shivered in the snowy cold, but the worst news came the next morning. The towering eucalyptus died. Or so the experts told us. Mile after mile of 150-foot-tall eucalyptus stood frozen, erect and imperturbable. Not a leaf stirred in the cold air. Rigor mortis, the stiffness of death, overtook each tree as surely as it does a corpse.

As you might imagine, politicians and conservationists argued about what to do with all those dead trees. Eventually they decided to cut them down. For months the buzz of chain saws irritated the air. Large stumps proliferated across the hillsides like tombstones. But the experts were wrong. Soon the tree stumps sprouted new growth. With seventy years of root systems infiltrating the ground, the new trees grew with frightening rapidity. The new trees were not the same as the old ones, of course. But every gardener understands that the garden changes from month to month, let alone from year to year.

But would you believe the worst challenge to those eucalyptus was yet to come? In 1991 during the worst wildfire we have ever known in Northern California, flames, fanned by forty-mile-an-hour gusts of wind, devoured neighborhoods as if they were kindling. Fiery torches of airborne branches blew across roads, even across freeways, to ignite home after home. At one point, the fire is said to have taken a house every second. There are no words to express the terror. I remember looking up into the black sky and feeling my stomach turn over as I tried to comprehend what I saw. Cars, gas lines, and houses suddenly exploded. Some of us were chased by thirty-foot-high walls of flame. Some of us did not escape. In the end, twenty-five people died and 3,354 residences burned.

Gardens were reduced to lumps of charcoal. In those nearby gardens that were not burned black, the heat of the fire ripened figs and turned grapes into raisins. Ashes drifted up to fifteen miles away. Even the firemen spoke of Nature having her way. Gardeners were humbled indeed.

We needed something to blame, something apart from ourselves. Six months after the firestorm, an interdisciplinary graduate class at the University of California looked at the physical and chemical aspects that sparked the blaze to pinpoint why and where it spread as it did. Among other findings, the students determined that the fire flank that rapidly consumed the first neighborhood was fueled by a two-acre grove of 120-foot-tall eucalyptus trees. The trees literally exploded into flames, sending millions of burning embers, which we have taken to calling firegrams, into the subdivision below. Within the first hour after the fire erupted, it had covered forty percent of the acreage that would ultimately be destroyed. The students concluded that the eucalyptus trees accounted for more than seventy percent of the energy released by burning vegetation during the firestorm.

In less than a century the mighty blue gum eucalyptus has gone from being officially favored to being regarded as the "dreaded fire carrier." Not only do we not know when it is really dead, but also we do not know quite how to kill it. As for the eucalyptus that were growing in the firestorm area, those that weren't burnt to the ground are, naturally, springing back to life.

The story gets back to the reason that gardening is so satisfying. No matter how many gardening books like this one are written, no matter how many clever discoveries experts make about horticulture, we simply cannot outfox Nature. She will have her way. We can cultivate the earth and make a home for ourselves and for other living creatures. But in the end we are both humbled and blessed by Nature. That is why I have spent an inordinate amount of time trying to put this gardening book in perspective. Gardening is not about following rules to get plants to grow. It is likely that something will volunteer to grow on your plot of earth if you do nothing at all. Gardening is about cultivating the earth because this is our home. This is where we belong. Gardening does more for the gardener than it does for the plants. If I sound daffy with enthusiasm, so be it. This book is intended to provide the sort of simple, practical advice you would get from an experienced and enthusiastic gardener who happened to live next door.

Get thee to a garden. Enjoy.

Katherine Grace Endicott

Gardening is our principal means of being connected to the earth. It is a great joy, so beware of becoming too caught up in the rules because they are constantly changing.

OLD RULES TO IGNORE

Old Advice: Put a heaping tablespoon of bonemeal in the bottom of the planting hole when setting out bulbs.

New Advice: Forget the bonemeal. As a result of technological refinements, most present-day bonemeal no longer contains enough protein to yield more than one-half percent of nitrogen. Research indicates that bulbs planted without bonemeal do just as well as bulbs planted with it.

Old Advice: Buy the largest, sturdiest plant you can buy; a five-gallon size is better than a one-gallon size.

New Advice: Buy the younger plant. In three to five years, the one-gallon-sized plant will be as large as the five-gallon-sized plant, and in seven to ten years, the one-gallon-sized plant will be better adapted and often larger than the five-gallon-sized. The younger plant develops a deeper, more widespread root system.

Old Advice: Dig a five-dollar hole for a one-dollar plant, and fill it with lots of soft soil amendments and a handful of fertilizer.

New Advice: Avoid creating too plush an environment for the new plant or the roots will simply curl around in the new hole and avoid sending roots out into the native soil.

Old Advice: When setting out transplants, encourage root development by adding vitamins, and spray the leaves with antitranspirants to minimize water loss.

New Advice: The only proven aid to new plants is weeding. Removing competing weeds encourages the plant to grow.

Old Advice: Cut back the branches of shrubs and trees when planting them so that the new root system has less to support.

New Advice: Do not prune. The leaves make energy (by photosynthesis) to grow new roots.

Old Advice: Make the roots of the new plant feel at home by tamping down the soil around the plant.

New Advice: Avoid compacting the soil around new plants (and old plants, for that matter).

Old Advice: When pruning trees, never leave a stub that you could hang your hat on.

New Advice: When pruning trees, leave the thickened branch collar (where the branch attached to the trunk). This juncture contains the highest concentration of phenols, the tree's own decay-resisting chemical.

Old Advice: Firmly stake a newly planted tree to prevent wind damage.

New Advice: The trunk will be strengthened by being blown in the wind, so support the root ball only, with low stakes and a tie, to prevent the tree from being pulled out of the ground by the wind.

HOW TO USE THIS BOOK

THE ADVICE BEGINS with the next section on Garden Basics, which covers gardening theory and techniques. I have tried to keep Part One, the Garden Basics section, to the bare essentials because I know busy readers would rather be out in the garden.

As much information as possible is put into Part Two, the month-by-month section, so that it can be absorbed naturally as the gardening year progresses. At the beginning of each month is a regional guide listing the key gardening tasks for that month. Several plants are featured each month so that readers can become familiar with the most popular plants in Northern California at the season of the year when they are most likely to be interested in them. The month-by-month guide is alphabetized; it is a snap to come up with pertinent information.

Naturally many areas of gardening overlap from month to month, and for that reason, significant information is occasionally repeated to save the reader the onerous task of constantly referring to other pages. This repetition has caused my poor editors immense aggravation, but I fought to keep the repetitions in the book because I want readers to have the information they need in the month they need it even if the same information was mentioned in another month, too. I know busy readers are going to skip a month or two, and the book is designed to keep the reader on track no matter what month the reader skips.

Alas, some cross-referencing is unavoidable, but the page number is always given to make that task easy, too. Color has been added to highlight sections that serve as a guide to that topic so that the reader knows at a glance that they have reached the most complete explanation of that topic and do not need to refer to other pages.

Part Three is the Reference Guide, which includes a glossary (somewhat opinionated, I must confess); a mail-order guide (with emphasis on local nurseries and seed houses); and a Gardening Resource section, which lists publications and organizations of interest to Northern California gardeners.

Of all the factors that influence whether a plant will grow or die in a garden, the first and most important is just how hardy the plant is. Put another way, the question becomes how cold does it get in your garden? Even this most basic question becomes complicated by the whimsical characteristics of Nature. Some winters are colder than others. Older plants are tougher and better able to survive than younger plants are.

As you garden, you will begin to see why we spent so much time in the introduction on the importance of not being bogged down by garden rules. What works one year may not work the next. What works with an older plant will not work with a young plant. Gardening rules are really sweeping generalities.

The best guide on climates in Northern California and on how hardy specific plants are is the *Sunset Western Garden Book*. However, it is relatively easy to find out what plants grow well in your area by looking at other gardens in your neighborhood. If a plant looks as if it has been growing for a long time, it is obviously well suited to that particular neighborhood.

At the beginning of every month in this book is a basic checklist of monthly garden tasks. These tasks are divided into the three broad climate zones in Northern California: the coastal, the Central Valley, and the high mountain. The climate pattern in your garden will probably be close to that in one of these areas even if the description is not entirely appropriate.

The coastal area is broadly defined as that regularly reached by fog, whether or not the garden actually overlooks the ocean. Frost strikes some parts of the coastal area with a vengeance, but typically it is not a danger after the beginning of March.

The Central Valley area is broadly defined by its longer frost period and higher summer heat. Technically it stretches from Redding to Modesto in Northern California but gardeners in both Santa Rosa and Gilroy have more in common with gardeners in the Central Valley than they do with coastal or high mountain gardeners.

The high mountain garden area differs from the Central Valley most obviously when snow falls. The danger of frost, as well as snow, limits the growing season in the high mountain area.

Besides the geographic area, other factors influence whether a particular plant will survive in your garden, among them: the slope of the ground, which drains away cold; the type of soil; whether the site is in full or partial sun; whether the wind is blocked by trees or buildings; and whether heat is reflected off walls or buildings.

A south-facing slope is much warmer than a north-facing one. A garden on a south-facing slope will burst into growth noticeably earlier in spring. This advantage comes bundled with a liability if the plants burst into growth before the frost season is truly over. New growth is particularly susceptible to frost damage.

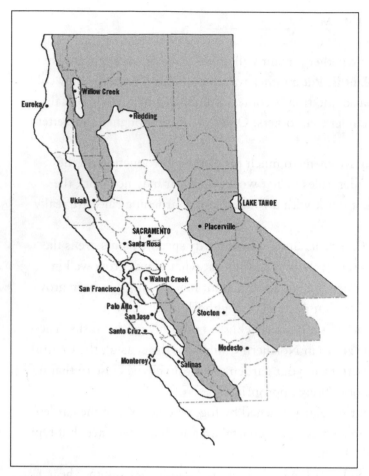

Climate Zones of Northern California

FROST

Any garden in a low point or hollow of land suffers from a higher risk of frost. The stillness of the sheltered air will also contribute to the risk. Cold air behaves like water and flows downhill until it is stopped by a barrier, and then it begins to fill the depression much as water collects and forms a puddle.

Plants that are native to warmer climates often cannot tolerate freezing temperatures. But air temperature is just one factor that determines whether or not plants will be damaged by a frost. When the temperature dips only a little below freezing but the air is moist from rain or fog, water vapor can condense and form ice crystals on both the ground and the plants. This condition helps warm the air around plants and protects them from extensive damage.

Experienced gardeners listen to the weather report and when near or below freezing temperatures are forecast, they dash outside to see if it is also a clear, windless, star-filled night. When there is no cloud cover, heat is lost rapidly and frost damage usually occurs. When temperatures fall more than a few degrees below freezing, no matter how moist the outside air, the frost will cause damage.

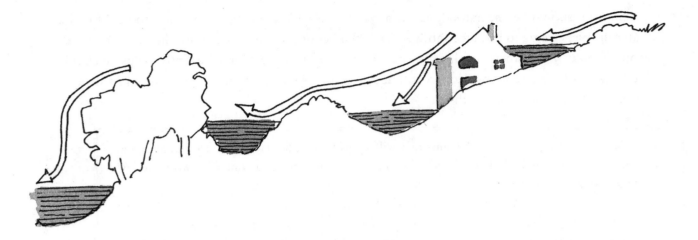

If you examine a frost-damaged plant, it is easy to see that the plant tissue has been affected. The water in the plant's cells freezes and then ruptures the cell walls. Some plants protect themselves from such damage by dropping their leaves in the fall or by dying back to the ground. Some plants have a natural antifreeze in their sap.

Deep frosts can also heave garden soil as the soil freezes, thaws, and refreezes. This heaving can push newly planted plants, that do not have established root systems, out of the soil. Mountain gardeners should mulch heavily around their plants immediately *after* the soil freezes to prevent sudden thawing during unexpected warm spells in early spring.

Coping with Frost

Gardeners have many tricks for coping with frost. Bougainvillea, citrus, fuchsia, seedlings, succulents, and new transplants are among the plants that need protection.

⊚ Cover tender plants that are open to the sky by setting stakes in the ground and draping burlap, plastic, old drapes, sheets, or newspaper over the stakes. Make certain that the covering does not touch the plant.

⊚ Cardboard boxes make good nighttime covers.

⊚ Remember to remove the covering the next morning when the temperature rises.

⊚ Wrap the trunks of young, tender trees, particularly citrus trees, in burlap or paper.

⊚ Spray plants with an antitranspirant. When roots freeze, the plant is unable to take up moisture. Leaves and stems continue, however, to transpire, taking moisture from living cells, which causes desiccation, and the plant turns brown or dies. An antitranspirant (sold in nurseries and often used to protect Christmas trees from excessive moisture loss) coats the leaves and stems so transpiration is reduced. This technique seems to work best in milder climates and when the antitranspirant is sprayed on in November and again in January.

Coping with Snow

Snow, it should be understood, has its advantages. When the temperature falls to near freezing, water droplets freeze to produce snow. A thick blanket of snow insulates both the plants and the ground and can keep them much warmer than the freezing air temperature. Snow helps ameliorate the heaving of soil caused by deep frost. But snow can also be hard on the garden, and gardeners have their tricks for coping with it.

⚬ The best technique is to select plants that will survive snow, but gardeners are a challenging lot and often plant marginal plants in the hope of getting them through a winter or two until they are large enough to survive on their own.

⚬ The weight of snow is its most harmful aspect. Gardeners should constantly knock the snow off new plants so that the weight does not build up and break fragile young limbs.

⚬ Pruning plants before winter to a shape that will shed snow is helpful. For example, prune hedges to a sharp arch on the top so that the weight of the snow does not collapse the hedge or wedge it apart.

⚬ An A-frame of cross-braced plywood will protect small shrubs from snow damage in their first few winters.

⚬ Plants can be packed with straw and then wrapped with burlap to protect them from snow and cold. There are many variations on this technique. The flexible branches of young trees or shrubs may be bound together with twine, surrounded heavily with straw, and then covered with burlap and tied with rope. Also a length of wire netting may be laid on a flat surface, covered with a layer of straw, and then topped with another layer of wire netting. This straw sandwich is then wrapped around a shrub and tied in place. Straw can be purchased from livestock supply stores.

WIND

Just as a garden at the bottom of a hill, where cold air puddles, will generate problems for plants, so does a garden at the top of a hill. Hilltops are often quite windy. Wind not only physically breaks plants, but also the force of the air dries out plant tissue. Some plants just cannot survive in windy sites.

In cities, buildings often function as mountains, forcing the wind to flow around them. The narrower the gap between buildings, the stronger the wind. In the streets of big cities such as San Francisco and Sacramento, skyscrapers create wind tunnels. The pattern of houses in a neighborhood can shelter a garden or create turbulent air patterns.

Coping with Wind

Naturally, gardeners have their tricks for coping with the wind. Be aware, however, that a solid fence is not the best protection because it rechannels the wind by forcing it up and over the fence only to dump it down violently on the area just behind the fence.

The best wind barrier allows some of the wind through, tempering its force rather than tackling the impossible task of stopping it cold. Even a slight barrier, such as that provided by a wire screen fence, can temper the force of the wind. Tall shrubs or fences with open spaces that let air through do a better job of softening the impact of the wind than does a solid wall.

The open spaces do not need to be even. It is only necessary to have occasional gaps for the wind to spill through, creating a counterforce to prevent the wind from dumping violently over the top. Redwood lattice fences have the advantage of allowing light as well as wind through. In a particularly cold garden, glass incorporated into your wind barrier allows both heat and light to collect on the opposite side.

Wind Barriers

There are general guidelines for creating an effective wind barrier. The barrier should be at right angles to the prevailing wind and be made of approximately two-thirds solid material to one-third holes. Many hedges and shrubs have these proportions. Such a wind barrier will reduce the force of the wind to almost nothing for a distance of about twice the height of the fence on the leeward side and will help reduce the impact of the wind on both plants and people for a distance of ten times the height of the barrier.

Plants as Wind Barriers

Plants that are strong enough to withstand gale force winds and that will work well as wind barriers in Northern California include: some acacias, cypress, eucalyptus, glossy privet, olive, and many pines (see the list on the following page).

The eucalyptus is the most commonly planted windbreak tree in Northern California, and there are many suitable, fast-growing varieties. Professional gardeners usually prune eucalyptus heavily during their first five years so that they do not become too top heavy and topple in the wind. The pruning also results in a thicker, denser windbreak.

Among the plants used as windbreaks:

- Blue–leaf wattle (*Acacia saligna*)
- ovens wattle (*Acacia pravissima*)
- Monterey cypress (*Cupressus macrocarpa*)
- Dwarf blue gum (*Eucalyptus globulus 'Compacta'*)
- Cider gum (*Eucalyptus gunnii*)
- Swamp mahogany (*Eucalyptus robusta*)
- Swamp mallee (*Eucalyptus spathulata*)
- Bird beak hakea (*Hakea orthorrhyncha*)
- olive (*Olea europaea*)
- Glossy privet (*Ligustrum lucidum*)
- Austrian black pine (*Pinus nigra*)
- Athel tree (*Tamarix aphylla*)

SOIL

A garden begins with a piece of land, a specific piece of land that is to be changed from whatever it is to something else. That specific piece of land is apt to give the gardener trouble because different plants like to grow in different soils.

Years ago, I moved into a brand-new house on the side of a mountain that overlooks the San Francisco Bay. Livestock may have once grazed those slopes, but there were no signs of cultivation in the native chaparral. It appeared as if no one had ever gardened there before. This seemed to be an opportunity, but others in the neighborhood took it as a challenge.

Shortly after I moved in, a large truck from a soil company arrived at the house next door. The driver took a quick look around him, shook his head and muttered, "Boy, you sure have your work cut out for you."

"What do you mean?" I asked.

"This is the worst soil I ever saw." He glanced scornfully at the hill behind my house. "Infertile." He pulled a few levers and soon several cubic yards of rich, black topsoil fell to the ground. I picked up a handful. It felt soft and crumbled between my fingertips.

I walked back to my house and stared at the soil. It was so pale that it was best described as tan rather than brown, and forget the notion of a rich, fertile black. If one could manage to scoop up as much as a handful, it felt hard—more rock than dirt. Nonetheless, behind my house grew a thicket of sage, chamise, coyote bush, and coastal live oaks. Infertile?

All that first summer I listened to the complaints of gardeners working nearby. Clearly, everyone thought the native soil a disaster. The ground was typically attacked with a pick axe. Once broken up, the rocky soil was hauled away and new fertile soil brought in.

I lamented the soil I had left behind in my former home—dark, heavy soil enriched by years of dropping pine needles. Rhododendrons, azaleas, camellias, and ferns thrived on that soil.

Fortunately, I was too busy to do anything about my new soil that summer. By the time the structural elements of my new garden were in place, it was October. Coincidentally, the California Native Plant Society held a sale not far from my home. A few of the plants offered for sale, such as ceanothus or manzanita, were familiar. Most were unknown.

"What kind of soil does this need?" I asked about this or that plant.

The volunteer's reply, inevitably, was "Well drained."

"What about rocky soil," I added tentatively, "with hardly any dirt?"

"Perfect."

It is odd how the obvious can come as a revelation. I carted home several dozen native plants. By the time I was ready to start digging, the rains had come, and to my amazement the soil that had been as tough as concrete during California's dry summer could now be easily dug with a shovel. Inspired, I bought five hundred dwarf coyote bushes (*Baccharis pilularis*), a cultivated variety of a bush native to coastal California, and covered the hillside with them.

By the following autumn, I had learned more about native plants and was amazed to discover what Nature had done while I was not watching. I had bought a native rush, the California gray rush (*Juncus patens*), and planted it along the slope above the boulder retaining wall. To my amazement, I saw that the rush now appeared of its own accord along the flagstone walkway. On the hillside, I saw blue eyed grass (*Sisyrinchium bellum*) blooming. I recognized the blue eyed grass and the rush only because I had bought identical plants in the fall. What might have been considered weeds now became valued because I had paid money for them.

Gardening in this lean rocky soil, which had once seemed so impossible, was becoming easy once I planted the appropriate plant. Not that I imagine for a moment that all other gardeners hearing of my success will be persuaded to grow plants appropriate to their own soil.

Gardeners, being a stubborn lot, do not always want to grow the plants that will thrive in their particular spot of earth. It is as pointless to argue that gardeners must make do with whatever soil they encounter in the garden as it is small minded to think that the only good soil is the fine tillable stuff that comes packaged from the nursery as potting soil. There are many ways to create a fine garden.

Whenever gardening friends despair of ever growing what they want on their native soil, I think of one bonnie fine Scotsman who created an exemplary park out of a sand dune. Few gardeners' landscaping problems compare to those faced by John McLaren when he took on San Francisco's Golden Gate Park in 1887. The 1,013 acres of sand dunes were regarded with much ridicule as something of a white elephant. One newspaper described the area as "a dreary waste of shifting sand hills where a blade of grass cannot be raised without four posts to keep it from blowing away."

Uncle John, as the stubborn gardener came to be called, was prepared for the challenge. After serving an apprenticeship at the Royal Botanical Gardens in Edinburgh, he tackled the dunes in the Firth of Forth in southeastern Scotland. In San Francisco, he tamed the sand dunes by planting seabent grass. He knew that, as the shifting sand piled up around the grass, the blades simply grew taller while the roots sank down deep to anchor the sand in place.

"Ye can gi' thanks for the seabent," he once said. "It's added 150 acres to the city in the past twenty years."

With the sand stabilized, he planted an impressive variety of trees and shrubs. When the wind and sand dared to bury his botanical prodigies, he had them dug out again, and stubbornly added more humus, manure, and seabent. The impressive results are an inspiration to any gardener touring San Francisco's magnificent park.

Whether it is a sand dune or a chaparral hillside, every plot of garden soil is perfect for growing a particular type of plant. Gardening is a lot easier when plant and soil are suited to each other. But with enough effort, a forest can be made to grow on a sand dune and a rose garden can thrive in a swampland. Each gardener brings a vision and creates a particular Eden.

My best advice to gardeners is to grow what will thrive in your particular soil, location, and climate. Soil is grouped into categories by its structure and texture. Sandy soil has large particles that allow water to drain rapidly; this is great for some plants, but it is a problem for most plants, which need more moisture and more nutrients than this fast-draining soil provides. Sandy soil feels coarse and gritty when squeezed together in the gardener's hand. Clay soil has very tiny particles that stick together like modeling clay when squeezed together. Clay soil drains too slowly for some plants, and it dries very hard in our rainless summer season. Gardeners with clay soil should avoid adding too much sand to the clay soil or they may end up with cement. *Loam* is a term used by gardeners for soil that combines both large and small particles so that it is easy to dig and it retains moisture without being soggy. Rocky soil is just what the name implies, a soil with lots of rocks, usually decomposed granite. Rocky soil is difficult to dig, but it usually drains well, and some plants prefer it. Many Northern California gardens contain a variety of soil types. The good news is that, no matter what the soil type, the advice for improving it is the same. Add nutritive-rich, fast-draining soil amendments—the very best being homemade compost. As if the reader had heaps of compost lying around! Amending soil can be helpful to the gardener, but it is important to realize that soil is only one component of a garden setting, and, in fact, you may not want to amend the soil because it is already perfect for certain types of plants.

Location, climate, and other garden plants combine with soil to create a type of habitat that is most useful to the gardener when selecting plants that will thrive in the garden. Gardeners in a forest setting of pines, redwoods, or oaks will find that the leaves of these trees fall to the ground and are worked into the soil by rain and by insects, creating an acid soil. A beautiful garden can be easily created by using plants that thrive on acid soil such as rhododendrons, azaleas, camellias, and ferns. Gardeners planting under huge old native oaks, however, should be careful not to plant within ten feet of the trunk.

Gardeners with sandy soil where salt drifts in with the ocean fog will concentrate on plants that thrive on fast-draining salty soil such as the cousin to the silk tree, the plume albizia (*Albizia distachya*), Monterey cypress (*Cupressus macrocarpa*), rugosa roses, and sea lavender (*Limonium perezii*). Nurseries located in coastal areas are well supplied with plants that thrive along the coast. Windbreaks are particularly important close to shore.

Gardeners with rocky soil will concentrate on plants that like lean, fast-draining soil, such as many pines, particularly the charming mugho pine (*Pinus mugo mugo*) or the tanyosho pine (*Pinus densiflora* 'Umbraculifera'), some heathers, junipers, succulents such as hen and chicks (*Echeveria imbricata*) or rosea ice plant (*Drosanthemum floribundum*), or the silky mat-forming sheep bur (*Acaena buchananii*), and the frothy, flowering fleabane (*Erigeron karvinskianus*). Classic rock gardens and alpine gardens are difficult to create on clay or sandy soil, but they are easy to create on soil that is already rocky. Gardeners with this type of soil may want to visit a rock yard to see the beautiful boulders, often covered with lichen and moss, that can be purchased and set in place in the garden.

The same principle of choosing the right plant applies also to the difficult spot or two that plagues every garden. Instead of cursing that low spot that collects water from the lawn sprinkler, make use of this small swampland by planting the stunningly beautiful Japanese iris (*Iris ensata*). Other gardeners, who go to great lengths to create a habitat for the Japanese iris, will be green with envy. Many coastal gardeners have trouble getting enough winter chill to grow fruit trees, or lilacs, or peonies; yet those same plants will bloom and thrive in the horrible gully that collects cold air and has killed off the citrus trees the gardener had fond hopes of growing there.

In some situations, the gardener deliberately chooses to concentrate only on the site to create a garden devoted to produce or flowers. Vegetable gardens are always amended with nutrient-rich, fast-draining materials. Gardeners who like to have lush perennial borders that they are constantly changing will need to heap compost and fertile soil amendments onto their garden plots constantly. This technique makes it very easy to dig in new plants and has much to recommend it from the gardener's point of view. I am not at all convinced, however, that plants are nearly as fussy as the gardener. But it does not matter. If lush, soft potting soil of the sort that comes out of a plastic bag from the nursery is the type of soil you want, then there is no reason not to spend the money and time to get that sort of soil. It would be a disservice to other gardeners, however, to insinuate that this is the only type of soil that is acceptable.

Gardeners who have the misfortune to live on land from which the topsoil has been removed, as sometimes happens in subdivisions, will have to have topsoil brought in. They may also have to have holes drilled through the hardpan. Hardpan is an impervious layer of soil that blocks water from draining. Plant roots need air as well as water, and plants growing directly above hardpan usually drown. Raised beds are an alternative for those gardening on impervious hardpan.

At the risk of driving the reader mad with repetition, I will again state that the easiest, most successful gardens are made by planting plants suitable to your soil and your climate. It is easy to tell what these plants are by looking at well-established plants in your neighborhood and by visiting local nurseries. If you are lucky enough to live near open space, see what Nature has planted. She always knows what she is doing. If, however, you have your heart set on growing plants that like a soil other than whatever is in your garden, add nutrient-rich, fast-draining amendments.

g a r d e n   b a s i c s

For suppliers who can deliver soil amendments by the cubic yard, look in the Yellow Pages under Soil Conditioners, or Topsoil, or Landscaping Equipment and Supplies.

⬤ Contact stables in your area to find manure. Sometimes they will even give it to you free, if you load and haul it away. Look for well-composted manure because hot, fresh manure will burn most plants or seedlings that come into contact with it. The manure should have composted for two or more months until it is no longer hot in the center of the manure pile and the manure has taken on an aged, gray appearance. Of course, the gardener can compost the manure at home before using it in the garden. Ideally the manure should be placed on a garden bed late in the fall and then the garden bed should be planted the following spring, allowing the manure to break down over the winter.

⬤ In the Sacramento area, gardeners may be able to find rice hulls inexpensively or even free for the hauling. Contact a rice-growers' cooperative for a source.

⬤ Elsewhere in Northern California, gardeners may find used mushroom compost from mushroom growers or sawdust that has been treated with nitrogen from lumber mills. Untreated sawdust needs to be composted until it is rotted before it is used in the garden.

Using Soil Amendments

The soil amendments may be dug into the soil or laid on top of the soil as a mulch. It may surprise some gardeners to learn that digging amendments into the soil is somewhat controversial. There are horticulturists who believe that digging the soil breaks down the beneficial, honeycomb-like structure made by worms and insects over hundreds of years. Amendments placed on top of the soil will find their way down into the soil through the combined forces of rain, worms, and insects. The speed with which this happens rates right up there with other great mysteries such as how socks manage to disappear between the time they are put into the washing machine and the time they are taken out of the dryer.

How Much Soil Amendment?

How much organic amendment should be added? Some horticulturists recommend an addition of one inch of material spread out evenly over the soil every year. This works out to about a five percent amendment to the top foot of gardening soil. Gardeners wanting rich, friable soil, of course, are going to add much more, up to fifty percent amendment to the top foot of gardening soil. There is a danger in adding too much amendment in that plant roots accustomed to rich, soft soil may wind around in the amended area rather than go deeper into the surrounding, unamended soil.

Compost is the best soil amendment. The technique of reducing organic material to decomposed, soft, small-sized material, called compost, can be complicated and time consuming or as easy as piling material and letting it decompose without much fuss.

Several types of compost units are sold in nurseries and hardware stores. Homemade units can be as simple as chicken wire formed into a three-foot circle.

Composting Simplified

Use only organic material; chop and shred larger material into pieces about half an inch in size.

1. Layer dry material, such as dried leaves, with an equal quantity of green material, such as grass clippings or kitchen vegetable trimmings. Six-inch layers work well. The ideal size for a compost heap is one cubic yard.

2. Keep the pile as moist as a damp sponge.

3. Turn the pile for faster decomposition. A well-constructed pile turned at least once every week will yield finished compost in as few as several weeks. Unturned piles take months, some up to a year. Turn from the top to the bottom and from the side to the center.

COMPOSTING MATERIALS

- Healthy plant parts
- Weeds without seeds
- Grass clippings
- Kitchen scraps such as vegetable or fruit waste, egg shells, coffee grinds, tea leaves
- Sawdust
- Straw
- Leaves
- Rinsed seaweed
- Horse manure or rabbit droppings

Commercial growers often have their soil pH analyzed by professionals in order to maximize their crops, whether they are tomatoes or zinnias. Soil pH ranges from 0 to 14 and indicates the range of acidity to alkalinity that affects the availability of soil minerals to plants. Most plants grow best in a pH range of between 5.5 and 7.5. Some plants prefer either alkaline or acid soil, but most ornamental plants tolerate a wide pH range. A soil's pH can be altered. But it is best to do so only after professional advice, because the altering may be difficult to correct. To have soil tested for pH, look in the Yellow Pages under Laboratories—Testing.

Soil laboratories will give very specific instructions about collecting soil from various parts of the garden. Send in the soil samples along with a list of what you want to grow there. You will receive not only an analysis of your soil but also instructions on what to add to get it perfect for what you want to grow. There are also home testing kits which give very limited (and sometimes inaccurate) advice. Friends who use home testing kits recommend the La Motte Kit, about $40.00 mail-order (La Motte Chemical Products, Box 329, Chestertown, MD 21620, phone 410-778-3100). Most gardeners may not want to go to this extreme, nor should they.

PLANTING

The backbone of a garden are the trees and shrubs. They are usually the first plants put into a garden. Autumn, October in particular, is the best time to transplant trees and shrubs in Northern California. Spring-planted trees and shrubs have to survive our long, rainless summer; fall-planted trees and shrubs can take advantage of our autumn rain and warm weather to become established before winter. By the following spring, those fall-planted trees and shrubs will have sufficient roots to burst into new top growth.

In the nursery, look for plants that have not already outgrown their pots. Although it seems as if the largest plant would produce the most vigorous growth in the garden, this is rarely true. A smaller plant with a younger root system will be better able to adapt to your garden soil and will overtake the larger plant in a few years. According to the East Bay Municipal Utility District in their *Water-Conserving Plants and Landscape Guide*, planting identical species from both one-gallon and five-gallon-sized containers in the same setting produced surprising results. In a period of three to five years, the one-gallon-sized plant was as large as the five-gallon-sized plant. In seven to ten years, the one-gallon-sized plant usually grew larger than the five-gallon sized plant. There are a few exceptions to this rule, particularly among slow-growing species such ginkgo, carob, crape myrtle, and olive.

1. Water the plant in the pot.

2. Dig a hole two to four times the width of the pot and a little deeper than the pot.

3. With the edge of the shovel or preferably a garden fork, loosen the soil at the bottom and up the sides of the hole.

4. Carefully remove the plant from the pot. Every gardener has a particular routine for doing this. I run an old kitchen knife around the inside edge of the pot to loosen the soil from the pot. Then I wack the bottom of the pot with my fist. Really big pots get wacked on the bottom with a shovel. Then I lie a large pot on its side (small pots are held upside down) and very carefully ease the plant out.

5. Gently pull free any roots that have wound around the pot. Loosen the roots at the bottom with your fingers.

6. Do not add any soil conditioners or amendments for trees and shrubs. Soil amendments would discourage the plant roots from growing out of the hole into the tougher soil.

7. Plant the tree or shrub at the same level that it was while in the pot, filling in the hole with the same soil that came out of the hole.

8. Water well. Cover the root area with a mulch to keep it free of weeds and to preserve moisture.

SEEDING

Seeds are intriguing. Some are so tiny that a million of them would nestle in a teaspoon. The largest seed is a coconut (*Lodoicea maldivica*) that the French call *coco-de-mer* or sea coconut. For centuries these immense sea coconuts washed up on French and English beaches from the Seychelles Islands, about one thousand miles east of Africa in the Indian Ocean. You would not want to be asleep on the beach when one arrived because the sea coconut can weigh up to forty-five pounds. (The record weight for a common coconut is only six pounds.)

Some seeds travel incredible distances; some wait interminable lengths of time before germinating, and still others germinate in the most improbable circumstances. With true long-term planning, Nature produces a portion of seeds much hardier than the rest in order to stagger and assure germination. In Northern California, certain species of manzanita and ceanothus have adapted to the periodic burning that occurs in our brushland by germinating when heated enough to scarify the seed coat. Only then can water penetrate and initiate growth. Propagators of the stately Matilija poppy (*Romneya coulteri*), see page 245, often burn straw over seed flats to encourage the seeds to sprout.

Seeds germinate under a wide variety of conditions. Take, for another example, common corn seeds. Planted in the spring garden with the temperature around 51°F, corn seeds will germinate in about twenty-one days. But placed in a warm spot, say the oven with just the pilot light on, they germinate in only three days. Or, to use the opposite extreme, consider lettuce seeds, which are dormant in the summer. During hot spells lettuce seeds prefer not to bother germinating at all. Given a two-week summer vacation in the freezer and then planted temporarily in a cool spot, say an ice chest in the basement, lettuce seeds may perform like troupers. See page 27 for techniques to encourage germination.

Seeding—Step by Step

1. Start with very fine soil. Most gardeners use a sterilized soil such as a potting mix. A few terrific gardeners believe that garden soil and compost are preferable because they contain beneficial soil microbes. They are doubtlessly correct, but most people still stick to sterilized potting soil because so many seedlings die from a fungus (actually a complex of microorganisms any one of which can be the culprit) popularly called damping off, which is carried in the soil. When a seedling dies by damping off, it keels over from a weakened stem right at the soil line. This is such a sad sight for an eager gardener that sterilized soil is usually preferred.

2. Use clean containers. Some gardeners use milk cartons with holes punched in them. I use small clay pots that have been run through the dishwasher. Some prefer growing seeds in flats. Nurseries and mail-order seed companies sell nifty plastic units that resemble miniature greenhouses. Old containers may be set out in the sun to help sterilize them and prevent the spread of fungal diseases.

3. Add water to the soil mix and stir or mush it about with your fingers until it is wet. Old, dried-out potting soil is amazingly difficult to get wet; so it is much easier to get the soil wet before you put the soil into containers.

4. Put the wet soil into the small planting containers and let excess water drain.

5. Place the seeds in the wet planting soil. Some seeds are very small and this can be tricky work. Do not place the seeds close together. Leave at least one-half inch between them, preferably more. The general rule in planting any seed is to cover it to a depth three to four times its size.

6. Cover the seeds very lightly with soil. This means only one-eighth inch of soil on top of each seed. Some English gardening friends tell me they use vermiculite to cover seeds because sunlight can be transmitted easily through vermiculite. However, some seeds germinate best in darkness. Read the seed packet to see if a need for light or dark is specifically mentioned.

7. Many seeds, and most vegetable seeds, do better when grown in warm conditions preferably with bottom heat, which emulates warm soil. Gardeners place seed pots on top of refrigerators, water heaters, or other appliances that produce a slightly warm surface. Remember to keep the soil damp.

8. Once the seedling has pierced the soil, it needs between four and six hours of sunlight a day. Remember to turn the pots regularly so that the seedlings do no grow lopsided as they bend toward the light. Also be sure to place a sturdy tray beneath the seedling pots to catch water runoff.

9. For the healthiest crop, thin plants so they do not crowd one another. The best way to thin is to snip off the unwanted seedlings with a pair of scissors. When pulling seedlings out you run the risk of disturbing or uprooting a neighboring seedling.

10. Seedlings are generally considered ready to transplant when they develop the second set of leaves. If the weather is not great outdoors or if you think the plant should be sturdier, transplant it to a larger pot and continue to nurture it indoors.

11. Acclimate seedlings grown indoors by moving them outdoors for a few hours a day for several days, a procedure called hardening off. This is an excellent technique for assuring the survival of the seedlings. However do not put the young seedling in direct sun during these visiting periods. Some gardeners leave the seedlings outdoors for an entire day and night before subjecting them to the rigors of transplanting.

12. Carefully transplant the seedlings into the garden. Be gentle. Do not press down hard on the soil around the seedling roots as this will compact the soil and deprive the roots of air. Roots need both air and water in the soil to thrive. Shield the seedling from bright sun for the first few days. A shingle makes a good shield for one seedling. An umbrella will shield several seedlings.

SCARIFY   Scarifying seeds is a method of enabling seeds with a tough outer coat to receive moisture. Care must be taken not to crush the embryo. (Botanically speaking, an embryo is the minute, rudimentary plant contained within a seed.) Large seeds may be notched on one side with a file. Medium seeds may be placed in a can with a few rocks, covered, and shaken until the seeds are slightly dented. Fine seeds, such as parsley seeds, are placed between layers of sandpaper and massaged, or placed between sheets of paper and pressed lightly with a rolling pin. Examples of seeds with tough outer coats are lupine, morning glory, okra, and to a lesser degree, spinach and parsley.

PRESOAK   At its simplest, presoaking is merely placing seeds to soak in water. The night before planting them, soak any seeds, but particularly such notoriously slow germinaters as parsley, carrots, and celery, in twice as much water as is needed to cover them. Many seeds will swell to twice their original size. Spread them on paper towels to dry for a few hours in the morning so that they do not clump together, which would make it difficult to plant them. Once presoaked, seeds must be planted promptly.

PRESPROUT   Presprouting begins with presoaking: cover the seeds with twice as much water as their depth and leave to soak overnight. After pouring off the water, place the seeds in a glass jar in a warm, dark cupboard. Rinse the seeds three times a day with lukewarm water. In a few days, when the seeds have begun to sprout, plant them very carefully in containers or in the garden.

The most gratifying method, to children and the impatient, is presprouting on newsprint, paper towels, or layers of toilet paper. Average-priced paper towels seem to have an edge over other materials. Whatever you use as the medium must hold up when wet yet allow the seedlings to break through. Place a strip of paper on a slightly longer strip of wax paper and mist it with a water sprayer until damp. Then place the seeds on the paper (spaced for planting), cover with another strip of paper, mist until that strip is damp, and cover very loosely with plastic wrap. Set these seed strips in a warm place, such as an oven warmed by the pilot light, or on the top of a clothes dryer or on an electric water heater. The strips of seeds may be stacked for easy handling. Keep the top strips slightly damp by misting occasionally but do not make them soaking wet. The combination of heat and moisture will promptly sprout many seeds. Flower seeds generally sprout better in the light.

Presprouted seeds should be gently planted into containers or into the garden. The seeds require careful nurturing until they have taken root in the soil.

PLANTING   The general rule in planting any seed is to cover it to a depth three to four times its size. Cover presprouted seeds with soft soil or compost. Seeds sprouted on paper towels are planted together with their paper-towel blankets. (But discard the plastic.) Presprouted seeds are very vulnerable to wind and sun during the first few days and should be protected from an intense dose of either. Keep the little seedlings well watered. You may need to mist them twice a day.

Plant cells, like the human body, are composed primarily of water. Sufficient water is essential to healthy plant life, and a lack of sufficient water not only wilts plants but also makes them susceptible to disease and to insects. But because plants need both water and air in the soil, overwatering can be as harmful as underwatering. Too much water may drown plants as well as promote soil diseases.

Plants vary widely in their need for water, but fortunately, most plants tolerate a variety of watering practices. One of the secrets of good gardening in Northern California is to group plants according to their water needs. Often water-loving plants are put close to the house where they can be fussed over and drought-tolerant plants placed further away where failure to water them will do no great harm.

Guidelines for watering certain plants are given throughout this book. In general, remember:

❀ Seedlings will die quickly without water.

❀ Young plants need more water because their root systems have not become extensive or established.

❀ Fruit trees and vegetables need water in the first half of the summer to become productive. Most plants will take a dry spell once they are established.

CONSERVING WATER

❀ Add organic amendments to the soil; they will help the soil to retain water.

❀ Mulch the soil surface to limit evaporation from the soil and to protect the soil from the sun's drying rays.

❀ Make watering basins. A water basin is a dam made of earth around the shrub or tree. The basin should extend to the outer edge of the plant where rain would naturally drip off the leaves onto the ground. This area, known as the drip line, is where the most productive roots grow.

❀ Use drip irrigation. Drip irrigation systems, by which small quantities of water are delivered directly to the roots of each individual plant, are widely sold at nurseries, hardware stores, and garden supply houses. Each system is a little different, and every company supplies an instruction booklet with the equipment.

❀ Water early in the day before the sun is bright and hot.

Fertilizing is the practice of supplying plants with nutrients; the three major or primary nutrients are nitrogen (N), phosphorus (P), and potassium (K). This gang of three are prominently displayed on fertilizer packages as a ratio, nitrogen : phosphorus : potassium (always in that order) such as 10N-10P-10K (the three nutrients are supplied in equal percentages) or 20-0-0 (only nitrogen is supplied), or many other combinations.

Nitrogen is the nutrient used most often in large quantities, and plants usually respond quickly to fertilizers high in nitrogen. Fertilizers sometimes also have macronutrients such as calcium (Ca), magnesium (Mg), and sulfur (S), and occasionally micronutrients (or trace elements) such as iron (Fe), manganese (Mn), boron (B), copper (Cu), zinc (Zn), molybdenum (Mo), and chlorine (Cl).

Plants have such slight needs for trace elements that too much can do them harm.

In Northern California, gardeners will occasionally encounter iron deficiency in citrus and acid-loving plants such as azaleas or camellias. This will appear as yellowing between the veins of the leaves, and it is easily corrected by an iron supplement that has been chelated to make it easily absorbed by the plant. Sometimes plants grown in subsoil (the topsoil has usually been scraped away by builders) will show a zinc deficiency by producing very small mottled leaves. It is easily corrected with chelated zinc. Fertilizers formulated for rapid growth will be high in nitrogens, and those formulated to stimulate flowering, fruiting, and strong roots will be high in phosphorous. There are also fertilizers formulated for special plants such as African violets (8-14-6) or roses (18-24-16). There are also all-purpose fertilizers, which can be applied to every garden plant.

Fertilizing can be a complicated process or a simple one. The gardener can apply one type of fertilizer to most plants once a year (generally early in the spring) or develop a complex schedule of applying a variety of fertilizers to different plants throughout the year. The gardener can also decide not to fertilize at all; the garden will continue to grow.

Some organic gardeners argue that enriching the soil with compost supplies all the nutrients that plants need, and that the use of commercial fertilizers should be avoided. Organic gardeners also argue that synthetic chemical (nonorganic) fertilizers acidify the soil and consequently repel earthworms. It is certainly true that when lots of fertilizer is supplied, some plants burst into an abundance of tender new growth that attracts insects. It is also true that rampant growth is not always desirable because it may need to be pruned.

In addition to the synthetic chemical fertilizers widely available in nurseries and hardware stores, there are organic fertilizers. The following are some of the more popular, along with the typical NPK ratio for each: alfalfa pellets (5-1-2), animal manure (0.6-0.1-0.5), blood meal (11-0-0), coffee grounds (2-0.3-0.2), compost (0.5-0.3-0.8), fish emulsion (4-1-1), fish meal (5-3-3), mushroom compost (0.7-0.3-0.3, but varies greatly), oak leaves (0.8-0.4-0.1), and sawdust (0.2-0-2.3). Organic gardeners also use as fertilizers inorganic minerals such as Epsom salts (ten percent magnesium, thirteen percent sulfur), and rock phosphate (0-3-0).

Organic fertilizers need to be applied in huge amounts. For example, to fertilize an area ten feet by ten feet would require two pounds of a synthetic chemical fertilizer (10-10-10) or five pounds of alfalfa pellets (5-1-2) or thirty-five pounds of mushroom compost (0.5-0.3-0.8). Organic fertilizers also improve soil texture, and some of them are used as soil amendments. Synthetic chemical fertilizers have the advantage in early spring when cold soil temperatures thwart the release of organic nutrients.

Fertilizers, both organic and synthetic, come in many different forms. The most popular form is dry; a dry, granular fertilizer is easily sprinkled evenly over the root area in the amount recommended on the fertilizer package and watered in well. Be careful to keep the dry fertilizer off leaves and stems to prevent burning.

Water-soluble fertilizers are dissolved in water and poured or sprayed on roots. The problem with water-soluble fertilizers is that the gardener needs to keep applying them because once they pass beyond the roots they are literally washed away.

Liquid foliar fertilizers are sprayed onto the leaves of plants. They are most effective early in the spring before a tough waxy coat forms on the surface of the leaf. Liquid fertilizers are mixed with water and can be applied to both roots and leaves. Fish emulsion and liquid kelp are liquid fertilizers that are often used as foliar sprays to give plants an extra boost.

Slow-release fertilizers are very popular with container gardeners because they release nutrients over a long period of time; often you will see the round grey capsules sprinkled on top of nursery-grown container plants. Slow-release fertilizers are also safer than water-soluble fertilizers that can burn roots if used in concentrations that are too high.

There are several general guidelines for using fertilizers. Fertilizers are usually applied before a plant blooms; for fruit trees this can mean very early in the year. Fertilize citrus with a high-nitrogen citrus fertilizer that includes iron because iron chlorosis (yellowing) is a common problem in Northern California. Other trees and shrubs often benefit from a high-nitrogen fertilizer with a formula such as 20-10-10. If you use granular fertilizer, make sure to water it in well. Not everything should be fertilized. Cacti, succulents, and some native plants should not be fertilized. Gardens with rampant, hard-to-control growth would be easier to handle with less or no fertilizer. When in doubt, it is far better to apply too little fertilizer than too much.

PRUNING

Pruning is the art of selectively cutting off branches in order to shape a tree or a shrub. In general, the best time to prune any woody plant is just before new growth starts, which is usually in late winter or early spring. The worst time to prune is right after leaves emerge in spring when the plant can ill afford to lose foliage. Prune dormant deciduous plants, such as fruit trees, roses, grapes, and cane berries, after their leaves have fallen and before their buds begin to swell. Of course, do not prune spring-blooming plants until they finish blooming.

Pruning Simplified

Two basic pruning techniques are used in general pruning. Thinning cuts remove entire branches. Heading cuts shorten branches and stimulate latent buds that produce new growth.

Begin pruning with thinning cuts and then use selective heading cuts.

Prune from the bottom up and from the interior of the plant to the exterior.

Thinning Cuts

Heading Cuts

Direct future new growth by cutting just above a bud that faces in the direction you want new growth to take. Hard pruning that removes a lot of old growth in winter will create a lot of new growth in the spring. Summer pruning does not tend to promote such vigorous growth.

Pruning Major Branches

The pruning off of a major branch requires still another technique that is relatively new to the horticultural sciences. In the past, gardeners were advised to cut the branch off flush with the tree trunk. Now gardeners are advised to protect the branch collar by leaving a very small stub. This collar protects the tree from disease and insects.

Small branches less than one inch in diameter can be removed with one straight cut using a pruning saw. Larger branches require several cuts; do not try to cut large branches with one cut because the first two cuts remove the weight of the branch. Although not all arborists agree, it is now believed that it is better to hold the pruning paint; wounds exposed to air are thought to heal better.

1. Begin by undercutting the branch slightly at a spot at least a foot away from the tree trunk.

2. Make the second cut just beyond the first cut; saw all the way through the branch from the top to the bottom, severing the limb.

3. Try to locate the natural branch collar with your finger tips. If you cannot find it, make your cuts at least an inch from the trunk. Make the third cut—an undercut—just beyond the branch collar to protect it from being torn.

4. Last, saw the limb through from above, making a slightly downward-sloping cut to meet the third cut, and sever the remainder of the limb.

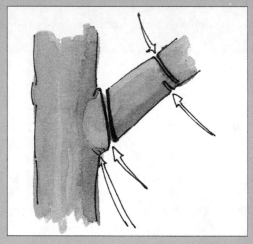

Branch Cut

Pesticides have been, without doubt, a boon to humankind. The synthetic insecticide DDT virtually eliminated malaria from many parts of the world. It took us a while to realize the downside to DDT. It is, after all, an unselective poison that remained in the food chain for many years and built up over time, resulting in the death of eagles and many other birds of prey. DDT has been banned since 1973. Since then we have learned more about the hazards of pesticides, including some that are still on the market. Diazinon, a broad-spectrum insecticide, is toxic to birds. Malathion is toxic to bees. But it is not just synthetic insecticides that are dangerous. Organic insecticides have to be monitored too. Even seemingly harmless sticky traps hung in trees kill hummingbirds whose tongues can get stuck when they go after the trapped insects.

A garden is a living habitat dependent upon birds, hummingbirds, butterflies, and many beneficial insects both for insect control and cross-pollination, so gardeners cannot afford to kill off their living allies. It takes a few years for a garden to find its balance with the right predators to dispose of harmful insects. Entomologists believe that it takes about three years for a favorable balance to be created once pesticides have been eliminated. Patience is part of successful gardening. A garden without butterflies and birdsong is much too high a price to pay to be rid of a few bugs.

PEST CONTROL GUIDELINES

❀ Many gardeners use chemical pesticides only if all else fails. Other gardeners do not use chemical pesticides at all, preferring to get rid of the insect-ridden plant rather than spend their gardening time spraying chemicals.

❀ Remember, it may take a few days or even weeks before the predatory beneficial insects arrive to destroy an overabundant insect invader. Have patience.

❀ The use of horticultural oils and insecticidal soap often significantly lowers the insect population without damaging the environment.

❀ If plants are plagued with aphids, switch from a soluble nitrogen fertilizer to slow-release nitrogen fertilizers such as compost. The rush of tender new growth that soluble nitrogen produces is very attractive to aphids.

❀ Release beneficial insects in the garden to control harmful insects.

❀ Only use pesticides believed to be harmless to the environment.

We are beginning to understand that the use of pesticides is actually self-defeating. Many insects build up a resistance or even an immunity to certain chemicals, eventually rendering the chemicals useless.

Pest Control: The Good

There are a number of living organisms that can be purchased and released to help control pests in the garden. These are known as beneficial insects. Many of these organisms live naturally in gardens and are killed by the unwise use of chemical and organic pesticides.

Today, biological controls are increasingly used in Northern Californian agriculture and are widely available. Although biological controls sound new, Chinese gardeners were using predatory ants to control beetles and caterpillars as far back as 300 A.D. To encourage these beneficial insects to stay in the garden, plant the wildflowers and small shrubs that they use for pollen and nectar.

LADY BUGS   Convergent lady beetles eat many insects that plague gardens, but be aware that lady bugs are notorious for moving on to neighboring gardens.

ENCARSIA FORMOSA   The encarsia is a small parasitic wasp that lays eggs inside developing whiteflies.

GREEN LACEWING   Known as the aphid lion, the green lacewing is commonly found in gardens. Both the larvae and the adults devour a range of insects and mites including aphids and spider mites. A single lacewing can eat up to eleven thousand spider mites.

GRASSHOPPER SPORE   *Nosema locustae* are grasshopper spore that cripple and kill many species of grasshoppers.

MITES   Predatory mites eat their cousins the spider mites but do not damage plants.

RED SCALE PARASITES   Red scale parasites are aphytis wasps that attack red scale insects, particularly in citrus orchards.

WASPS   Trichogramma wasps are widely used parasitic wasps that attack the eggs of caterpillars. Repeated applications usually achieve the desired control.

Pest Control: Attracting the Good

You do not have to buy beneficial insects; you can lure them into the garden with their favorite plants. Favored plants include many flowering bedding plants such as cosmos, sweet alyssum, and yarrow. The greater the variety of favored plants, the greater the variety of beneficial insects your garden will attract.

ANNUALS

⊛ Baby blue eyes (*Nemophila menziesii*) has blue flowers on small plants from March to May. It attracts parasitic wasps.

⊛ Coriander (*Coriandrum sativum*) has small white flowers on a lacy-leafed plant in May and June. It attracts parasitic wasps.

⊛ Cosmos (*Cosmos bipinnatus*) has many colors of flowers from spring to fall but white flowers are the most effective in luring beneficial insects. It has willowy, ferny foliage and attracts lacewings and lady beetles.

⊛ Sweet alyssum (*Lobularia maritima*) has white flowers on small, ground-hugging plants that are in bloom most of the year in mild winter areas. It attracts lacewings and parasitic wasps.

⊛ Tidytips (*Layia platyglossa*) is a cheerful wildflower with gaily painted yellow and white flowers from spring to fall. It attracts parasitic wasps.

◉ Common fennel (*Foeniculum vulgare*) has billowy foliage and flat yellow flowers from spring to fall. It attracts lacewings, lady beetles, and paper wasps. (Paper wasps make wonderful decorative hives if you can manage to keep rock-throwing adolescents from using them for target practice.)

◉ Coreopsis (*Coreopsis gigantea* or *Coreopsis grandiflora*) has yellow, orange, or maroon flowers from late spring to early fall. It attracts lacewings, lady beetles, and parasitic wasps.

◉ Crown-pink (*Lychnis coronaria*) is a soft gray plant that sends up tall shoots of magenta, pink, or white flowers in spring and summer. It attracts parasitic wasps.

◉ Yarrow (*Achillea*) has ferny foliage and flowers in many shades; new cultivars have wonderful dusty pastels. It blooms from spring to fall and attracts lady beetles and parasitic wasps.

Pest Control—Recommendations

The pesticides listed below are currently accepted for use on many types of organically grown produce in Northern California.

◉ *Bacillus thuringiensis* (known as BT) is a microbial control for many caterpillars. After eating treated plants, the caterpillars die within three days. BT can be used on all food crops up to harvest. It is sold under several trade names. Note: Be careful when using BT. Many gardeners will not use it because it kills the caterpillars that result in butterflies.

◉ Diatomaceous earth is an inorganic desiccant dust derived from the skeletons of microscopic marine organisms. It controls cockroaches and ants as well as some plant pests. Use carefully; some forms can be hazardous when breathed.

◉ Horticultural oils are highly refined oils used to control aphids, psylla, scale insects, mites, and mite eggs and to smother overwintering insects and their eggs.

◉ Lime sulfur, an inorganic control for mites and some plant-sucking insects, is commonly used on fruit trees.

◉ Neem oil is a derivative from the neem tree (*Azadirirachta indica*). It is considered to be only slightly toxic to mammals and does not persist in the environment. It is the pesticide I usually reach for on the few occasions that I use a pesticide. It is effective against many garden pests including aphids, caterpillars, mealybugs, thrips, and white flies and is also effective against diseases such as mildew and rust. Some gardeners use neem oil and insecticidal soaps alternately to kill insects over a broad range of stages. Neem oil was only recently approved for use in California so you may not find it listed in older gardening books. A popular brand of neem oil is Safer's BioNeem.

◉ Nicotine sulfate is a plant derivative that controls aphids, thrips, leafhoppers, and other sucking insects. Be careful; it is toxic to mammals, including household pets.

◉ Pheromones are attractants applied in lures to monitor the presence of insects so that other controls can be applied. In small areas they are used to disrupt insect mating and reduce future generations.

◎ Pyrethrum is a derivative from pyrethrum daisies. It kills many insects including aphids, beetles, flies, mealybugs, moth larvae, mosquitoes, and thrips. It loses its effectiveness within a few hours of exposure to sunlight.

◎ Rotenone, another plant derivative, is usually used as a dust to kill chewing insects such as beetles, slugs, loopers, mosquitoes, thrips, and flies.

◎ Sabadilla is a plant derivative that kills leafhoppers, caterpillars, and citrus thrips. Unfortunately it also kills honey bees.

◎ Soap (particularly insecticidal soap) is used to control aphids, mites, and other plant-sucking insects. It is best to test soap on part of the plant before spraying the entire plant because it is phytotoxic to a few plants under certain conditions. Several insecticidal soaps are mixtures of special fatty acids that are not toxic to most beneficial organisms but are toxic to most small insects.

WEEDING

A weed is simply a plant growing in the wrong place. One of my favorite stories is told by a friend who was hiking in the Himalayas. Knowing that she was interested in plants, the guide took her on a lengthy trek to see a rare plant. The plant was indeed interesting, even fanciful. But it was very familiar to her and is commonly known at home as the dandelion.

Weeding is an important aspect of gardening, because weeds steal moisture and nutrients from cultivated plants. Weeding is best done as soon as the weed is recognized as unwanted. The longer the weed remains in place the deeper its root structure becomes and the more difficult it is to remove. You want to get the weed up before it sets seed because a single weed can yield two hundred fifty thousand weed seeds. Gardeners usually develop the habit of pulling up weeds as they encounter them no matter what else they happen to be doing at the time.

Serious weeding is done with a tool that looks like a long screwdriver or with a weeding fork. Grab the weed with one hand and, with the other, push the tool down alongside the roots and pry them up as you pull the top up. Many weeds will grow back, so it is important to extricate the root.

Hoeing is done by moving a hoe back and forth over the surface of the soil to root up small weeds. Hoeing is most effective in early spring to eliminate small annual weeds. Care must be taken not to damage the surface roots and growth of cultivated plants growing nearby.

Weeding is also done with chemicals that work in one of three methods. Some chemicals, called pre-emergents, kill weed seeds as they sprout. Other chemicals kill whatever they touch by being absorbed into the leaves and stems or through the roots. Still other chemicals are selective—killing only broad-leafed plants or narrow-leafed plants.

Many gardeners in health-and-environment-conscious Northern California do not like the idea of chemical weed killers because many of the chemicals remain in the environment and do not break down quickly. I am one of those people, so you are not going to read a lot about chemical weed killers from me. After reading authoritative horticultural journals I have concluded, however, that there is one chemical weed killer that is believed to be relatively harmless to the environment. This is a chemical known as glyphosate, which acts on foliage and translocates down to the roots, killing many difficult weeds. It is strong enough to do in poison oak. Fortunately, glyphosate does not persist in the soil. A popular trade name for glyphosate is Roundup.

New to the market are several organic weed killers based on soap. Safer makes an herbicide called Superfast that destroys a leaf's cuticle layer with fatty acids that dehydrate the plant and cause it to die. These herbicides are quick and effective for spot control of annual weeds.

Of course you would not want to use chemical weed killers on a windy day. Be sure to read the label carefully. The weed killer does not know a rose bush from a perennial weed.

Reducing Weeds

Mulching is a way of cutting down on weeds because it eliminates their access to light and air.

Newly disturbed soil almost always produces a new crop of weeds because cultivation brings new weed seeds to the surface. One method of reducing weeds is to sprout weed seeds deliberately, hoe them down, water the bed again, and hoe the ground again a week or two later when new weed seeds have sprouted. This two-step process can be repeated and is often employed in creating wildflower gardens.

Sometimes black plastic is laid over the soil of a new bed and left in place for a few months. The theory is that the plastic heats up in the sun and cooks the weed seeds. Sometimes plastic is laid down along a path to eliminate weeds, and soil or gravel is placed on top of the plastic. I do not recommend this method of weed reduction because, in my experience, the plastic breaks down and pokes through the soil in unsightly tufts.

You should know that not all gardeners believe in weeding. Some feel that weeds draw beneficial insects and should be left in the garden. And that brings us back to where we started. There are many ways to create a fine garden, including one that makes room for weeds.

Part Two: Month-by-Month Guide

JANUARY GARDENING

FEBRUARY GARDENING

MARCH GARDENING

APRIL GARDENING

MAY GARDENING

JUNE GARDENING

JULY GARDENING

AUGUST GARDENING

SEPTEMBER GARDENING

OCTOBER GARDENING

NOVEMBER GARDENING

DECEMBER GARDENING

... J a n u a r y ...

January is a month for curling up in a cozy armchair with a stack of garden catalogs within reach. With rain slashing at the windows, it is a time for dreaming of the resurrection of spring. When perusing a garden catalog, look for plants from climates similar to our own, plants that will endure our long summer drought season. The full-color photographs in many of the more elaborate catalogs make plant buying easy. Some of the choicer, rarer plants, however, are sold through small mail-order nurseries that cannot afford to publish a full-color catalog. Some of the most interesting catalogs are listed at the Reference Guide starting on page 301. Order from catalogs promptly to avoid having to accept substitutions later in the season.

It is difficult to image droughts on January days when one storm after another is piling up off the coast and the sky does not clear for days. Alaskan storms drop snow in the high Sierra Nevada; Hawaiian storms bring warm rains that melt the snow and bring the danger of flooding. Central Valley gardeners will also have to contend with radiation fog (also known as tule fog) as airborne moisture from the rain-soaked earth condenses into a fog so thick that it closes down airports.

The cold wet month of January with the danger of frost or heavy snow is not a favorite one for gardeners. Yet, oddly, some of the year's most important gardening tasks occur in the cold winter months. On the rainless days gardeners attend to the tasks of dormant spraying and pruning, and they buy bare-root plants.

KEY GARDEN TASKS

All Gardeners

◉ Order now from seed catalogs. If you wait too long, you may have to accept substitutions later in the season.

◉ Order bare-root roses and fruit trees from specialty nurseries. They will usually stop shipping bare-root plants by the end of March.

◉ Move garden plants brought indoors for the holidays back outside if they will not be subject to frost or snow.

◉ Make sure you have adequate drainage for heavy rain storms, see page 56.

◉ Constant dry heat from heating systems stresses indoor plants. Check them for signs of yellowing or wilting; they may need more water and an occasional misting. Fertilize indoor flowering plants that are in bloom now.

▲ ▼ ▲

Coastal Gardeners

In addition to the tasks listed for all gardeners, watch out for frost. Be ready to cover susceptible plants or move them to a sheltered location. See page 47.

◉ Prune roses, deciduous fruit trees, and ornamental shrubs. Work from the inside of the plants toward the outside. Remove diseased or dead branches as well as branches crossing or rubbing each other. Then prune the exterior for an attractive form. Leave the pruning of spring-flowering trees and shrubs until after they have bloomed. See page 49 for more complete instructions.

If desired, spray deciduous shrubs and fruit trees with a dormant spray to kill overwintering insects; see page 47.

◉ Shop for bare-root plants and plant them when the soil is dry enough to dig properly. See page 45.

◉ Cymbidiums should be in bud now. Protect them from frost (see page 47) or bring them indoors to a cool location.

In nurseries, look for bedding plants such as cinerarias and primroses to give an instant color boost to the entryway or window boxes.

▲ ▼ ▲

Central Valley Gardeners

In addition to the tasks listed for all gardeners, watch out for frost. The weather is likely to be truly cold this month. Be ready to cover susceptible plants or to move them to a sheltered location. See page 47.

◉ Prune roses, deciduous fruit trees, and ornamental shrubs. Work from the inside of the plants toward the outside. Remove diseased or dead branches as well as branches crossing or rubbing each other. Then prune the exterior for an attractive form. Leave the pruning of spring-flowering trees and shrubs until after they have bloomed. See page 49 for more complete instructions.

If desired, spray deciduous shrubs and fruit trees with a dormant spray to kill overwintering insects; see page 47. It is particularly important to use a lime sulfur spray for peach and nectarine trees to prevent a fungus commonly known as peach leaf curl, which causes distorted leaves and scarred fruit.

◉ Shop for bare-root plants and plant them when the soil is dry enough to dig properly. See page 45.

◉ Look for colorful bedding plants such as calendulas and chrysanthemums in the nursery to give an instant color boost to the entryway or window boxes.

▲ ▼ ▲

High Mountain Gardeners

In addition to the tasks listed for all gardeners, pay attention to the damage snow may do to the garden. Lighten the weight on shrub and tree branches by knocking the snow off.

◉ When a sunny day breaks through the winter storms, walk around the garden inspecting broken limbs and branches. When the sun melts the ice, get out your pruning shears or saw and recut torn branches to remove damaged areas. Now that the branch pattern is clearly visible on deciduous trees and shrubs, prune them to attractive shapes. For more on pruning, see page 43.

◉ Consider placing a potted cotoneaster with its colorful red berries or a carefully pruned potted pine in the entryway for a visual feast on wintry days.

APPLES

For buying bare-root apples see the section on Bare-Root plants, page 45.
For winter pruning of apple trees, see the section on Pruning, page 50.

Bare-root apple trees are sold in January; the apple is probably the most widely grown fruit in the home gardens of Northern California. Apples do well in areas with winter chill and mild summers. In areas that are not prime for growing apples (apples need five to seven weeks when the temperature is below 45°F), select more adaptable varieties. In hot areas, such as around Sacramento, green-skinned apples do better than red-skinned varieties. High mountain gardeners should do well with 'Sierra Beauty' and 'McIntosh.' Remember that many apples need another variety of apple that blooms at the same time as a pollinator; a nurseryperson or charts commonly found in apple catalogs will simplify buying apple trees that will pollinize one another. Some apple trees are self-fertile and do not require another tree to produce apples.

All apples have an interesting genetic history since they are among the oldest cultivated fruits. Apple seeds and apple cuttings crossed the Atlantic with the Pilgrims. Over the next two hundred years, apple trees spread across the continent. Although folklore has Johnny Appleseed with a bag slung over his shoulder randomly scattering seeds across America, the actual Johnny Appleseed, also known as John Chapman (1774–1845), knew that apples grown from seeds do not necessarily resemble their parents. Mr. Chapman established a chain of nurseries that grew apple saplings. By the time of his death, his nurseries had reached as far as Indiana.

The home gardener can grow a wide variety of apples. Through the miracle of grafting, several varieties can be grown on a single tree. Grafting is like going back in a time machine. You can, for example, taste exactly the same classic dessert apple, 'Calville blanche d'hiver' that grew in the gardens of King Louis XIII in 1627. You can taste the apple with the longest history—the 'Api' (now known as the Lady apple), first developed by the Etruscans and later cultivated by American colonists.

Those unaccustomed to home-grown varieties may be surprised to discover how widely apples vary in taste. Commercially grown varieties are usually chosen for a neutral taste and a uniformly blemish-free, shiny skin that will please almost anybody except for those fussy gardeners who have tasted just how complexly flavored apples can be. Having tasted the pleasures of the varieties available to home growers, gardeners may soon discover that they want one of that and that and that. Growing your own apples means that you can indulge in a flavor not suited to everyone's taste. I am very fond of the 'King of Tompkins', which has several qualities that do not endear it to others. This apple can grow very large, as big as a grapefruit, and its texture is very crisp and to some palates coarse. Sometimes it develops an odd quality called water core, which makes the flesh translucent and quite sweet. Its origins are unknown but records of it date to at least 1804.

Unusual apples are the province of the gardener. Another one of my favorites is a sweet apple with pink flesh called 'Pink Pearl.' It was introduced in 1944 by the apple breeder Albert Etter, who lived in California near Garberville. He hybridized it from 'Surprise,' a cultivar introduced in the states from Europe about 1850. It is thought that 'Surprise' was derived from *Malus pulila* var *Niedzwetzkyana,* whose name indicates its own more distant origin.

For Northern California nurseries that sell antique apple trees, see page 302.

Apple Growing Simplified

Botanical name: *Malus.* Apples have been bred for so long that it is difficult to assign modern cultivars to any one species of *Malus.*

Common name: Apple.

Site preference: Plant apple trees in full sun, in a site sheltered from the wind.

Soil conditions: Many soils are suitable, particularly deep soil.

Water: Water regularly.

Nutrients: Fertilize moderately with nitrogen in spring.

Problems: Paint the trunk of the tree with a diluted white latex paint to discourage borers and prevent sunscald.

Special care: Take care to select an apple that is self-fertile or have a suitable apple called a pollinator available for cross-fertilization.

Hints: Except in areas where apples thrive, it is essential to find out which cultivars are known to do well locally before ordering and planting apple trees.

Apple Favorites for Northern California

LATE-SUMMER HARVEST

'Red Astrachan'—Many consider this old Russian apple (introduced from England in about 1825) to be the very best pie apple. It is medium-sized with a red blush over a yellow skin.

'Rosebrook Gravenstein'—This crisp, juicy variety is considered to be the prettiest red-striped Gravenstein. It needs a pollinator.

FALL HARVEST

'Ashmead's Kernel' (about 1700)—This golden russet English apple is a favorite of many for its sugary, aromatic qualities.

'Cox's Orange Pippin' (1830) —The English consider this their favorite dessert apple. It does well in cool climates and when espaliered.

'Tompkins King' also called 'King of Tompkins' (1750)—A large, classic apple that is an excellent keeper with an amazingly crisp texture.

'Pink Pearl' (1944)—The pink flesh surprises everyone. It tastes as good as it looks. Very pretty, dark pink blossoms make it ornamental.

'Sierra Beauty' (year unknown)—A handsome apple that is known for its crisp texture and tart, juicy taste.

'Winter Banana' (1876)—A mild, pretty apple beloved by kids. It is an excellent pollinator and will survive heat better than most apples.

WINTER HARVEST

'Calville blanche d'hiver' (1598)—A favorite of the French, this apple has a sweet flavor.

'Api' or Lady (before 1600)—A very small, decorative apple that is very old.

'Spitzenberg' (1700s)—A flavorful apple that was Thomas Jefferson's favorite.

BALCONY AND ENTRYWAY GARDENS

Gardeners limited to the small spaces of a deck or balcony and those wishing to enhance an entryway should continue to transplant winter-flowering plants into pots. Azaleas, calendulas, cyclamen, and primroses are good choices. Be sure to keep potted plants that are sheltered from rain well watered.

BARE-ROOT PLANTS

In January bare-root plants and trees (see list below) are available. These are plants that are dug up while dormant and sold without any soil clinging to their roots, which makes them easier to handle and hence less expensive—about half the price—than container-grown plants. Bare-root plants tend to adjust quickly to a new location because they do not have to make a transition from nursery container soil to your garden soil.

Now is the time to buy bare-root plants from your nursery or a mail-order catalog. When buying a bare-root plant from the nursery, look for smooth, well-developed, knot-free roots, unblemished bark, plump buds, and a healthy, well-branched top. Many bare-root plants will have a swollen section above the roots where one variety has been grafted onto a more vigorous rootstock.

> ### BARE-ROOT PLANTS INCLUDE:
>
> - Roses, both modern and antique
> - Shade trees
> - Vines, such as clematis, wisteria, and grapes
> - Fruit trees such as apples, pears, and plums
> - Flowering shrubs, such as lilacs
> - Berries, both blueberries and cane berries
> - Strawberry plants and asparagus plants
> - Artichokes and rhubarb

If your garden soil is too wet and heavy for planting, cover the roots of the bare-root plant with damp soil for planting later (see instructions on the following page). As long as the plants are in a cool, shaded area with their roots protected, they will wait a few weeks. Do not wait too long, however. Soon they will start sending shoots out and burst into leaf.

Bare-root Planting Directions

1. Soak the bare-root plant in a bucket of water for a few hours. Dig a hole a little deeper than the roots of the plant. Pack some of the dirt from the hole into a cone that reaches almost to the top of the hole.

2. Place the bare-root plant over the cone of dirt so that the bud union (a thickening where the roots meet the plant trunk) is just above the soil level. Drape the roots over the cone. Backfill with dirt and water well.

 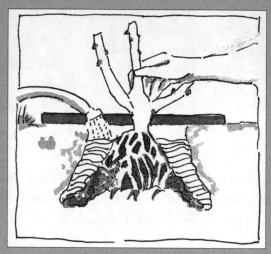

BIRDS

Even gardeners who do not normally feed birds may want to help them survive the hardships of winter. What do birds want? Their favorite foods include black-striped sunflower seeds, oil-type sunflower seeds, sunflower kernels, red and white proso millet, and peanuts. A winter treat that offers birds a source of quick, high energy is suet (a form of fat available from a butcher) held in a nylon mesh bag (of the type often used to sell bulk produce) or stuffed into a pine cone. Suet is offered only in winter when cooler temperatures keep it from turning rancid. Commercially packaged combinations of suet and birdseed are available. Place the bird foods where feeding birds will not become cat food.

CLIVIAS

Buy clivias from nurseries now while they are in bloom. In addition to the familiar bright-orange-flowered standard, there are many new varieties, including a white one. Clivias bloom in areas too dark for most other flowering plants.

CYMBIDIUMS

Cymbidiums should be coming into bloom soon. It is a good time to purchase them. Feed plants that have not yet bloomed with a bloom-promoting fertilizer. Do not feed blooming plants but con-

tinue to water them. Watch out for snails around the flower spikes. Once the buds have reached full size, bring the cymbidium indoors where the warm temperatures will encourage the blooms to open. Many cymbidiums have a sweet fragrance that is much appreciated in winter. In most areas of Northern California, cymbidiums should be protected from frost. See page 87 for more information on growing these lovely plants.

DORMANT SPRAYING

Dormant spraying is done in two or three doses. The first application is made in December or January (see page 279). Dormant spraying with horticultural oils kills overwintering insect eggs, mites, softbodied insects, and some scales by blocking the supply of oxygen and suffocating the pests. Deciduous fruit trees, some deciduous shrubs, and rose bushes should be sprayed after they have lost their leaves. Horticultural oils (also called dormant oils) are highly refined petroleum oils that are manufactured specifically for use on plants. Follow the directions on the horticultural oil, use a good sprayer, and aim the fine spray onto the bare branches and limbs. Spray only when the temperature is above 45°F. Dormant spraying is usually limited to fruit trees and roses.

Note: Do not spray Japanese maples or blue spruce with horticultural oil.

Mineral solutions of lime sulfur or hydrated lime and copper sulfate are also sometimes used for dormant spraying to control specific pests on specific trees. Mineral solutions can be combined with horticultural oil for broader coverage. Some of these sprays are caustic, so be sure to wear protective clothing, goggles, and rubber gloves.

Lime sulfur controls anthracnose, apple scab, brown rot, peach leaf curl, and powdery mildew. It is frequently used on peach trees and on other fruit trees as well. Peach leaf curl, a water-activated fungus, attacks during the blossoming stage; it is important to spray peach trees with lime sulfur and oil just before the pink buds open, when they resemble popcorn about to pop. Note that lime and sulfur are very caustic, so protect yourself.

Bordeaux mixture (hydrated lime and copper sulfate) controls brown rot, peach leaf curl, some grape diseases, some apple diseases, downy mildew, and many fungal diseases.

Sulfur controls fungal spores, brown rot, peach scab, apple scab, and powdery mildew.

FROST

January is one of the coldest months of the year in Northern California. Gardeners should watch for signs of approaching frost: a cloudless sky, still air (no wind), cold (less than 45°F by 10 P.M.), and dry (no moisture condensing on windshields).

Plants that need to be protected from frost include bougainvillea, citrus, fuchsia, and succulents. Susceptible plants in containers should be moved under the eaves of an overhanging roof or beneath a leafy tree. Plants that cannot be moved should be covered with burlap, plastic, old drapes, or newspaper arranged over stakes set in the ground. The covering, particularly if it is plastic, should not touch the plants. Remove the covering the next morning when the temperature rises.

In most of coastal Northern California, where the temperature does not go much below freezing and the frost is short-lived, you can also protect vulnerable plants by spraying them with an antitranspirant. Available at nurseries, antitranspirants are commonly used on indoor Christmas trees and greens to form a protective coating on foliage to hold in moisture. This is probably the easiest method of frost protection, as the gardener does not need to monitor the weather each night. Each application lasts several months, so antitranspirants are usually sprayed on twice during the cold season.

When a plant is injured by frost, it is best to leave the damaged portions on the plant to protect the portion below the damage until the cold season has passed. For more information see Frost, page 14.

FRUIT TREES

Fruit trees are dormant in January. Many fruit trees are sprayed with horticultural oil to kill overwintering pests (see Dormant Spraying, this month, page 47), and some are pruned (see Pruning Fruit Trees, this month, page 49). New fruit trees are sold as bare-root plants (see Bare-Root, this month, page 45). For suggestions on selecting apple trees for Northern California, see Apples, this month, page 43.

HOLIDAY PLANTS

January is the time to deal with outdoor plants that were brought indoors for the holidays. Living Christmas trees should be outdoors by now. The dry indoor air may have caused the soil in the container to dry out to the point where wetting it again is difficult. The easiest method of soaking the container is to plunge it into a tub of water until the bubbling stops. Alternatively, you can add a wetting agent (available in nursery stores) to the water. If you intend to plant a living Christmas tree in the ground, remember that most grow very large.

Flowering holiday plants such as azaleas, cinerarias, cyclamen, and poinsettias should have the florist's wrapping removed to allow for better drainage. Trim away dead blossoms and keep the plants moist while indoors. Outdoors, put them in a sheltered spot until you are ready (and the soil is ready) to give them a permanent home.

HOUSEPLANTS

Winter heating systems are hard on houseplants. The gardener may be so caught up in the holiday activities that plants go unwatered and then wilt. Fortunately, a number of houseplants will politely endure neglect. The best houseplants for forgetful gardeners are piggy-back plants (which recover miraculously from water stress), Swedish ivy, mother-in-law's tongue, golden pothos, and the rubber plant.

PRUNING

Pruning fruit trees is covered below.

Pruning roses is covered later in this month, page 51.

Woody plants are generally pruned just before new growth starts; which is usually in late winter or early spring. The worst time to prune is right after leaves emerge in spring, when the plant can ill afford to lose foliage. Prune dormant deciduous plants, such as fruit trees, roses, grapes, and cane berries, after their leaves have fallen and before their buds begin to swell. Of course, do not prune spring-blooming plants until they finish blooming.

Two basic pruning techniques are used in general pruning. Thinning cuts remove entire branches. Heading cuts shorten branches and stimulate latent buds that produce new growth.

Begin pruning with thinning cuts and then use selective heading cuts.

Prune from the bottom up and from the interior of the plant to the exterior.

See page 31 for details on these techniques.

Pruning Fruit Trees

I strongly recommend that gardeners with fruit trees invest in a good book on the art of pruning fruit trees; a very young fruit tree requires formative training, which is not covered here. Also a good pruning book will illustrate a variety of styles for training fruit trees from the classic urn-shaped tree in a small orchard to the espaliering of trees along wires against a wall. Fruit trees are pruned to encourage fruit. Fruit is formed either on spurs, which resemble short, stubby twigs, or on new growth. Sometimes fruit is formed on both. Depending upon where the fruit is formed, the tree is pruned either to encourage spurs or to force new growth.

⚜ Apple trees are pruned to open the interior and lower branches to light—often by shortening upper branches. This helps decrease susceptibility to mildew. Mature apple trees are pruned to remove crossing branches and overly vigorous branches.

It is very important to know *where* your apple tree bears fruit—improper pruning could severely curtail the crop. Most apple trees bear fruit on short stubby shoots called spurs that bear for up to twenty years. They are pruned to encourage spurs.

Apple trees that bear fruit at the tips of shoots grown the previous summer are pruned to force new growth. The gardener can always observe the tree during the summer to see where the fruit is carried.

⚜ Apricot trees bear fruit on both one-year-old wood and on spurs that bear annually for about four years. One method of pruning is to head back some of the older branches to force new growth in the spring. The idea is to prune enough to produce new fruiting spurs and to prune away old spurs that have lost their vigor.

⚜ Cherry trees have fruiting spurs that bear for a long time. Prune only to shape and remove dead or diseased wood.

⚜ Citrus trees do not require much, if any, pruning in the winter. Prune only to remove dead or diseased branches. See page 153 for a description of summer pruning.

⚜ Fig trees need only a light pruning in winter to remove crossing branches and dead or diseased wood.

⚜ Peach trees and nectarine trees are pruned heavily each winter because their fruit is produced on new wood. Mature trees may be pruned by shortening each branch of the previous year's growth by two-thirds, or by pruning out two of every three branches formed in the previous year, or by shortening some branches by two-thirds and removing other branches.

Alternatively, prune off half of the new growth by cutting out short branches and heading back long branches by one-third.

⚜ Pear trees are pruned lightly each year, using thinning rather than heading cuts, to remove crossed branches and any branch or twig that looks scorched, withered, or has black, sunken cankers.

⚜ Plum trees bear fruit on spurs. Japanese plum trees produce much more new growth each year than European plum trees do. (The popular 'Santa Rosa' is a Japanese plum.) Prune the vigorous growth of Japanese plum trees each year by shortening excessive vertical growth, cutting back new vertical growth by half and making the cut above one of the small outside (out-facing) branches. The half that remains will form fruit spurs during the summer and will bear fruit the year after that. Be sure and prune away the suckers, those spindly shoots that grow from the tree trunk at soil level.

Prune mature European plum trees only to remove overly vigorous and crossing branches and to thin new shoots.

Pruning to encourage spurs

1. Cut back a young side branch leaving between three and six buds (bumps under the thin bark).

2. The next winter cut the same branch back to the top flower bud. A flower bud is fatter than a slender branch bud. These flower buds will bear fruit.

3. The flower buds form spurs that will bear fruit year after year.

Pruning to force new growth

1. For the first winter leave the young side branch alone.

2. In the second winter cut back to the last top bud.

3. In the third winter cut back the entire branch, leaving only a stub.

4. In the fourth year start the cycle over again, by leaving the one-year-old branch intact until the following winter.

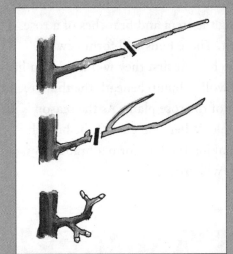

Spurs

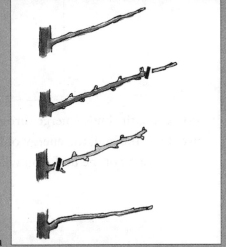

New growth

Pruning Roses

January is a good month to prune hybrid tea roses. Remember that they bloom only on new wood, so you want to promote as much healthy new wood as possible. Generally, roses should be cut back by between one-third and one-half, leaving canes at least eighteen inches long. Cut above a swelling bud pointing outward, away from the center of the bush. Remove all suckers and dead wood. Because climbing roses bloom on second-year wood, they should only be trimmed of twiggy growth and weak shoots.

Antique roses, also known as old garden roses, are very individual—unless you know where to prune, do not prune them. Because most antique roses are pruned after blooming, instructions on pruning them is given in the July section on page 187.

If you want to see rose pruning demonstrated, contact the nearest public rose garden and ask if consulting rosarians give demonstrations there. Nurseries and botanical gardens often offer pruning classes. Do not fret too much, however, over the proper technique. An astonishing study was done by the British Royal National Rose Society in which roses were essentially sheared back to a uniform eighteen inches high with little regard for the placement of the cuts.

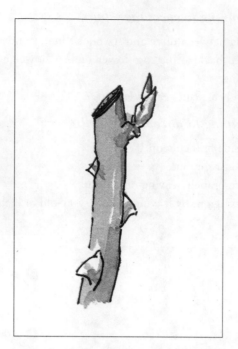

After three growing seasons this draconian pruning technique seemed to have caused no harm. Doubtless this is good news for the gardener who annually hacks away haphazardly at the rose garden. The rest of us will go on with our careful pruning, confident that California's benign climate favors those who leave as much healthy wood as practical. Rose pruning is easy once you learn how to recognize the buds that lie along the stem and branches of a rose plant. These buds will form new branches. At first they will feel like a little swollen bump beneath the thin green skin of the rose plant. As the season progresses, the buds emerge through the skin and are plainly visible. When you cut off the branch just above the bud, the energy of the rose plant is directed into making the bud form a branch. By the placement of the bud, you will see just where the new branch will grow.

Pruning Roses Simplified

Arm yourself with good-quality pruning tools. Loppers that can reach into a thorny rose bush are excellent. (A lopper has two relatively small blades and long fifteen-inch to thirty-inch handles.) A pair of sharp hand pruners will do most of the work. The shears should fit comfortably in your hand. Gloves, preferably thick leather gloves, are also useful. Very thick plastic gloves made just for pruning thorny shrubs are effective.

1. Begin by cutting away any dead, diseased, or puny-looking twiggy growth. Also remove any cane (branch) that rubs against or grows very close to another cane—always saving the more vigorous, healthy cane.

2. Now step back and look at the rose bush to picture the next few essential pruning cuts. Ideally you want a rose bush with vigorous canes radiating from the central bud union, that tough swollen joint that should be just above the soil. (The bud union is where the flowering variety was grafted onto another variety with more vigorous rootstock.) The center of the bush should be left open to let in air and light.

3. Reduce the length and the number of remaining canes to create a vigorous, balanced framework. Make each cut just above an outward growing bud (see illustration) to direct the new growth. Remember that in Northern California we try to save as many canes as possible—at least three and as many as ten canes should remain.

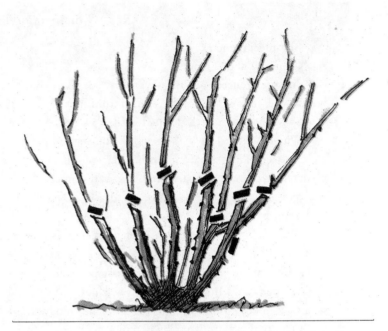

Pruning a Hybrid Tea or Grandiflora Rose

ROSES

For buying bare-root roses, see page 45.

Northern California is a prime rose-growing region. Advice on rose growing in this book is given on two levels, one for the casual grower and a more complex level for the rose fanatic.

Currently the fashion is for antique roses. New rose growers should know that antique roses, also called old garden roses, typically have a limited season of bloom. Modern roses bloom in Northern California from spring to early winter. Antique roses often look more like camellias or peonies than like hybrid tea roses. The new rose enthusiast should also know that there are modern roses that look like antique roses but bloom repeatedly throughout the growing season. Ask for these new "old garden roses" at the nursery or ask to see the David Austin hybrids. David Austin is an Englishman well known for breeding modern roses that look like antique roses.

Modern roses have been bred for different purposes. Hybrid tea roses are the hands-down favorite for cut flowers. They are bred to have long stems with a beautiful blossom at the end of each stem. Floribundas have been bred to create attractive shrubs with beautiful flowers in sprays of bloom at the end of each stem. Everything is relative: Floribundas are prettier shrubs than hybrid tea roses, but they are still known for their flowers rather than for their leaves or their splendid form. Grandifloras are larger shrubs than floribundas. They have flowers either in sprays of bloom or as a single bloom on each stem. Climbing roses are used to cover walls or trellises, but they do not really climb, they lean.

Rose Growing Simplified

Botanical name: *Rosa.*

Common name: Rose.

Site preference: Full sun for at least six hours, but inland gardeners should note that roses do not do well in areas where the temperature rises above 100°F.

Soil conditions: Well-drained fertile soil; mulch to keep down weeds and retain moisture.

Water: Water deeply and regularly during dry periods.

Nutrients: Roses bloom much better with heavy fertilizing, so feed them regularly with a complete fertilizer from spring to mid-fall. Add iron chelate or iron sulfate if the leaves turn yellow but the veins remain green—this is a condition called chlorosis. More specific instructions are given each month.

Pests: I do not believe in spraying insecticides or fungicides in my garden. Most rose growers, however, spray with a fungicide to control the three banes of Northern Californian rose growing: blackspot, mildew, and rust. The most popular fungicide is called Funginex. The same manufacturer combines fungicides with pesticides and calls the product Orthinex. Many rose growers spray with one of those products every eighteen days or so.

I try to avoid problems by planting my roses in full sun with lots of room for the wind to dry them out. I also water early in the morning, and spray the leaves with water to blast off aphids.

Planting: For the proper planting of bare-root roses, see the illustrations and instructions on page 46. Plant container-grown plants at any time except during really cold weather.

Pruning: Modern roses, especially hybrid tea roses, are pruned now; see page 52 for complete instructions and illustrations. Antique roses are generally pruned in the summer; see page 187.

Special care: To promote flowering during the blooming season, always cut a rose stem back to a branchlet with five leaves.

Bouquets: For terrific homemade rose preservatives, see page 142.

Antique roses are discussed on page 118. In January nurseries and even some supermarkets have many bare-root modern roses for sale, but the gardener will have to seek out a source for most antique roses. For mail-order nurseries, see page 306.

ROSE FAVORITES FOR NORTHERN CALIFORNIANS

The best advice on selecting roses will come from a local rosarian familiar with those roses that do best in your neighborhood. Write the American Rose Society (Box 30000, Shreveport, LA 71130) and ask for the name of consulting rose experts in your area. Their advice is free.

For mail-order nurseries, see page 306.

Modern Roses

These choices are based on vigor, bloom, and disease resistance in Northern California.

The best reds are 'National Trust,' for its beautifully formed petals and disease resistance, and the fragrant 'Mr. Lincoln.'

The best pinks are 'Bewitched' for its fragrant, large blossoms, and 'Queen Elizabeth.'

The best yellow is 'Gold Medal,' for its abundance of bloom.

The best whites are 'Honor,' for its vigorous growth and long-stemmed, large blossoms, and the nicely shaped 'Pascali.'

The best exhibition rose is the creamy pink 'Touch of Class,' for its dramatically superior flower form.

My own favorite is 'French Lace,' for its disease resistance and its profusion of exquisite ivory blooms blushed with shell pink and a pale green.

Fragrant Roses

Fragrant modern roses include 'Fragrant Cloud,' 'Mr. Lincoln,' 'Sutter's Gold,' 'Perfume Delight,' and 'Pink Peace.'

Fragrant antique roses include 'Belle de Crécy,' 'Comte de Chambord,' 'Ferdinand Pichard,' 'Maiden's Blush,' and 'Rosa Mundi.'

Antique Roses

'Old Blush' dates from 1752. It has fragrant, pink flowers resembling cabbage roses, and it blooms in summer through fall.

'Austrian Copper' dates from 1590 and blooms once a year in a brilliant orangish yellow.

'Reine des Violettes' dates from 1860. It is a tall, nearly thornless bush with repeated waves of dusky blue violet flowers.

'Rosa Mundi' dates from 1581 and blooms once a year with pink flowers striped with red.

See page 118 for fuller descriptions of these roses.

Notably Tough Rugosas

High mountain gardeners and seaside gardeners will do well with very hardy rugosa roses.

'Frau Dagmar Hartopp' is spectacular with crepe-paper textured, pink petals and bright yellow stamens. It is also fragrant, blooms repeatedly, and makes an excellent cut flower.

'Robusta' is a long-blooming, scarlet-flowered, fragrant shrub.

Heavy rain can create havoc in the garden. If damage has already occurred, examine the area to determine where drainage needs to be improved. Remember to direct water flow from drainspouts away from the house foundation and away from the roots of trees or shrubs that cannot tolerate swamp life. Also remember not to walk on heavily saturated lawns and planting areas because it compacts the earth too much.

Potted plants should be tipped over on their sides to allow water to drain out. Look plants over for signs of fungus or mildew. Some landscapers wash black sooty mildew away with Ivory soap and water.

Succulents should not be cold and wet simultaneously because the water in their fleshy tissue may turn into ice. If parts of a succulent have already turned to mush, cut those parts away and allow the cut to heal over. Succulents that have rotted away at the bottom should be gently uprooted. Cut away the rot, let the cut heal over, and then replant the succulent in a moist, well-draining medium such as sand or perlite. It will probably develop new roots.

Be sure to pull away any muddy soil that has collected around the base of a shrub or a tree or the trunk may begin to rot.

VEGETABLES

In January, cold weather usually limits growth in the vegetable garden. Coastal gardeners with the milder weather can grow and harvest through the winter. But, frankly, most gardeners put the vegetable patch to rest for the winter because few gardeners seem to enjoy gardening in the rain. Enthusiasts, however, may want to continue the vegetable garden with winter crops. Plant seeds of arugula, bok choy, fava beans, lettuce, mizuna, radish, and spinach. Also plant garlic, onions, and shallots. From flats, plant out cold-tolerant lettuces and cabbage.

WATERING AND SPRINKLER SYSTEMS

January and February are typically rainy months in Northern California, so turn off your automatic watering system and let the weather dictate when you turn the system on again. Remember to water plants underneath house eaves.

WILDFLOWERS

Although it is easier to sow wildflower seeds in the warmer, drier fall season, it is possible to sow them in January. The complete description of growing wildflowers, including many recommendations, is in the November section under Wildflowers on page 269. Here is a quick review of the basics: Begin by removing all weeds and grasses. Do not add fertilizer to the soil. Mix wildflower seeds with sand so that the seeds can be scattered more evenly.

Lightly rake the seeds into the soil, pushing the rake back and forth to make certain the seeds are worked in well. Then use your hand or a piece of cardboard to tamp down the seeds and improve germination.

Hide the seeds from birds by broadcasting a light layer of compost over the seeds. Sprinkle the ground with a fine spray of water. Seed germination depends upon moisture, so if the rains do not fall, water weekly with a fine spray to keep the ground moist.

... february ...

What bulbs are in bloom?

February is a month of heavy rain and freezing temperatures in much of Northern California. The weather does not beckon gardeners outdoors. There are, however, usually one or two days of false spring—days so gloriously bright and unseasonably warm that thoughts turn quickly to the garden.

Now is the time to complete winter pruning of deciduous trees, vines, fruit trees, and roses. Finish shopping for bare-root plants. By the end of March, bare-root plants in nurseries will be potted up and sold at higher prices. And send in catalog orders before the merchandisers run out of stock in the springtime rush.

The coming of spring is evident in the buds forming on early blooming deciduous shrubs. Bring some of the winter prunings indoors to force those buds into bloom. It usually takes between ten to fourteen days in a warm room for the buds to open. The gardening season is about to begin—by the end of this month, we will have gained a precious hour of daylight, which is good news for both plants and gardeners.

All Gardeners

Purchase bare-root plants. Cover the roots until you have the time and the weather is right for planting.

❀ Order bare-root fruit trees from specialty nurseries. They will usually stop shipping bare-root fruit trees by the end of March.

❀ Send in orders to seed companies before they run out of stock later in spring.

❀ Clean and repair garden tools. Sharpen the blades of pruning tools and shovels. Service the lawn mower.

▲ ▼ ▲

Coastal Gardeners

In addition to the tasks listed for all gardeners, finish pruning deciduous trees, shrubs, vines, fruit trees, and roses (see page 70).

❀ If desired, and deciduous plants have not leafed out yet, apply a final application of dormant spray to kill overwintering insects (see page 65).

❀ Select and plant azaleas, camellias, and rhododendrons while they are in bloom.

❀ Cyclamen, cineraria, and primroses purchased in bloom from the nursery make a handsome display in coastal gardens.

▲ ▼ ▲

Central Valley Gardeners

In addition to the tasks listed for all gardeners, complete pruning of deciduous trees, shrubs, vines, fruit trees, and roses (see page 70).

❀ If desired, and if deciduous plants have not leafed out yet, apply a last application of dormant spray to kill overwintering insects (see page 65).

It is particularly important to use a lime sulfur spray for peach and nectarine trees to prevent a fungus commonly known as peach leaf curl that causes distorted leaves and scarred fruit.

❀ Select and plant azaleas, camellias, and rhododendrons while they are in bloom. Particularly well suited to Central Valley gardens are the camellias 'Ballet Dancer,' 'Elegans,' also known as 'Chandler Elegans,' 'Shiro-Chan,' 'C. M. Wilson,' and 'Mathotiana.'

▲ ▼ ▲

High Mountain Gardeners

In addition to the tasks listed for all gardeners, keep clearing away heavy snow that may be building up on tree branches and shrubs.

❀ When a sunny day breaks through the winter storms, walk around the garden inspecting broken limbs and branches. When the sun melts the ice, get out your pruning shears or saw and recut torn branches to remove damaged areas. Now that the branch pattern is clearly visible on deciduous trees and shrubs, prune them to attractive shapes. For more on pruning, see page 70.

❀ If you use insulating plastic-foam covers (often called rose cones) around roses, remember to remove them temporarily during bouts of warm weather. The cones act like greenhouses on mild sunny days, and roses are likely to prematurely sprout. Be sure to put the cones back around the roses when cold weather returns.

During the height of the pollen season, from late February to June, there are often thousands of pollen grains in every cubic meter of air. Only about twenty-five to thirty popular landscape plants are responsible for most plant-related allergies in California, so the gardener can alleviate much of the misery. Grasses, particularly Bermuda grass, are the worst culprits. Pollen from the trees listed on the right is known to aggravate allergies.

- Acacia
- Almond (*Prunus*)
- Ash (*Fraxinus*)
- Birch (*Betula*)
- Cottonwood (*Populus*)
- Elm (*Ulmus*)
- Fruitless mulberry (*Morus alba*), male
- Oak (*Quercus*)
- Olive (*Olea europaea*)
- Pecan (*Carya illinoensis*)
- Privet (*Ligustrum*)
- Sycamore (*Platanus*)
- Walnut (*Juglans*)
- Willow (*Salix*)

Most colorful and showy flowers are safe, because they are pollinated by insects. Avoid flowering plants that are pollinated by the wind. The latter usually have drab, inconspicuous flowers often in clusters or tassels, such as grasses, cattails, and ragweeds.

AZALEAS

Now is an excellent time to purchase azaleas. They are in bloom and they are also dormant, which is the best time to plant them. They grow slowly, so look for pleasing form and leaves as well as for pretty blooms.

You may want to try a tip I learned from a neighbor whose azaleas seemed to bloom much longer than anyone else's azaleas. Every morning, she emptied used coffee grounds as a mulch around the azaleas.

Be sure and look for one of our most beautiful native shrubs, the Western azalea (*Rhododendron occidentale*), which produces fragrant, showy flowers each spring and bronze leaves in fall.

See also Rhododendrons, page 71.

BALCONY AND ENTRYWAY GARDENS

Place pots of blooming tulips or daffodils where they can be readily enjoyed. A potted flowering quince is one of the most charming and picturesque of the early bloomers.

BARE-ROOT PLANTS

February is the second month that bare-root plants are likely to be sold in nurseries in Northern California. If you have not already done so, now is the time to purchase bare-root plants and trees before supplies run out. Here is what you need to know if bare-root plants are new to you. Bare-root plants are dug up while dormant and sold without any soil clinging to their roots, which makes them easier to handle and hence less expensive—about half the price—than container-grown plants. Bare-root plants tend to adjust quickly to a new location because they do not have to make a transition from nursery-container soil to your garden soil. They were discussed in January; please see page 45 for directions on how to select bare-root plants, illustrated instructions on planting them, and a list of common bare-root plants.

BULBS

Fertilize spring-blooming bulbs as the foliage emerges. Some growers recommend dried blood meal; follow the directions on the package, sprinkling the blood meal around the emerging foliage. If you wait to feed bulbs until after they bloom, as is sometimes recommended, the foliage may die before the fertilizer reaches the root system, and then the whole effort will be wasted as the bulb will not be able to take up the fertilizer.

Cut off the heads of tulips that have already bloomed and are starting to fade. It is not necessary to remove the fading blooms of other bulbs.

CAMELLIAS

Favorites of Northern California gardeners, camellias are also magnificent container plants, well suited to the city garden with limited space. They should be sheltered from strong wind and hot sun. They like rich, organic soil and must be planted high with their trunk base slightly above the soil level. Mulch camellias to keep the soil moist. Despite these pampering instructions, camellias positively thrive in the hot Central Valley; Sacramento, where more than eight hundred varieties bloom, is famous for its annual Camellia Festival. Camellias are in bloom now so this is an excellent time to select them.

CAMELLIA FAVORITE VARIETIES

These are all *Camellia japonica* varieties. *Camellia sasanqua*, which blooms in the fall, is discussed in the November section on page 258.

'Guilio Nuccio' is considered by many experts to be the finest camellia in the world. It has very large rose coral flowers with two layers of petals and fluted inner petals.

'C. M. Wilson' has very large, pale pink flowers that resemble anemone blossoms.

'Glen 40' has flowers with many deep red petals. It is an especially good container plant.

'Kumasaka' makes a profusion of deep pink flowers resembling roses in full bloom.

'Mrs. D. W. Davis' is a showstopper with its immense pale pink flowers.

Camellia Petal Blight

If the camellia blossoms are turning a ghastly brown, suspect the dreaded camellia petal blight. Pick a fallen brown blossom. Try to feel (then see) tiny, hard black masses like small grains that indicate disease. To prevent the spread of petal blight, pick up all the fallen blossoms. Then remove all the ground mulch beneath the infected plants. Discard both blossoms and mulch.

CLIVIAS

The dark days of winter can be brightened with a flowering clivia (*Clivia miniata*) also known as a kaffer lily. They actually grow better without direct sunlight. Visit a nursery to select one of the newer French or Belgian hybrids that bloom from December to April.

CYMBIDIUMS

Standard cymbidiums should be in bloom now through April. February is a good time to purchase these easily grown orchids. Feed plants that have not yet bloomed with a bloom-promoting fertilizer. Do not feed blooming plants, but continue to water them. Protect them from frost. Cymbidiums are divided after they are finished blooming, which will be by March for the miniature varieties and by May for the standard varieties. See Cymbidiums in March, page 87, for more information on growing and dividing cymbidiums.

DAFFODILS

Daffodils (*Narcissus*) make fine bouquets. Cut them with a sharp knife just as their blossoms begin to open, and then leave them in a deep pail of warm water for several hours. Some gardeners add a teaspoon of sugar to the vase when they are arranging them to preserve them longer. Be sure to leave the tall green leaves outside still attached to the bulb. This foliage provides nutrients for next year's bloom. Let the foliage wither and yellow. If you cut the foliage too early, you may not get bloom the subsequent year. Daffodils are planted in the fall; see page 224 for more information.

DORMANT SPRAYING

If deciduous plants have not leafed out yet, and you did not apply the final application of dormant spray in January, then apply it now to kill overwintering insects. Dormant spraying with horticultural oil is particularly helpful to gardeners who grow roses and fruit trees. See page 279.

FORCING BLOOMS

The approach of Valentine's Day brings a longing for great masses of bloom to herald spring on a glum winter day. The good news is that branches of apple, cherry, forsythia, and quince can all be forced into early bloom indoors. Other early bloomers such as witch hazel, winter honeysuckle, pussy willow, and star magnolia are also good for forcing. Forsythias are so easy to force into bloom that they often grow roots while in the vase.

1. Select branches on which the flower buds have already begun to swell and cut off a two- to three-foot length.

2. Smash the cut ends with a hammer (to increase absorbency) and place the branches in a deep container of water.

3. Change the water every few days and keep the container in a bright place indoors where the room temperature is between 60°F and 70°F.

The buds should open in about two weeks. Some gardeners add copper pennies to the water. Others dip the ends of the branches in wax after the flowers have opened.

FROST

February is one of the coldest months of the year in Northern California. Although this information on frost was covered in January, it is repeated here because frost protection of vulnerable plants is essential, and the same measures taken to protect plants in January must be repeated in February. Gardeners should watch for signs of approaching frost: a cloudless sky, still air (no wind), cold (less than 45°F by 10 P.M.), and dry (no moisture condensing on windshields).

Plants that need to be protected from frost include bougainvillea, citrus, fuchsia, and succulents. Susceptible plants in containers should be moved under the eaves of an overhanging roof or beneath a leafy tree. Plants that cannot be moved should be covered with burlap, plastic, old drapes, or newspaper arranged over stakes set in the ground. The covering, particularly if it is plastic, should not touch the plants. Remove the covering the next morning when the temperature rises.

In most of coastal Northern California, where the temperature does not go much below freezing and the frost is short-lived, you can also protect vulnerable plants by spraying them with an antitranspirant. Available at nurseries, antitranspirants are commonly used on indoor Christmas trees and greens to form a protective coating on foliage to hold in moisture. This is probably the easiest method of frost protection, as the gardener does not need to monitor the weather each night. Each application lasts several months, so antitranspirants are usually sprayed on twice during the cold season.

FROST DAMAGE

When a plant is injured by frost, it is best to leave the damaged portions on the plant to protect the portion below the damage. When you see regrowth on other parts of the plant, it is safe to prune off the damaged section. Have patience. Frequently plants look quite dead, but make an astonishing recovery.

FRUIT TREES

Continue to prune fruit trees, grapes, and cane berries. When the leaves appear, dormancy is broken, and it is too late to prune.

In general, the best time to prune any woody plant is just before new growth starts. That is usually in late winter or early spring. The worst time to prune is right after leaves emerge in spring when the plant can ill afford to lose foliage. Of course, you may want to bring branches of fruit trees indoors to bloom.

Pruning stimulates new growth and increased fruiting. Prune out dead wood that looks gray and brittle. Prune out branches that rub against each other. Pruning opens the interior of a plant to sunlight. Before shaping a fruit tree, learn its habits—some fruit only on old branches, others only on new growth.

See page 49 for a detailed description and illustrations of pruning.

HOUSEPLANTS

In February the gardener is likely to become restless. The weather is not conducive to gardening but the green thumbs are itching. Naturally, the gardener turns to houseplants. Like hemlines, houseplants cycle in and out of fashion. Following the renewed popularity of lava lamps and Fiestaware, houseplants are due for a second coming.

This time around, life ought to be a little easier for the indoor gardener. New cultivars, new potting mediums, and self-watering pots go a long way toward easing the chores. The standard Boston fern *(Nephrolepis exaltata* 'Bostoniensis') has been upgraded with a cultivar 'Dallas'. Although it is often described only as a miniature Boston fern, 'Dallas' is practically indestructible.

Even the durable African violet comes in preferred cultivars. The African Violet Society of America has an honor roll for cultivars that have appeared on lists of favorites for the past five years. Among the winners are:

- 'Boca Grande' (pink)
- 'Emilie Savage' (lavender blue)
- 'Frances Young' (light pink)
- 'Hart's Snow White'
- 'Melodie Kimi' (purple and white)
- 'Ming Blue' (light blue)
- 'Pay Dirt' (bright pink)
- 'Wrangler's Jealous Heart' (light pink)

Houseplant—Streptocarpus

Indoor gardeners looking for a flowering plant as easy as the African violet but more distinctive should consider its cousin, the streptocarpus. Larger and more dramatic than an African violet, it is still small enough to serve as a table centerpiece, growing between six and twelve inches high. At first glance, with its long sword-shaped leaves and brightly colored flowers, the streptocarpus looks more like the outdoor primrose.

There are many hybrid streptocarpus varieties. Some of them are in bright lipstick colors; others are in cool shades of lavender, blue, and purple. Many streptocarpus have dark stripes running down the throats of their trumpet-shaped flowers. There is even a white hybrid streptocarpus with red stripes.

Streptocarpus Growing Simplified

Botanical name: *Streptocarpus.*

Common name: Cape primrose; streptocarpus.

Site preference: Bright indoor light, but no direct sun, preferably a spot with additional humidity. Like African violets, they do well under fluorescent lights.

Soil conditions: Use a rich, fast-draining potting soil such as a mixture of sphagnum peat moss, perlite, and vermiculite. Use a wide clay pot rather than a deep pot, which would keep the roots too wet.

Water: Water evenly with tepid water, then let the soil dry out between weekly waterings. Constantly soggy soil leads to root rot.

Nutrients: Fertilize with high-phosphate liquid fertilizer to promote bloom, but do not mix it too strong or the plants will suffer. Fertilize every month from April through September.

Special care: Water promptly if the plants start to wilt.

Houseplant—Phalaenopsis

Ever since 1818, when William Cattley, an import merchant and amateur horticulturist, found a few bulbous stems used as packing material in a shipment of tropical plants, the world has been daffy about orchids.

Cattley had no idea what those bulbous stems were. He simply potted them up, and to the delight of future prom queens, the unknown bulbous stems developed gorgeous ruffled lavender flowers that were named *Cattleya labiata autumnalis*. Ever since, orchids have represented the unattainable—the ultimate in gardening expertise.

In truth some orchids are almost as easy to grow as weeds. Of my many houseplants, my favorite is the moth orchid. For all its refined elegance, it is the most dependable of indoor bloomers. I have one moth orchid that is in bloom six months of the year.

Like buying real estate, the secret to growing a moth orchid is location, location, location. Find the right spot, and then do not fuss too much. Weekly watering, regular fertilizer, and annual repotting is all the care a moth orchid requires for magnificent blooms.

Phalaenopsis Growing Simplified

Botanical name: *Phalaenopsis.*

Common name: Moth orchid.

Site preference: This is the important part. Phalaenopsis need bright light with little or no direct sunshine on the plants. Fluorescent light can be useful. Moist air is also helpful. The higher the temperature, the moister the air should be. Try growing a phalaenopsis in the bathroom or near the kitchen sink where the air is naturally moister. In really hot weather, phalaenopsis should be misted in the morning. They like the same temperatures as humans do, although these orchids also like temperatures as high as 85°F, which most people would find too hot.

Soil conditions: Special orchid bark.

Water: This is not as critical as you might think. A phalaenopsis grows in bark because its roots need air as well as water. Water once or twice a week, letting the water drain away completely.

Nutrients: Fertilize about every third watering with an orchid fertilizer or a houseplant fertilizer formulated for blooming plants. The timing of the applications is not critical but do fertilize regularly.

Hint: There is a trick to getting a phalaenopsis to bloom twice in one year. When the last bloom is beginning to wilt, cut the stem off just above the next swollen bud (feel along the stem for the raised bumps, if you do not see them). Weeks later the top bud will start to form a new bloom.

IN BLOOM IN FEBRUARY

⚘ Annuals: anemone, calendula, Iceland poppy, pansy, and sweet William

⚘ Perennials: abutilon, bergenia, clivia, cineraria, cyclamen, primrose, and violet

⚘ Bulbs: hyacinth, narcissus, and tulip

⚘ Flowering trees: acacia and magnolia

⚘ Shrubs: camellia, daphne, quince, salvia, and Scotch broom

⚘ Natives: Dutchman's pipe, barberries, and fuchsia-flowering gooseberries

⚘ Cymbidiums

IN THE NURSERY IN FEBRUARY

⚘ Annuals: forget-me-not, snapdragon, stock, and sweet William

⚘ Perennials: cineraria, candytuft, gazania, and primrose

⚘ Shrubs: azaleas, camellias, quince, and rhododendron

⚘ Bare-root plants: cane berries, fruit trees, and roses

⚘ Bulblike: tuberous begonia, calla, gladiolus, and lily

Some of the most magnificent magnolias are or soon will be in bloom. This is an excellent month to see what appeals to you. Two favorites are the saucer magnolia (*Magnolia soulangiana*) and the star magnolia (*Magnolia stellata*). Both do very well in Northern California where they get enough chill to be in their best form. These magnolias do not resemble the Southern magnolia (*Magnolia grandiflora*) that leaps to mind when most people think of magnolias. The Southern magnolia, with its forcefully fragrant huge white flowers, blooms in summer and is discussed in the July section on page 186.

The saucer magnolia is often referred to as a tulip tree because the flowers resemble stiff, upright tulips. There are many varieties available, ranging in color from pure white to a pale pink and then through the pink scale to a deep purple burgundy. Visit the Japanese Tea Garden in San Francisco's Golden Gate Park to see just how artistically saucer magnolias (*Magnolia soulangiana* 'Burgundy') can be pruned.

Several superb varieties of the star magnolia (*Magnolia stellata*) are commonly available. Many people consider 'Centennial' to be the finest example. It has five-inch white flowers blushed with pink and a fine texture to the foliage that makes it a handsome ten-foot shrub. 'Dawn' has pink flowers with an exceptional number of petals, some forty to fifty to each bloom.

Magnolia Growing Simplified

Botanical name: *Magnolia*.

Common name: Magnolia.

Site preference: The site is very important because magnolias are difficult to move once they have become established. They need an uncrowded location in full sun. Remember that they grow to be large trees.

Soil conditions: They prefer rich, moist, well-drained soil.

Water: They need summer water but do not do well in swamp conditions.

Nutrients: Feed regularly with a high-nitrogen fertilizer. Iron chelates should be part of the fertilizer in many areas of Northern California where chlorosis (yellow leaves, or yellow between the veins of the leaves) is a problem.

Problems: The eventual large size of most magnolias can cause difficulties.

Hints: Magnolias are good trees to plant in lawn areas where their magnificent flowers are shown off to advantage. Many magnolias also have a handsome branch pattern when their leaves drop off in the fall.

PRUNING

(See page 30 for a detailed description and illustrations of winter pruning.)

Early spring is the time to prune many trees and shrubs. Many nurseries offer classes on pruning in February. Do not delay too long because warming weather will soon send plants into a vigorous growth spurt which you want to direct by pruning. Of course, wait to prune spring-blooming plants until they have finished flowering. Also avoid topping trees by lopping off the central branch. Topping weakens the tree, shortens its life, and looks awful.

Gardeners used to be advised to prune large branches close to the trunk. Now it is believed that, by leaving the slightly thickened bulge where the branch meets the trunk, the tree will form a callus over the cut more rapidly. Also hold the pruning paint; wounds exposed to air are believed to heal better, but not all arborists agree.

Cast a critical eye at the shrubs growing next to the house. Chances are they have become overgrown and are covering windows and hiding some of the best features of the exterior. Selectively cut away branches to shape the plant to a form that is both pleasing and complimentary to the house. Do not shear them as you would a hedge or you will end up with dense, twiggy growth and a dead center. To determine where new growth will occur, feel along the skin of a branch and find the buds (small bumps). Cutting just above such a bud stimulates new growth in the bud.

RAIN DAMAGE

The heavy rain in February can create havoc in the garden. While inspecting for damage, remember not to walk on heavily saturated lawns and planting areas because it compacts the earth too much. Pay particular attention to the areas near drainsprouts. The water should be channeled from drainspouts away from the house foundation and away from the roots of trees or shrubs that cannot tolerate swamp life.

Look plants over for signs of fungus or mildew, and wash black sooty mildew away with Ivory soap and water. Since February is cold as well as wet, this is a dangerous month for succulents because when they are cold and wet simultaneously, the water in their fleshy tissue may turn into ice. If this has already happened and parts of a succulent have turned to mush, cut those parts away and allow the cut to heal over. Succulents that have rotted away at the bottom should be gently uprooted. Cut away the rot, let the cut heal over, and then replant the succulent in a moist, well-draining medium such as sand or perlite. It will probably develop new roots.

Potted plants should be tipped over on their sides to allow water to drain out. To prevent their trunks from rotting, pull away any muddy soil that has collected around the base of a shrub or a tree.

RHODODENDRONS

Northern California has some of the most favored rhododendron growing areas in the west. When the rhododendrons bloom, nothing can compete with them for intense, brilliant displays. They seem to explode with color, an entire shrub pulsating with vivid magenta, or a small tree flaming with a pure, deep orange.

Rhododendrons are dormant while blooming, so February, when they are budding, and March, when many are in full bloom, are excellent months to select and plant rhododendrons.

Be sure to consider native American rhododendrons. It was a native *Rhododendron canadense* that moved Emerson to write:

> *Rhodora! if the sages ask thee why*
> *This charm is wasted on the earth and sky,*
> *Tell them, dear, that if eyes were made for seeing,*
> *Then Beauty is its own excuse for being.*

The rhododendron tribe is a very large group of approximately eight hundred species and ten thousand varieties of evergreen or deciduous shrubs and a few trees. In their native southeast Asia, rhododendrons have measured eighty feet tall. There are also dwarf rhododendrons that form a soil-hugging ground cover only inches high. The emphasis in hybridization recently has been upon dwarf plants. 'Shamrock,' for example, grows only eighteen inches high.

Some of the most popular rhododendrons are azaleas. Linnaeus, the Swedish naturalist who developed a system of classifying natural objects, believed that azaleas were different from rhododendrons. Later botanists corrected his error, but gardeners ever since have tended to side with Linnaeus. Azaleas do seem to be different.

For one thing, most rhododendrons are evergreen; many of the most spectacular azaleas are deciduous and their autumn leaves turn glorious shades of maroon and yellow orange. As they grow older, many deciduous azaleas form distinctive tiers. One of the most highly regarded is the Royal azalea (*Rhododendron schlippenbachii*)—a vivid rosy pink blossoming plant with purple red leaves and intense fall colors of scarlet, orange, and yellow. The native California, or Western azalea, (*Rhododendron occidentale*) is particularly attractive.

Rhododendron blossoms come in a variety of colors: scarlets (from an intense red to a pale whisper of a pink), vivid orange to soft apricot shades, yellows, and bluish purples. Although many rhododendrons bloom in March, April, and May, there are cultivars that bloom at almost any time of the year. Malaysian cultivars bloom off and on throughout the year.

When choosing rhododendrons, remember to consider the appearance of the foliage. The flowering season is relatively short—a month or two—but you will have to live with the foliage for the rest of the year.

RHODODENDRON CHOICE VARIETIES

FOR CENTRAL VALLEY GARDENS:

◎ 'Blue Ensign' is a four-foot shrub with lavender blue flowers and a compact, well-branched form.

◎ 'Cunningham's White' does best in partial shade where its white blooms tinted with greenish yellow marks are spectacular.

◎ 'Pink Pearl' is smothered with rose pink blooms. It needs pruning to keep its six-foot form attractive.

FOR HIGH MOUNTAIN GARDENS WITH TEMPERATURES TO −25 DEGREES:

◉ 'Laurie' has a compact three-foot form, white flowers marked with pink and gold, and a coppery bronze winter leaf color.

◉ 'Nova Zembla' is a handsome five-foot shrub with extremely showy red flowers and vigorous growth habits.

◉ 'Ramapo' is considered outstanding. Its compact three-foot high form holds plentiful trusses of pale violet flowers.

FOR COASTAL GARDENS, ANY OF THE VARIETIES LISTED ABOVE AND THE FOLLOWING:

◉ 'Anna Rose Whitney' is a well-formed, densely branched, six-foot shrub with large rose pink blooms.

◉ 'Gomer Waterer' is considered one of the very best. It is a six-foot shrub with white blooms blushed with lilac.

◉ 'Jean Marie de Montague' is a five-foot shrub with showy, bright red trusses.

◉ 'Lem's Monarch' is a compact, seven-foot shrub with huge flower trusses of white flowers blushed with intense pink.

Rhododendron Growing Simplified

Botanical name: Rhododendron.

Common names: Rhododendron; azalea.

Site preference: Filtered shade or full sun. The myth that rhododendrons are deep shade-loving plants has resulted in lots of leggy, ragged-looking plants searching for sun. True, a rhododendron will tolerate shade, but where the shade is really needed is underneath the plant to keep its top roots cool and moist.

Soil conditions: Rhododendrons like well-drained, moist, acid soil. Accustomed to the furies of a monsoon storm, they will settle for frequent mistings and damp (but not soggy) topsoil. Rhododendron enthusiasts, hoping to imitate a Himalayan forest, plant them under large spreading trees.

Water: Rhododendrons should be kept moist but not soggy.

Nutrients: Mulch with acid-producing compost such as pine needles, oak leaves, or redwood or fir chips. Enthusiasts will fertilize with an acid fertilizer monthly from the blooming period to the cooler days of autumn. Other gardeners will forget to fertilize or fertilize only when they are fertilizing everything else—their rhododendrons will still bloom just fine.

Special care: Plant rhododendrons with the top of their root mass slightly above soil level. Then be sure and mulch well.

Tip-pinch young plants to make them full and lush. Prune older, leggy plants to a pleasant shape by cutting back to a side branch or leaf whorl or to dormant buds. After blooming, pinch off faded flower heads; this is a time-consuming task, but the reward is a much prettier plant next blooming season.

For buying and planting bare-root roses see page 45.

If you did not do it in January, complete the pruning of hybrid tea roses. For detailed instructions and illustrations of rose pruning, see page 51. Here are the basic rules: Remember that hybrid tea roses bloom only on new wood; so prune to promote as much healthy new wood as possible. Generally, roses should be cut back between one-third to one-half, leaving canes at least eighteen inches long. Cut above a swelling bud pointing out from the center. Remove all suckers and dead wood.

Climbing roses are pruned differently. Trim only the twiggy growth and weak shoots; climbing roses bloom on second-year wood.

Unless you know where to prune, do not prune antique roses (also known as old garden roses) because they are very individual. Generally antique roses are pruned after blooming. See the July section under Roses, page 187.

To see rose pruning demonstrated, contact the nearest public rose garden and ask if consulting rosarians will give demonstrations there. Nurseries and botanical gardens often offer pruning classes.

SNAILS

Snail alert! Warming nighttime temperatures will soon lure the slimy regiments into destructive garden maneuvers. Slugs and snails are easiest to find at night and on overcast mornings. Destroy them.

Lest you take snails too lightly, consider the following. The common garden snail is a mollusk belonging to the class *Gastropoda*, a word meaning stomach-foot. That description alone should forewarn you. Each has twenty-five thousand teeth and eats dead snails. Conveniently, the anus of the snail is located right next to its mouth. The snail is a hermaphrodite. As well as reproducing as part of a male and female couple, a snail can reproduce all by itself, laying up to one hundred eggs! Worse news is still to come. The snail, crafty fellow that it is, can fill up on your tender young plants, seal off its shell with mucus, and go dormant for as many as four years. Then, like a sleeping nightmare, it awakes and all but cries out, "I'm back!"

The only solution is to keep after those darn snails, so that they do not reproduce. They have been sleeping the winter away in a patch of weeds or under an overturned clay pot. As they begin the invasion into your garden, stop them. A long list of snail-preventing measures is given in the March section under Snails on page 98, because in March they will become even more of a problem. The basic tactic for dealing with snails is to constantly pick them off by hand. Of course commercial snail baits are also handy but be careful when using them so that small animals or children do not have access to the bait. Put copper strips around commonly attacked plants, shrubs, and trees. Snails dislike crossing rough surfaces, so crushed egg shells and cedar bark will discourage them. A swift boot stomp seems the kindest way to kill them. Salting them seems cruel, and it is bad for the garden soil.

STRAWBERRIES

Bare-root strawberries are sold in February. These are dormant plants with the soil removed from their roots. Gardeners living in the Central Valley and the warmer portions of high mountain areas will want to plant strawberries as early as possible in spring. Coastal gardeners can plant strawberries in the spring, but the best time is November; see the November section on Strawberries, page 266.

Strawberries are regional plants and local nurseries carry appropriate varieties. One plant will produce about one quart of strawberries each year. Figure on ten plants per person.

A favorite is the 'Sequoia,' an everbearing variety with large, sweet strawberries in spring, summer, and fall. 'Sequoia' was developed especially for coastal California. 'Lassen' and 'Tioga' are better choices for the warmer Central Valley. Also look for the great-tasting, everbearing 'Fort Laramie' and 'Quinault'.

Store plants in a cool, damp place (wrapped in plastic in the refrigerator, for example) until the ground is suitable for digging. Remember that soil should not be too wet or you will compact it too much by working it. To make the plants easier to handle, some gardeners cut the roots to about five inches in length before planting.

Many gardeners plant strawberries on eight-inch-high mounds and spread the roots out before filling in around the hill. Use a fertilizer high in nitrogen one inch beneath the roots. Watch out for snails.

Note: it is important to place the crown (the center where the roots meet the stem) just above the soil level: lower and the crown will rot; higher and the roots will dry out.

TOOLS AND MACHINERY

The approach of spring will beckon gardeners outdoors soon, so now is the time to prepare the garden tools and machinery. Use a wire brush to clean them and then sharpen tools with cutting edges such as shovels, spades, hoes, pruning shears, hedge trimmers, and trowels. To prevent rust, apply oil lightly to the cutting edges.

Lawn mowers and rototillers should have their spark plugs cleaned or replaced. You may also want to replace the air and oil filters on some machines. Run the engine until the oil is hot, then drain the oil and replace it.

VEGETABLES

Harvest cauliflower, Brussels sprouts, broccoli, and cabbage. When you have cut off the head of cauliflower, it is time to add the plant to the compost bin. Do not plant another member of the cabbage family in the same place for several years because they share the same diseases.

Thinking ahead to summer's vegetable gardens prompts gardeners to sow tomato, eggplant, and pepper seeds indoors to get a head start on the growing season. A heating cable speeds sprouting. Some gardeners get similar effects by placing containers with seeds on top of water heaters or other slightly warm surfaces. Seedlings such as broccoli, cabbage, cauliflower, lettuce, green onions, spinach, and peas, that like cool weather, can be set out now. Remember to enrich the vegetable garden soil with an organic compost before setting out next year's seedlings.

VIOLETS

Spring-blooming violets should be fertilized now in preparation for their bloom. Violets thrive in Northern California. Even gardeners who did not plant violets may soon discover them blooming in some sheltered, moist corner of the garden. They have a habit of spreading from neighbor to neighbor with no help from the gardener.

The violet most often associated with the name is the English variety, *Viola odorata* 'Royal Robe.' But I often find myself contending with a particularly endearing variety that blusters its way through from one bed to the next. It appeared quite of its own accord, so I do not know the variety for certain, although I suspect it is a native Western dog violet (*Viola adunca*). I curse it in summer when it aggressively attacks the perennial bed, but I bless it each spring when its sweet fragrance floats in the air.

Northern California gardeners are frequently surprised to learn that there are many native varieties of violets. There is a low-growing native violet, the redwood violet (*Viola sempervirens*) that forms a ground cover in shady woodland gardens and has the delightful habit of popping up bright yellow blooms for much of the year. There is a species of violet well suited for every garden condition, except for a few extreme habitats such as salt marshes and dry deserts.

All native species of violets are among the most fragrant of wild flowers. Hence the classic nosegay of violets and Shakespeare's description of true excess, "to throw a perfume on the violet."

The oil that gives the violet a fragrance has a peculiar chemical called ionone that soon short-circuits the sense of smell. The violet flower exudes its cloying fragrance and then our ability to smell it disappears, but within a minute or two we will once again smell the violets until the ionone strikes once more, and the cycle is initiated again.

The appeal of the violet is a quality apart from its singular sweet, pervasive scent. Its allure derives from the violet's apparently universal and ageless ability to delight and please the viewer.

"Charm" wrote the novelist Francis Marion Crawford, "is what the violet has and the camellia has not."

Violet Growing Simplified

Botanical name: *Viola.*
Common name: violet.
Site preference: In the mild regions of Northern California violets grow well in either full sun or partial shade. In hot areas, they need shade from the afternoon sun. They are frost hardy to 14°F.
Soil conditions: Varies by species, many types prefer rich, organic compost.

Nutrients: It is not necessary to fertilize violets, but a feeding in late winter with an all-purpose fertilizer will produce profuse spring flowers.

Special care: Plants spread by runners. When the violets have spread as densely as desired, snip the runners for superior bloom. Shearing the lank top growth in late fall will also promote lush blossoms although it ruins the appearance for a few months.

WEEDS

The winter rains lead, as night follows day, to sprouting weed seeds. Unfortunately, the best method of weeding is by hand. This requires you to grasp the tiny unwanted plant by the stem, as close as possible to the ground, and then gently pull it up out of the soil, roots and all. Do not yank. Yanking usually only pulls the top growth off and leaves the roots to sprout again. Some gardeners give a little twist as they pull. Some weeds are more easily pulled when a digging fork or a screwdriver is edged down beside the long taproot and the tool used to pry the weed up. The younger the weed, the easier it is to pull up.

WILDFLOWERS

Although it is easier to sow wildflower seeds in the warmer, drier fall season, it is possible to sow them in February when the rain will help germinate them. Complete directions for sowing wildflower seeds, including recommendations for Northern California, are found in the November section under Wildflowers, page 269. If you sowed seeds in the last several months, remember to water if the rains do not fall. Seed germination depends upon moisture.

Calville
Blanche
d'hiver

JANUARY

FEBRUARY

MARCH

SEEDS

... March ...

Frost this month?

Shrubs and flowering trees in bloom?

◄◉◄ *March Features* ◉►►

The fierce winds that blow in off the Pacific Ocean are called westerlies. These are the winds that heap the sand into dunes and batter the cypress into artistic contortions. In March, these westerlies whisk through the garden, increasing the wind-chill factor and making the hapless gardener feel even colder as body heat is literally blown away.

Not all March days are so brusque, however. There are some calm, rainless days when the gardener prepares for spring—days of digging compost into the vegetable garden, completing the winter pruning, planting out the bare-root plants. The ambitious gardener may want to start seeds indoors to plant out later. The leisurely gardener will want to enjoy the wildflowers coming into bloom and perhaps a freshly picked bouquet of daffodils or fragrant lilacs.

Be sure to continue to watch out for frost, which is particularly dangerous when plants are leafing out with new growth. If frost has already damaged plants, leave the plant alone until the frost danger has completely passed. When new growth begins, prune away the old damaged growth.

KEY GARDEN TASKS

All Gardeners

◉ Sow seeds of summer vegetables and annuals indoors.

◉ The bare-root season is almost over. Buy soon and plant when the weather is right for planting. Complete those orders for bare-root fruit trees from specialty nurseries, which usually stop shipping bare-root fruit trees by the end of March.

◉ Send in orders to seed companies before they run out of stock later in spring.

◉ Wet weather is good for indoor gardening chores such as cleaning and repairing garden tools. Do not forget to sharpen the blades of pruning tools and shovels, and to service the lawn mower.

▲ ▼ ▲

Coastal Gardeners

In addition to the tasks listed for all gardeners, begin weeding while the weeds are young and the ground is still wet.

◉ Fertilize roses, citrus, and all flowering plants that are about to bloom. Trees, shrubs, and cool season lawns could use a high-nitrogen fertilizer.

◉ Fertilize azaleas, camellias, and rhododendrons when they finish blooming.

◉ Prune spring-blooming plants as they finish blooming.

◉ Watch out for snails and earwigs.

◉ Use a strong spray from the hose to wash away aphids.

◉ After the danger of frost is past, prune hydrangeas, fuchsias, and bougainvilleas.

◉ Plant out summer bulbs such as callas, cannas, dahlias, gladiolus, lilies, tigridia, tuberous begonias, and watsonia.

◉ For spring bloom, you can still plant cool-weather bedding plants such as cinerarias, dianthus, and Iceland poppies. To cover the fading bulb foliage, set out six-packs of lobelia and sweet alyssum.

◉ There is still time for a cool season vegetable crop. Set out nursery-grown broccoli, celery, and lettuce.

▲ ▼ ▲

Central Valley Gardeners

In addition to the tasks listed for all gardeners, begin weeding while the weeds are young and the ground is still wet.

◉ The rice growers in the Sacramento Valley remove the fibrous hulls from the grains. Rice hulls are an excellent, inexpensive soil amendment. Contact a rice growers' cooperative to find the nearest local source.

◉ Fertilize roses, citrus, and all flowering plants that are about to bloom. Trees, shrubs, and cool-season lawns could use a high-nitrogen fertilizer.

◉ Fertilize azaleas, camellias, and rhododendrons when they finish blooming.

◉ Prune spring-blooming plants as they finish blooming. Toward the end of the month (but before new growth begins), prune back both oleanders and crape myrtles to produce new flowering wood.

◉ Watch out for snails and earwigs.

◉ Use a strong spray from the hose to wash away aphids.

◉ After the danger of frost is past, prune hydrangeas, fuchsias, and bougainvilleas.

◉ Plant out summer bulbs such as amaryllis, callas, cannas, gladiolus, lilies, and tuberous begonias.

▲ ▼ ▲

High Mountain Gardeners

The weather is the key to when mountain gardeners can get into the garden and begin digging. In some high mountain areas, the growing season is so short that the only way to be sure of getting a crop of vegetables to mature is by starting seeds indoors or by planting out nursery starts later in the year. A sunny window can serve as temporary greenhouse for sprouting seeds of vegetables and annuals.

◉ When the weather permits, sow seeds of the drought-tolerant native wildflowers outdoors in a well-drained planting area. The following wildflowers are recommended for high mountain gardens.

◉ Lewis flax (*Linum perenne lewisii*) has small blue flowers from May to September. Soak the seed in tepid water for twenty-four hours before planting; sow in a sunny area.

◉ Gray's lupine (*Lupinus grayi*) has blue and violet flowers with yellow centers from May to July. Soak the seed in tepid water for twenty-four hours before planting in a sunny or partially sunny area.

ALLERGIES

During the height of the pollen season, from late February to June, there are often thousands of pollen grains in every cubic meter of air. Only about twenty-five to thirty popular landscape plants are responsible for most plant-related allergies in California; so the gardener can alleviate much of the misery. Grasses, particularly Bermuda grass, are the worst culprits. For a list of trees known to aggravate allergies, see the February section on Allergies, page 63.

AZALEAS

When azaleas finish blooming, fertilize them with an acid-type fertilizer. (At the same time fertilize camellias, blueberries, and rhododendrons with the same fertilizer.) Tidy up azalea plants after they bloom by pruning back uneven growth.

BALCONY AND ENTRYWAY GARDENS

Place pots of blooming tulips or daffodils where they can be readily enjoyed. Pots of tuberous begonias or fuchsias should be watered and fertilized this month. Fuchsias should be trimmed back only when the danger of frost has passed.

BAMBOO

On March days when the wind blows and the rain slashes against the roof, I have often stood at the window and wished I'd had the good sense to plant a clump of bamboo where I could see it. Few plants react as magically to weather as bamboo. When pruned to show off the slender wooden culms, the bamboo presents an unusually graceful silhouette that sways in the wind and glistens in the rain.

The Sung poet, Su Shih, wrote, "Without meals one becomes thin, without bamboo one becomes vulgar."

Some bamboo grows so fast that you can literally watch it grow. A bamboo culm has been recorded gaining fifty inches in twenty-four hours. Each individual culm lasts for up to several years. As it dies, it should be cut away. Unlike a tree trunk, which increases in diameter with age, a culm emerges from the ground with the diameter it will always have. Within weeks, it grows to its ultimate height. As the plant itself ages, fatter culms emerge from the ground and grow taller. Some bamboo reach one-hundred and thirty feet in the tropics but in Northern California ninety-five feet is about tops.

When selecting bamboo, it is important to remember that there are two basic types—running and clumping. The running bamboo often gets away from the gardener. The shoots run underground to pop up several feet away from the original planting site. Some gardeners control running bamboos by surrounding them with a concrete barrier several feet deep. Clumping bamboo, which merely increase in girth, are much easier to handle. Many bamboo make excellent container plants.

Of the three hundred varieties he grows, Gerald Bol of Bamboo Sorcery Nursery in Sebastopol (see page 303 for the address) particularly likes the Mexican weeping bamboo (*Otatea acuminata aztecorum*) for its finely textured, plentiful leaves. He is also fond of the twelve-foot-tall *Himalayacalamus falconerii* for its gracefully arching culms.

Bamboo Growing Simplified

Botanical name: Giant grasses with woody stems are all members of the grass family, *Gramineae*, but have been classified into many different genera, among them *Arundinaria*, *Bambusa*, *Chimonobambusa*, *Phyllostachys*, and *Sasa*.

Common name: Bamboo.

Site preference: Provide a sheltered site that is protected from wind. In hot climates, select a site that provides afternoon shade.

Soil conditions: Bamboo prefers rich, moist soil, but it will grow in other types of soil.

Water: Bamboo, like other grasses, loves water, but it will not grow in soggy ground. Once established, bamboo is drought tolerant.

Nutrients: For rapid lush growth, use a high-nitrogen fertilizer or a lawn fertilizer every month. To control growth, cut back on the fertilizer.

BLUEBERRIES

Apply an acid fertilizer (the same as that used for azaleas and rhododendrons) to blueberry bushes. Pine needles or other acid mulch should be added on top of the soil around the berries.

BOUGAINVILLEA

Because bougainvillea blooms on new wood, prune it as soon as the danger of frost in your area is likely to have passed.

BULBS

See also Summer-Flowering Bulbs, which should be planted this month, on page 99.

Continue to fertilize spring-blooming bulbs as the foliage emerges. It is important to do so when the foliage emerges because if you wait to feed the bulbs until after they bloom, as is sometimes recommended, the foliage may die before the fertilizer reaches the root system, and then the whole effort will be wasted as the bulb will not be able to take up the fertilizer.

When the bulbs finish blooming and begin to wilt, do not cut off the foliage. It provides nutrients for next year's bloom. Let the foliage wither and yellow before cutting it off or you may not get bloom the subsequent year. Cut off the heads of tulips that have already bloomed and are starting to fade. It is not necessary to remove the fading blooms of other bulbs—only tulips.

CAMELLIAS

Fertilize camellias with an acid fertilizer. Mulch with pine needles or oak leaves if they are available. Continue to pick up fallen camellia flowers to prevent the spread of camellia petal blight.

If the camellia blossoms are turning a ghastly brown, suspect the dreaded camellia petal blight. Pick a fallen brown blossom. Try to feel (then see) tiny, hard, black masses like small grains that indicate disease. Gather up all the fallen blossoms, then remove all the ground mulch beneath the infected plants. Discard both blossoms and mulch.

After blooming, prune leggy camellias at a point where the branch swells; this encourages a fuller, more attractive growth pattern.

CEANOTHUS

If Walt Whitman had lived in California he might have written, "When ceanothus last in the dooryard bloomed," for in California, it is the ceanothus that marks the "ever-returning spring." A native ceanothus, sometimes referred to as California lilac, dazzles the viewer with its intensity and profusion of blue or purple flowers that resemble small lilacs. The range of intense blues in the ceanothus is considered to be unrivaled in any other genus of shrubs. To come upon a ceanothus in full bloom is to become momentarily spellbound by a plant that is entirely saturated with sprays of bloom.

Ceanothus begin blooming in our coastal and foothill regions in February, and the mountain varieties do not finish blooming until May. Naturally the stunning splendor of the ceanothus was not lost on early plant explorers, and long before gold-rush fever brought California to the world's attention, ceanothus cultivars were being grown in European nurseries and planted in gardens there.

Eventually, about ten years into this century, local gardeners became interested in the native ceanothus. Unfortunately many of those early plants were just average specimens. To this day, many of the best-known varieties are probably not the best examples, aesthetically speaking.

COMPOST

Composting is the technique of reducing organic material to decomposed, soft, small-sized material for the garden. There are books written on composting, and it can be complicated and time consuming or as easy as piling material and letting it decompose without much fuss. Several types of compost units are sold in nurseries and hardware stores. Homemade units can be as simple as chicken wire formed into a three-foot circle.

Composting Simplified

Use only organic material; chop and shred larger material into pieces about half an inch in size.

1. Layer dry material, such as dried leaves, with an equal quantity of green material, such as grass clippings or kitchen vegetable trimmings. Six–inch layers work well. The ideal size for a compost heap is one cubic yard.

2. Keep the pile as moist as a damp sponge.

3. Turn the pile for faster decomposition. A well–constructed pile turned at least once every week will yield finished compost in as few as several weeks. Unturned piles take months, some up to a year. Turn from the top to the bottom and from the side to the center.

CYMBIDIUMS

Cymbidiums are large, impressive orchids that are easy to grow in Northern California, particularly in the coastal areas. The British imported them from the tropical jungles of Asia and have been growing them in greenhouses for the past two hundred years. During World War II many cymbidiums were sent from England to Santa Barbara to protect them from bombing raids. In Santa Barbara it was soon discovered that the cymbidiums did better outdoors than in the greenhouse. When the war ended, the cymbidiums had multiplied and thrived so well in California that many divisions were kept when the originals were returned. They have been favored by California gardeners ever since.

When I first encountered cymbidiums growing under the protective branches of a friend's oak tree in Santa Cruz, I refused to consider them as orchids. After all, I imagined that orchids were difficult greenhouse plants. Perhaps because of my reluctance to give them full orchid status, cymbidiums behaved in a contrary and unaccountable manner in my own garden. Other doomed plants die in a forthright fashion, so that I can toss them in the compost heap and get on with growing plants of a

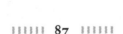

more agreeable disposition. But my cymbidiums persisted with an infuriating obstinacy. They would not bloom, mind you, but neither would they die. Not that it is always easy to gauge a cymbidium's health.

Cymbidiums are deceptive. A nice, lush, green cymbidium indicates too much shade—it probably will not bloom. The ideal is a golden green, what might be called a "pasty" or even "sickly" green. If your lawn were that color, you would fertilize it. Eventually, I said, "The heck with those orchids." From then on the cymbidiums were on their own. I watered them with the rest of the plants, and I fertilized them with whatever I used on the roses. So it followed one fine March morning, I turned the corner in the garden, intent on fertilizing the roses, and discovered the cymbidiums in full bloom. I quickly forgave them all the trouble they had caused me.

Cymbidium Growing Simplified

Botanical name: *Cymbidium*.

Common name: Cymbidium.

Site preference: Cymbidiums should be grown outdoors in pots located in close to full sun along the coast and in filtered sun inland. If the leaves are burning, give them more shade. If the leaves are a deep green, give them more light. In periods of light frost, move them underneath an overhang or high branches. When the temperature drops below 28°F, move them to a warmer location.

Soil conditions: Redwood bark prepacked for orchid growers is widely available.

Water: From spring to fall, they should be watered one or more times a week. In the winter, water every other week.

Nutrients: Fertilize them with a liquid fertilizer high in nitrogen from March to July, then switch to a liquid fertilizer low in nitrogen and high in phosphorus until the following January.

Special care: Cymbidiums bloom best when crowded. When they absolutely bulge out of their pots, it is time to repot them.

Cymbidiums, Repotting

1. Water the plant well.

2. Remove the orchid from the pot; often it is easiest to break the container first.

3. Use a sturdy knife to divide the orchid into two or more parts. Leave at least three healthy pseudobulbs (with leaves) and several back bulbs (they have no leaves) in each part.

4. Cut away the dead, shriveled roots, which will probably account for about one-third of the plant. Pull away and discard the old potting mix.

5. Place the division with a leafless back bulb to the back of the new pot. Holding the plant up, gently tuck a commercial cymbidium potting mix in around the roots. The most common mix, in Northern California, is redwood bark. Do not bury the pseudobulb.

6. Water well and place the plant in the shade for a few weeks.

Repotting Cymbidiums

DRIP SYSTEMS

Now, in preparation for the end of rainy season, inspect drip systems for leaks. Clean the filters of sediment and inspect screens for algae. A toothbrush is a handy cleaning tool. Walk the length of your lines, making sure all the emitters are working. Sometimes it is easier just to add a new emitter rather than to remove and repair the old clogged emitter.

EASTER LILIES

As soon as you bring an Easter lily (*Lilium longiflorum*) home, fill the pot with water once or twice and let it drain. To avoid root rot, water thereafter only when the surface of the soil is dry to the touch. Do not fertilize. While it is in bloom, the plant prefers bright, indirect light and daytime temperatures of around 70°F. At night, it prefers temperatures between 40° and 45°F. Put the pots outdoors in a sheltered location at night if your home is warm. Each flower will last about a week. Remove both the faded flower and its stem.

The Easter lily is not likely to bloom again indoors; however, it should survive several years if planted outdoors in light, filtered shade or in full sun in foggy areas. Lilies need good drainage. Plant the lily a little deeper than it was when growing in the pot.

FERTILIZE

When the weather begins to warm, it is time to apply fertilizer to many plants.

Blooming or fruiting plants particularly need fertilizer to produce large crops. Fertilize citrus with a high-nitrogen citrus fertilizer that includes iron. Iron chlorosis (yellowing) is a common problem in Northern California.

Trees and shrubs benefit from a high-nitrogen fertilizer with a formula such as 20-10-10. If you use granular fertilizer, make sure to water it in well. The water from drip lines is usually not enough to dissolve fertilizer cast around plants.

In areas with warming daytime temperatures and little danger of frost, foliar feed the new growth. Until they get waxy and tough, brand-new leaves will readily absorb fertilizers. Mix water-soluble foliar fertilizers according to directions and spray on new growth once a week.

Not everything should be fertilized. Cacti, succulents, and some native plants should not be fertilized. Gardens with rampant, hard-to-control growth would be easier to handle with less or no fertilizer.

FLOWERS

Pinch off the dead or dying flowers to keep new flowers coming. This is particularly effective with cool-season plants such as calendula, cineraria, Iceland poppy, snapdragons, and stock.

FROST DAMAGE

Leave the frost-damaged parts on the plant to protect the parts below the damage. When you see regrowth on other parts of the plant, it is safe to prune off the damaged section. Have patience. Many times plants look quite dead, but make an astonishing recovery.

FRUIT TREES

Codling moths, which make those infuriating holes in otherwise perfect fruit, are common pests in apple, pear, and walnut trees. The suburban home gardener with only a few fruit trees can control this pest by using pheromone traps. Male codling moths are attracted by the pheromone lure and get caught in the trap. Set out these traps now. If your nursery does not carry the pheromone lure, try the mail-order garden supply sources listed on page 310.

Beware of late rains that can promote a fungal disease in fruit trees called phytophora or, more descriptively, crown rot or collar rot. There is no cure, so prevention is the best policy. Particularly in the heavy clay soils that are common in Northern California, plant fruit trees high, that is, the area where the trunk of the fruit tree goes into the soil should be higher (by at least six inches) than the surrounding soil. This slope will drain water away from the trunk. Also keep a twelve-inch circle of ground around the trunk clear of any growth.

FUCHSIAS

When the danger of frost is past, prune fuchsias by removing last summer's growth, but leave two swelling leaf buds on each pruned branch. This is an important task because fuchsias bloom only on new growth. Pruning stimulates the new growth that produces bloom. Prune hanging baskets back to the edge of the container. Prune the branches of upright standards back to the wires of the form. Prune upright bushes back to about six inches off the ground. Severe pruning helps control fuchsia mites. Later, when active growth starts, pinch off the tips to make the plant fuller. Fertilize. For more information on fuchsias, see page 110.

GLADIOLUS

In selecting gladiolus corms, choose nice, high-crowned corms rather than the older, flatter, larger corms. The high-crowned corms are more productive.

The newer varieties of gladiolus have several advantages. The taller, new strains, which grow up to five feet tall, stand upright without staking, have twenty to twenty-six florets on each spike, and fourteen florets or more open at the same time. Each floret is between four and five inches wide.

If you plan to cut gladiolus for flower arrangements, choose the miniature varieties. They grow spikes about three feet tall with between fifteen and twenty florets on each spike. Each floret is between two and three inches wide.

Gladiolus Growing Simplified

Botanical name: *Gladiolus* x *hortulanus*.

Common name: Gladiolus.

Site preference: Full sun.

Soil conditions: They grow deep roots and need well-drained, deeply prepared soil.

Planting: Space corms every six inches apart, setting them between four and six inches deep. Plant corms every fifteen days through May for a succession of flowers.

Water: After the spikes emerge, water regularly until the flowers fade.

Nutrients: Add a complete fertilizer, such as 5-10-10 or 4-12-12 at planting time, but keep the fertilizer away from direct contact with the corms. Then, when a half-dozen leaves appear on the new plants, fertilize them again, placing the fertilizer a few inches away from the tender young plant and watering it in well.

Problems: Plant gladiolus corms early to minimize damage by thrips. Thrips puncture and lay eggs in the tissue of the corms underground. Some gardeners dust gladiolus corms with a bulb dust that is both an insecticide and a fungicide. Thrips are difficult to see because they are very small. To check for thrips, hold a white sheet of paper under a blossom (thrips prefer pale-colored blossoms) and tap the blossom. Thrips will appear on the paper as elongated specks. Overhead watering discourages thrips.

Special care: Cut the spikes when the first flowers open. Leave at least five leaves at the bottom to nourish the corm for next year's blossoms. Place a spike in water in a cool room for a day to let it develop before using it in an arrangement.

Hints: Gladiolus combine well in the garden with delphiniums and Shasta daisies.

Storing: When the foliage begins to yellow, about four weeks after the plants bloom, dig up the corms, cut off the tops just above the corms (throw the tops away), and dry the corms in a cool, well-ventilated area for about three weeks. Dust them with a bulb dust to protect them from insects and then store them in a single layer, preferably in a well-vented container such as an old garden flat in a dry area such as a garage.

Prune back vigorous species, such as the smooth hydrangea (*Hydrangea arborescens*) and peegee hydrangea (*Hydrangea paniculata*), which bloom on current year's growth, down to several buds per stem. This will result in huge blooms. Left unpruned, the plants will produce more but smaller blooms. Many gardeners grow the garden hydrangea (*Hydrangea macrophylla*), which blooms most heavily on the stems formed the year before. **When in doubt, prune only stems that have already bloomed.** See page 156 for more information on hydrangeas.

IN THE NURSERY IN MARCH

- Annuals: ageratum, impatiens, lobelia, marigold, snapdragon, and stock
- Perennials: cineraria, gazania, geranium, and primrose
- Bulblike: amaryllis, tuberous begonia, calla, canna, dahlia, gladiolus, tigridia, and watsonia
- Shrubs: azalea and camellia

IN BLOOM IN MARCH

- Annuals: calendula, Iceland poppy, sweet alyssum, and pansy
- Bulbs: hyacinth, daffodil, and tulip
- Perennials: cineraria, candytuft, gazania, primrose, and violet
- Trees: acacia, fruit, hawthorn, and tulip
- Shrubs: azalea, camellia, ceanothus, and Scotch broom
- Natives: redbud, pink flowering currant, California poppy, trillium, wallflower, fawn lily, and pussy willow

LAWNS

The large green lawn is an object of some controversy in Northern California. Given our long dry summers and frequent droughts, many horticulturists think gardeners should turn to other alternatives. On the one hand, lawns use a very high proportion of household water and require regular fertilization and mowing. On the other hand, for recreation nothing is quite as satisfying as a lawn.

The question boils down to usage. Households with need of a large play place for children and adults who like to play games outdoors should have lawns. Those who consider a lawn only as an easy solution for a large space should rethink their garden plans. They may be happier with a ground cover that requires less maintenance. Certainly when the drought years come (as they always do), they will be ecstatic with their alternative.

Many new ground covers have entered the marketplace. One that I am particularly fond of is *Dymondia margaretae.* (You can tell how new it is by the lack of a common name.) It forms a ground-hugging mat of tiny whirls of green-and-white striped leaves. It is drought tolerant but spreads rapidly with water. It is virtually maintenance free once established. It even survives modest foot traffic with no ill effects. It is well suited to all of the coastal areas and to areas of the Central Valley where the winters are warmer.

If nothing but a lawn will do and you are new to the business of owning a lawn, the best way to find out what sort of lawn is most suitable is to talk to your neighbors. Their first-hand experience under the local growing conditions and under the regulations your water department is likely to impose during the drought years is the best advice available.

Lawns come in basically two varieties: warm-season lawns and cool-season lawns. Both types are grown in Northern California. Cool-season lawns look most like those lush green lawns in the eastern part of the United States. They stay green all year round, but they take a lot of water; without water they die. Warm-season lawns such as those of Bermuda and zoysia require about half the water that a cool-season lawn needs. They can survive some drought (although they will not look very good) and that same indestructible quality makes them invade the flower beds. Warm-season lawns turn brown in the winter. Some lawns are mixtures of cool-season and warm-season grasses.

Lawn grass can be grown from seed or brought in as sod. Fall is usually a better time to plant lawns than spring, but spring will do fine as long as you know that water rationing will not be in effect over the long dry summer. New lawns must have water to become established. Preparation is very important in putting in a new lawn, and proper preparation will cut down on maintenance in the future. It is important to consult a book devoted to lawns when installing a lawn yourself, and it's probably wise to consult one even if you are hiring someone else. Some of the key tasks in lawn preparation are: digging the lawn area and amending the soil, very carefully leveling the soil to provide for proper watering, installing drains for the runoff, installing the sprinkling system, selecting the lawn grass and then either seeding or laying down the sod, and finally coddling the brand-new grass.

Lawn Tasks

Bluegrass, fescue, and ryegrass lawns have an active growth spurt this month. Fertilize them lightly with lawn food and reseed bald patches. Do not overfertilize. The latest research in lawn care suggests that too early or too rapid growth in lawns leaves the grass weak and less able to survive the heat and stress of summer.

Nursery Plants

By March the gardeners' green thumbs are itching. In many areas it is a little early to be setting plants out because there is still a danger of late frost that would damage many young plants. Use the following guidelines when selecting new plants.

Look at the bottom of the container. Roots curling vainly around in circles indicate that the plant has been kept too long in the container.

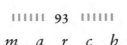

Look for yellowing leaves. When the leaves below the top leaves turn yellow and start to fall off, the plant has used up its nitrogen. Leaves that are turning purple indicate that the plant has used up its phosphorus.

Look for indications that leaves have already fallen off or that the newest leaves are abnormally small. And heaven forbid that the tiny plant should be trying to fruit or flower. That is a last-ditch effort on the part of the plant to continue the species, probably because it has lacked sufficient water.

It comes as a surprise to many new gardeners that the healthiest plant is often the smallest one. For plants well suited to Northern California, see below.

OAKS

Around March, the oak-moth larvae hatch and send troops of worms down the trees on silky threads. These tiny but hungry pests can be so numerous that they defoliate a tree, but the trees do survive. Spraying with BT (*Bacillus thuringiensis*) will help. For more details on this organic pesticide see page 35; and for information on Oaks see page 140.

ORCHID CACTUS

Epiphyllums, popularly known as orchid cactus, need feeding as soon as the danger of frost is past in your area. Feed with a bloom-promoting fertilizer such as 0-10-10. Orchid cactus absorb moisture through their stems, so pour the fertilizer solution on their stems as well as their soil.

PLANTS SUITABLE TO NORTHERN CALIFORNIA — THE NEW CALIFORNIA GARDENS

When spring arrives, Northern California gardeners want to start planting even though it is better to plant most shrubs and trees in the fall. Now that the urge to plant is strong, it is also a good time to consider what sort of plants are best suited to Northern California. In the past, many of our gardens were based on the English park model, with sweeping green lawns and beds of plants that need a lot of summer water. Drought and water rationing demanded a new model. After all, drought is a regular feature of our climate, and we cannot ignore California's dwindling water supply. Clearly, we needed to change our vision of what a garden should look like in California.

What we needed was a garden of drought-resistant plants that was so gorgeous that we all wanted to copy it. Wonderfully, gardeners and landscapers have been evolving just such a new garden style using loose, billowing perennial flowers and grasses that are drought tolerant.

Plants for a new Northern California style come from our own native plants and from plants native to climates similar to ours. Local nurseries offer a number of flowering plants suitable to our dry-summer, wet-winter climate that will supply attractive year-around form with little or no water once established. The following is a short list of flowering plants that should convince even the most skeptical gardener that drought-resistant does not mean drab.

◉ Amethyst eryngium (*Eryngium amethystinum*) is a good example of the unusual plants being used to create the new style in the Northern California garden. This stiff-branched, three-foot shrub has a distinctive thistlelike quality. The long-lasting metallic-looking blue gray blooms with touches of amethyst are stiff bursts of spiny color. This plant will grow in a well-drained, sunny location anywhere in Northern California. It blooms from summer into fall. *Eryngium variifolium* is similar, with branches of star thistles in lavender and gray and tidier leaves at the base of the plant that have interesting white veins.

◉ Fleabane (*Erigeron karvinskianus*) is a low-growing tangle of narrow leaves and small, fringed, white daisies tinged pink. It is almost always in bloom and has a carefree country-garden appearance. It can also be used in hanging baskets.

◉ Fortnight lily (*Dietes vegeta*, also called *Dietes iridioides*) is a three-foot-high plant with narrow irislike leaves and open, waxy, white flowers blotched gaily with a touch of yellow orange. It has a sculptural appearance and is good planted singly or in groups. Do not cut off the long flowering stalk because additional flowers will form on the same stem.

◉ Golden shrub daisy (*Euryops pectinatus*) is a four-foot, rounded shrub that is covered with bright yellow daisies from late winter to early summer. It should be trimmed after bloom. It tends to be a bit leggy so you may want a lower-growing plant in front of it.

◉ Lavender cotton (*Santolina chamaecyparissus*) is a two-foot, rounded, gray shrub with yellow button flowers. The best part of this plant is the lovely gray foliage, which should be clipped to keep it full and lush. Try combining it with other gray-foliaged, drought-resistant plants such as English lavender and artemisia.

◉ Jerusalem sage (*Phlomis fruticosa*) is an old-fashioned garden plant that has staged a comeback in the new California garden. Like many plants in the new garden style it has gray-green leaves that set off the unusual tiers of yellow flower clusters that form whorls along four-foot stems. It takes full sun, lean soils, and drought conditions. With water it will bloom repeatedly throughout the summer. Cut back the plant each fall by about one-third.

◉ Lion's tail (*Leonotis leonurus*) is a striking shrub that grows between three and six feet wide in full sun. Its common name derives from the unusual orange flowers that form dense whorls covered with a furry coat that looks like fine hair. It should be pruned to the ground in winter to keep it looking well groomed.

◉ Many other sages have become quite popular because they are suitable to our climate. Mexican bush sage (*Salvia leucantha*) is a three-foot to four-foot gray-green shrub with long velvety purple spikes that reach dramatically for the sun. It should be planted at the back of a garden bed, and the old stalks should be trimmed to the ground because it will bloom almost continuously on new stalks.

◉ A choice cultivar of our native *Salvia clevelandii* is 'Allen Chickering,' which grows into a dense four-foot shrub with fragrant leaves and deep lavender blossoms. The leaves are so fragrant that one sniff of a crushed leaf and the gardener will half-believe she has gone to heaven in spite of herself.

◉ Russian sage (*Perovskia* 'Blue Spire') is a wispy shrub with ghostly plumes of lavender blue flowers that seem to hover over the bed. The plant prefers well-drained soils in full sun.

◉ Tree lavatera (*Lavatera thuringiaca*) is grown for its showy flowers of dusty pinks or lavender with beautifully textured petals. Despite the common name, this is a willowy, graceful shrub. It grows in many soils, rich or lean, in full sun with water or in drought conditions.

(continued)

> Yarrows are native to California, growing in dry scrub where their low, flat clusters of tight-knit bloom come as a surprise to the traveler. Many new cultivars have soft sunset colors perfect for the California garden. One of the best is 'Moonshine,' which has finely dissected, fernlike, gray-green foliage and soft lemon yellow flower heads. Sun-loving and drought-tolerant, yarrow should be divided every few years and cut back after bloom.

POTATOES

For gardeners who would like to try home-grown potatoes, there is a local saying: Potatoes planted by Saint Patrick's Day will mature by the 4th of July—just in time for potato salad. Considering our current culinary passion for the pink fingerlings of Ruby Crescent, the pale nuggets of Yellow Finn, and the blue orbs of Viking Purple, the potato's slow rise to popularity may seem astonishing.

The potato arrived in Europe from Peru in the 1500s. In was regarded as food for the poor, or worse, as poisonous. By 1750, Frederick the Great was ordering Prussian peasants to grow potatoes. Unfortunately those early potatoes contained enough solanine in the green skin to cause an occasional skin rash that the peasants mistook for the dreaded leprosy. The peasants pulled up their potato crops. Frederick tried posting soldiers in the field. When that failed, he set an example by eating potatoes publicly on his palace balcony.

The Irish, presumedly, needed no encouragement. The potato became so well established, that when a potato blight struck in 1845 and 1846, a million people perished and a million more migrated to the United States. Because of the great Irish migration, the potato is considered to be one of the plants that changed the course of history. Irish Americans increased the popularity of the potato in the United States, and it is now a standard in our cuisine.

Potato Growing Simplified

Botanical name: *Solanum tuberosum.*

Common name: Potato.

Site preference: Full sun. Ten square feet will yield eighty pounds of potatoes. One eighteen-inch-deep half-barrel will grow one vine yielding up to fifteen pounds of potatoes.

Soil conditions: Sandy loam—that is, a well-drained, compost-rich soil. Loose soil also makes it easier to harvest potatoes.

Water: Moisture throughout the season.

Nutrients: Do not use fresh manure, which causes scabs. Use compost or composted manure.

Starting: Potatoes are best grown from certified disease-free seed potatoes that can be purchased inexpensively from some nurseries, farm-supply houses, and mail-order companies. Home gardeners are usually spared the many diseases and pests that plague professional growers who must use the same ground year after year.

Special care: Plant potatoes in early spring for an early crop. For a fall harvest, plant potatoes successively from mid-May to mid-June. For an early spring harvest, plant in the fall. Cut seed potatoes into chunks with at least two eyes per chunk. Plant seed potatoes (sprouting eyes up) not more than four inches deep. When the emerging shoots reach about five inches, cover all but the top inch with more soil. Continue to hill up (cover with soil, dead leaves, or straw) whenever the shoots reach about ten inches high. Do not expose the tubers (potatoes) to light because it turns their skins a mildly toxic green.

Hints: For the best flavor, harvest potatoes when they are young. New potatoes are ready to harvest when the tops begin to flower. Mature potatoes are ready to be dug after the tops die down. Before harvesting them, first leave the mature potatoes in the ground for another two weeks to set the skins.

PRUNING

If you did not complete your winter pruning chores in January and February, do so now because warming weather will soon send plants into growth spurts that the gardener can control by careful pruning. For those who still have pruning to do, the basic concepts are repeated here. Pruning stimulates new growth and increases flowering and fruiting. Prune dormant deciduous plants such as fruit trees, roses, grapes and cane berries as their buds begin to swell. In general, the best time to prune any woody plant is just before new growth starts, usually in late winter or early spring. The worst time to prune is right after the leaves emerge in spring when the plant may suffer from losing growth.

Again, as in February, prune out dead wood, which looks gray and brittle. Prune out branches that rub against each other. Pruning opens the interior of a plant to sunlight. Before shaping a tree or shrub learn its habits—some bloom or fruit only on old branches, others only on new growth.

Pay particular attention to what are called foundation plants growing next to the house—shrubs that are often overgrown and ill-shaped, covering windows and hiding some of the exterior's best features. Trim these shrubs by thinning them—selectively cutting away branches to shape the plant to the desired size. Do not shear them as you would a hedge or you will end up with dense twiggy growth and a dead center.

Remember that one of the basic techniques in pruning is to feel along the skin of a branch to find the buds (small bumps) where new growth will sprout. Cutting just above such a bud stimulates new growth.

For more information and illustrations of pruning, see page 30.

RHODODENDRONS

Pick off all withered rhododendron flowers, taking care not to injure the growth just below the flower. Fertilize with an acid type of fertilizer.

Fertilize roses when they begin to leaf out. Cover the ground around roses with a mulch but leave a mulch-free space around the rose canes.

Roses need lots of fertilizer to produce an abundance of bloom. Gardeners in a hurry can apply any high-nitrogen fertilizer with a formula such as 16-5-5. I am fond of a fertilizer suggested by a president emeritus of the American Rose Society: a coffee can full of plain alfalfa pellets (formulated for rabbits and available at pet-food stores) sprinkled around each rose bush. Evidently as alfalfa decomposes it produces an alcohol called triconetal, which is high in nitrogen. Roses seem to thrive on it and it makes a wonderful, weedless mulch.

A friend who grows roses commercially near Petaluma uses granular, water-soluble fertilizers with a high concentration of nitrogen such as 21-0-0 (ammonium sulfate). Shrubs take in nutrients along their drip line, which is where the rain naturally drops off the leaves, so sprinkle the fertilizer there. Be sure to water well. Rose fanatics will wait a week or two after the nitrogen feeding and then apply half a cup of Epsom salts (magnesium sulfate) around each rose bush—and again, water well. It is believed to activate plant enzymes that are essential to growth. Epsom salts can be purchased at a drug store.

SLUGS AND SNAILS

The secret to controlling the snail and slug problem is to begin trapping them now and prevent a population explosion later. Many homemade devices may be used as traps. Flower pots placed in the shade and propped up on one side make snails easy to find the next morning. Lettuce or other large leaves will attract snails.

A notoriously effective trap is a shallow container of beer placed level with the earth. Snails are attracted by the yeast, crawl in, then drown. Some gardeners in Eugene, Oregon, have discovered that a homemade recipe is more effective than beer. They dissolve a tablespoon of granulated yeast (active dry yeast) in three cups of water, add two tablespoons of sugar, and pour the brew into a shallow pan with a lip half an inch above ground level so that beneficial beetles do not take the bait and drown.

Handpicking either early in the morning or at night by flashlight quickly diminishes the snail population. Some commercial baits work by paralyzing snails so that the sun will finish them off. If the snail makes it into the moist shade, it may survive the ordeal.

If you are inclined to use commercial snail bait, place it inside a flattened milk carton or tin can so that it is accessible to slugs and snails and inaccessible to children, birds, pets, and other mammals.

After your own snail and slug population has been largely eliminated, the next step is to create barriers to prevent neighboring snails from invading the garden. The sharp-edged grains of diatomaceous earth deter snails, as do crushed eggshells or wood ashes. Expensive but effective are copper collars that snails refuse to cross. Use them around citrus trees, kiwi vines, and other valuable trees, shrubs, and vines.

Also be sure to cut off all low-growing branches that serve as bridges for snails. Remember that just as our common snail (*Helix aspersa*) is a gourmet treat to many Europeans and a few Americans, it is also a treat to other mammals. Do not be too quick to discourage natural predators such as skunks, snakes, some birds, frogs, toads, opossums, and even the common roof rat. Ducks are known to relish snails. Unfortunately that is not all they relish and more than a few choice flowers may disappear along with the snails.

SUMMER-FLOWERING BULBS

Dahlias bloom from summer until the cold and frost do them in in the fall. To see a wide range of dahlias and to dispel any doubt that they can be grown even in foggy conditions, make a summer visit to the area adjacent to the south side of the grand, Victorian glasshouse in Golden Gate Park. The very showy flowers come in a variety of styles from pomponlike to spiky and cactuslike to open and daisylike. Plant dahlia tubers about seven inches deep in full sun in rich, well-drained soil. Plant so that the eye (the growth bud on the tuber) is up. When the dahlia has three sets of leaves, pinch off the top set to force the plant to make branches. Fertilize with an all-purpose fertilizer every two weeks.

Gladiolus, see page 91.

Lilies are the regal queens of the bulbs. Florists depend upon their bloom for the most dazzling displays. Many of the fancy hybrid lilies are somewhat difficult but not impossible to grow. Plant lily bulbs as soon as you obtain them. They prefer a light soil with good drainage and they are planted about three times as deep as the bulb is high; a two-inch bulb is planted four inches deep. Most of them like their roots cool, so they are often placed where another plant will shade their roots while the stems grow tall into the bright sun. Protect them from gophers. See page 185 for more complete directions for growing.

Tuberous begonias are favorites along the coast, and the small seaside city of Capitola in Northern California holds an annual begonia festival. There are new heat-resistant varieties that are suitable for growing away from the moist coast. Tuberous begonias form amazing, iridescent blooms that have an other-worldly quality. They are often used in hanging baskets and window boxes. Plant tuberous begonia tubers in rich soil (add lots of wet peat moss) with the bumpy, concave side up. Place them in a partially shaded area and keep them damp. When the tubers have sprouted and are about three inches high, begin fertilizing with a balanced liquid fertilizer. Water and fertilize regularly. See page 303 for the address of a begonia grower in Northern California.

One of the tasks most loved by gardeners is spring planting. When the weather begins to warm, gardeners can hardly wait to rush outside and begin planting. California gardeners are no different in this instinct from other gardeners in the northern hemisphere. However, this instinct is inappropriate for Californians.

Please repeat softly, "I will remember that fall is the best season to plant shrubs and trees in California so that the rainy season can promote a healthy root structure." Having done this, feel free to rush outside right alongside me and get down to that satisfying task of planting.

One more caveat before you begin digging those holes. According to horticultural research, trees and shrubs rarely benefit from the myriad products used to aid them during transplanting. Researchers have examined different products (including antitranspirants, root dips, soil conditioners, and amendments) and concluded that none of them actually helped transplanted trees and shrubs do better, and some actually hindered growth. What did work was good old-fashioned weeding. What may surprise gardeners is that pruning at transplanting time had a negative effect on establishment and growth.

TOPSOIL

Buying topsoil for an organic garden can present a problem because it is difficult to obtain information from a commercial supplier about the precise source of the soil. Obviously, a visual inspection is in order for clues such as clods of old pavement. There is a simple test for herbicides. Take a sample of the soil home and plant a few cucumber seeds in it. If the seeds take longer than a week to sprout or if the seedlings die, the topsoil may well be tainted with herbicides.

VEGETABLES

There is still time to get in a crop from cool-season seedlings of cabbage, cauliflower, celery, and green onions. From seed, plant arugula, escarole, frisée, radishes, and lettuce. Also set out artichoke plants and asparagus roots now.

Do not be in too much of a hurry to set out summer-crop plants and seeds because a frost could kill off young seedlings and cold, wet soil could rot seeds. You can speed things up outdoors by growing crops under a row cover, which offers protection from frost and cold. Reemay, a featherlight spun polyester fabric, fits over entire beds, insulating young seedlings from the cold (the manufacturer says down to 28°F). As the plants grow, the fabric rises along with the plants, protecting the young seedling from the weather and many garden pests. Be sure to allow room for growth by cutting the fabric larger than the garden bed. Secure the fabric to the ground with the wire loops designed for use with drip irrigation. Note that there is a downside to this marvelous invention. After a few seasons of use, it will become too torn to be used again and must be disposed of.

For a more permanent solution, some gardeners build a mini greenhouse a foot or two high using an old window frame or a sheet of clear acrylic for the top. Technically called a cold frame, this shelter speeds up the growth of seeds in poor weather. The seedlings are later transplanted out into the garden.

Indoors, sow tomato, cucumber, and squash seeds to plant out later.

Vegetable Garden Pests

If you plan to put in a vegetable garden or a new bedding plot, you will have less trouble with the bugs if you start preparing the soil a few weeks ahead of time. After you have removed the old mulch and other garden debris, you will notice a lot of hungry little pillbugs (those tiny bugs that roll up into a ball when touched) milling about. With any luck they (along with hungry snails, slugs, and earwigs) should mosey on to greener pastures before you sow seeds or put in a few transplants. Sowbugs, which are also hungry little devils, are identical to pillbugs except that they do not roll up. Normally pillbugs and sowbugs are friends to the gardener because they break down organic material, which is good for the soil. Unfortunately tiny pillbugs can devour seedlings and transplants overnight.

Vegetable Gardening Preparation

1. Select a site that drains well and receives a minimum of six hours sunlight each day.
2. Weed it well.
3. Dig the soil at least one foot deep. Add organic amendments such as compost, leaf mold, peat moss, aged manure, rice hulls, and mushroom soil. Add as much as you can; there is no such thing as too much compost in the vegetable garden.
4. Create a watering system. Soaker hoses are good. Irrigation trenches work well with established plants. Overhead sprinklers waste water and promote disease.

For planting the vegetable garden, see page 121. For most of Northern California in years with typical weather patterns, March is too cold for planting summer vegetables outdoors. They will simply wait until the soil warms to grow or, worse, they may freeze.

WEEDS

The easiest weeding is accomplished by doing away with the weed while it is still too small to matter. Once it is large enough to be yanked out by hand, the plant is big enough to have a considerable root. Weeds compete with garden plants for moisture, sun, nutrients, and space. Whatever you do, be sure to weed before those weeds set seed. Heed the gardener's warning, "One year's seeding makes seven years' weeding."

...april...

Frost this month?
Trees and shrubs in bloom?

──•◄◎ April Features ◎►•──

In April in the areas that are now frost free, the gardening season begins in earnest. Although certain seeds will not sprout until the soil temperature rises, it is time to renovate the vegetable garden soil. Provided that the soil and air temperature are warm enough, the sooner plants are placed in the garden, the sooner they will fruit or flower. The key to good gardening in April is to weed and then plant vegetables and summer flowers.

Cool-season plants should still be in bloom. But do not buy new cool-season flowering plants from the nursery such as calendulas, chrysanthemums, forget-me-nots, Iceland poppies, or pansies. No matter how beguiling they are right now, in most of Northern California their season is just about over. It is wiser to set out summer-flowering plants now such as cosmos, delphiniums, impatiens, lobelia, marigold, hollyhocks, nasturtium, nicotiana, petunia, portulaca, sunflowers, verbena, and zinnias.

All Gardeners

When the garden soil is dry enough to work in without the soil clinging to the shovel, dig in lavish quantities amounts of compost or other organic amendments. This is particularly important in the vegetable garden.

◉ Before digging into the spring gardening season, clean and repair garden tools; sharpen the blades of pruning tools and shovels; service the lawn mower.

◉ When spring-blooming bulbs fade, leave the dying foliage intact to draw nutrients down into the bulb for next year's bloom. To cover the fading bulb foliage, set out six-packs of lobelia and sweet alyssum.

◉ Take cuttings from last fall's chrysanthemums to root for new plants that will bloom this fall.

▲ ▼ ▲

Coastal Gardeners

In addition to the tasks listed for all gardeners, continue weeding.

◉ Take cuttings for new plants from azaleas, carnations, chrysanthemums, geraniums, and succulents.

◉ If you did not fertilize last month, fertilize citrus, flowering plants about to bloom, trees, shrubs, and cool-season lawns. Fertilize azaleas, camellias, and rhododendrons when they finish blooming.

◉ Fertilize roses.

◉ Prune spring-blooming plants as they finish blooming. After all danger of frost is past, prune hydrangeas, fuchsias, and bougainvilleas.

◉ Plant out summer bulbs such as callas, cannas, dahlias, gladiolus, lilies, tigridia, and tuberous begonias.

◉ Set out summer-flowering plants.

◉ Watch out for snails and earwigs, both of which devour seedlings. Use a strong spray from the hose to wash away aphids. Wrap fruit tree trunks with a sticky tape to control ants, wrapping low so that birds, particularly hummingbirds, will not be attracted.

▲ ▼ ▲

Central Valley Gardeners

In addition to the tasks listed for all gardeners, begin weeding while the weeds are young and the ground is still wet.

◉ In preparation for the coming hot, dry season, apply a mulch.

◉ Take cuttings for new plants from azaleas, carnations, chrysanthemums, geraniums, and succulents.

◉ Fertilize roses and crape myrtles. Fertilize azaleas, camellias, and rhododendron when they finish blooming. If you did not fertilize them last month, fertilize citrus, flowering plants about to bloom, trees, shrubs, and cool-season lawns.

◉ Prune spring-blooming plants as they finish blooming. Prune hydrangeas, fuchsias, and bougainvilleas.

◉ Plant out summer bulbs. Set out summer-flowering plants.

◉ Watch out for snails and earwigs, both of which devour seedlings. Use a strong spray from the hose to wash away aphids. Wrap fruit tree trunks with a sticky tape to control ants. Wrap low so that birds, particularly hummingbirds, will not be attracted.

◉ For sweet corn try the superb 'Breeder's Choice' or 'Double Treat.'

High Mountain Gardeners

In addition to the tasks listed for all gardeners, sow wildflower seeds outdoors, when the weather permits, in a moist location in full or part sun. Among the wildflowers that do well in mountain areas:

⚙ California columbine, also known as Western columbine (*Aquilegia formosa*), which has delicate red and yellow, deer-resistant flowers from June to August. It will bloom next spring.

  Sierra lupine (*Lupinus confertus*), which has violet blooms from June to August.

⚙ A sunny window can serve as temporary greenhouse to give you a head start on the planting season by sprouting seeds of vegetables and annuals you intend to grow later. In some high mountain areas, the growing season is so short that the only way to be sure of getting a crop of vegetables to mature is by starting plants indoors by seed or planting out nursery starts later in the year.

⚙ Finish pruning deciduous trees before new growth appears.

⚙ Apply a dormant spray (horticultural oil sometimes mixed with either lime sulfur or copper; see page 279) to fruit trees after pruning. This will help control aphids, mites, scale, and other insects.

ANNUALS

See Bedding Plants, below.

BALCONY AND ENTRYWAY GARDENS

Transplant summer-flowering plants into pots. Cosmos, fuchsias, geraniums, gerberas, impatiens, marguerites, petunias, tuberous begonias, and zinnias are all dazzling bloomers.

BEDDING PLANTS

Set out summer-flowering annuals and perennials. Nurseries are well stocked with them now.

In shady areas you will get lots of quick, bright, colorful bloom from impatiens and lobelia. This can be accented with the intensely colored leaves of coleus and the speckled leaves of begonias. Hanging baskets of begonias and fuchsias do well in semishaded areas.

Sunny areas planted from six-packs and pony packs of ageratum, cosmos, marigolds, salvias, sweet alyssum, and petunias will fill in very quickly. Wait until the weather warms before planting heat-loving plants such as aster, dwarf dahlia, or zinnia.

For a more permanent planting try the perennials: agapanthus, campanulas, columbine, daylilies, dusty millers, marguerites, statice (sea lavender), and Shasta daisies. For perennials that require little water, plant coreopsis, English lavender, Mexican evening primrose, Mexican bush sage, and yarrow.

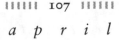

BERRIES

Plant berries now. Strawberries, which prefer full sun but will tolerate some shade, will give you a crop this year. Plant cane berries in full sun and do not expect much in way of berries until the summer after this one. Easiest are the bush berry plants such as blueberries, currants and gooseberries. Do not plant currants or gooseberries near pine trees that have five needles bundled together because they can infect one another with white pine blister rust. For a berry that packs an intense flavor into its petite size, try the Alpine strawberry, also called *fraise de bois*. These woodland berries will naturalize in partially shady gardens that receive regular water.

BOUGAINVILLEA

The lovely bougainvillea should be pruned because it blooms on new wood. It is safely pruned when the danger of frost has passed.

BULBS

When spring-blooming bulbs fade, leave the dying foliage to draw in nutrients to the bulb for next year's flowers. Some bulb growers recommend taking off the dead flowers, which of course removes the seed pod so it cannot draw nutrients away from the bulb. Some gardeners like to cover the browning foliage with another plant such as forget-me-nots, lady's-mantle, or California coral bells. There are always the old-standbys, sweet alyssum and lobelia, for covering bulbs or use spreading annuals such as petunia or verbena.

CHITALPA

In a botanical laboratory at the Uzbek Academy of Sciences in Uzbekistan in 1964, two American genera were being studied by the Soviets. One was the southern catalpa (*Catalpa bignonioides*), a tall, robust southern beauty that sheds her leaves at the first hint of winter but oddly has a tropical aura. The other was a small, stalwart fellow known as the desert willow (*Chilopsis linearis*), which is very drought tolerant. Both Americans produce beautiful flowers.

A Soviet geneticist, Nikolai F. Rusanov, hoped to engineer a cross between the two. And before too long he did it, creating a new plant—a marvelous plant that flowers and thrives even under drought conditions: the *x Chitalpa tashkentensis*. The shiny green leaves, which are slightly larger than those of an oleander, are smaller than those of the catalpa but larger than those of the desert willow. The flowers, which bloom from spring to fall, resemble the flowers of a pale and frothy rhododendron. The variety known as 'Pink Dawn' is a pale pink with a delicate yellow throat etched with thin burgundy stripes that serve as nectar guides to pollinating insects. The variety known as 'Morning Cloud' is white with a pale lime throat and burgundy stripes which serve as nectar-guide lines.

The chitalpa grows quickly to thirty feet and sometimes grows an amazing fifteen feet in three years. It may be pruned to a single trunk or left as a multitrunked tree. It may also be pruned to the size of a large shrub.

It will tolerate frost and temperatures down to about 10°F. The blooms, which first appear when the tree is at least three years old, come from late spring to fall in large, abundant tresses of between fifteen and forty flowers. In the fall, the leaves drop off. Fortunately, the tree does not produce the long pods characteristic of both parents, so there is little problem with litter.

It is said that when the California wind whistles through the wavering branches of a chitalpa tree each spring, the mournful sound of the Russian mandolin is heard—a remnant, no doubt, of the tree's birthplace in a foreign land near Samarkand.

Chitalpa Growing Simplified

Botanical name: *x Chitalpa tashkentensis*.

Common name: Chitalpa.

Site preference: A wide variety of sites is acceptable, but the tree grows best when sheltered from fierce winds.

Soil conditions: Chitalpa is not fussy about soils.

Water: Water in summer until the tree is established; thereafter it is drought tolerant.

Nutrients: Fertilize in early spring.

Problems: Fast growth may produce brittle branches that may snap in a high wind.

Special care: If a single-trunk tree is desired, prune away sprouts from the base of the tree.

CUTTINGS

Take cuttings for new plants from azaleas, carnations, chrysanthemums, geraniums, and succulents. See page 135 for illustrated instructions.

1. Snip off a four-inch length from the supple growth at the tip of a branch. Use healthy nonblooming stems for the cuttings.

2. It helps to dip the cut end in a rooting hormone, available at nurseries.

3. Root the cuttings in damp sand or in vermiculite.

CYMBIDIUMS

When cymbidiums have finished blooming, fertilize them every two weeks with high-nitrogen liquid fertilizer formulated for orchids. See page 88 for repotting cymbidiums, but remember that they bloom best when crowded.

EARWIGS

Set out rolled newspapers at night to trap the earwigs. The next morning collect and dispose of the newspapers in a covered garbage can.

EASTER LILIES

To avoid root rot, water potted Easter lilies only when the surface of the soil is dry to the touch. Do not fertilize. For more information see Easter lilies in the March section, page 89.

FERTILIZE

If you did not fertilize citrus, roses, or other summer-blooming shrubs last month apply fertilizer now. As the air warms, new shoots appear on trees and shrubs. The soil, however is still cold, which slows the ability of roots to absorb nutrients. In areas with warming day-time temperatures and little or no danger of frost, this is a good month for foliar feeding the new growth. Brand-new leaves will readily absorb fertilizers until they get waxy and tough. Mix water-soluble foliar fertilizers according to directions and spray on new growth once a week.

FRUIT TREES

Fruit trees develop fruit now. Thin the fruit when it is as big as a dime to produce larger fruit. Thinning also reduces the weight and consequent stress on young branches.

FUCHSIAS

Not so very long ago, you could stroll through almost any coastal town in Northern California and see hanging baskets of flowering fuchsias. Everyone seemed to grow fuchsias. Central Valley gardeners took great pains to get fuchsias to grow in the dryer inland areas.

Then a gardener from Northern California went to South America and, knowing that fuchsias are fairly easy to grow from tip cuttings, clipped a few and tucked them into the suitcase. At the airport in San Francisco the fuchsia cuttings were conveniently forgotten when the traveler passed through the agricultural inspection station. At first the cuttings grew and flourished. Then they developed a strange condition that caused the leaves and the flowers to curl in the most grotesque fashion.

Whether those particular fuchsias were discarded is not recorded. We know that many coastal gardeners did toss their fuchsias in the garbage when they suddenly, and quite unexpectedly, became disfigured. Slowly the tiny little fuchsia gall mite (*Aculops fuchsiae*), which hitched a ride from South America in the suitcase of a Northern California gardener, spread from one garden to the next. Many gardeners stopped growing fuchsias, figuring it was not worth the trouble.

The fuchsia has made a comeback in recent years, as predacious mites have also swelled in population by feeding on the fuchsia gall mite.

Fuchsia Growing Simplified

Botanical name: *Fuchsia.*

Common name: Fuchsia.

Site preference: Fuchsias need filtered sun. Except in true coastal areas with lots of midday fog, avoid growing them in full sun. Also avoid deep shade. Protect fuchsias from hot drying wind.

Soil conditions: Provide a light, fast-draining potting soil.

Water: Potted plants need to be watered twice weekly in most areas. Fuchsias like to be moist but not soggy. Avoid letting fuchsias sit in water or root rot may develop.

Nutrients: Fertilize early in the season with a fertilizer high in nitrogen. Switch to a fertilizer high in phosphorus when the plant has developed many branches. Continue to feed with a high-phosphorus formula every month until the winter dormant season.

Problems: The dreaded little fuchsia gall mite causes the leaves and flowers to curl and shrivel. Pinch off affected foliage and throw it away in the trash. I prefer to grow species fuchsias and small-flowered fuchsias, which are not bothered by the mites.

Special care: If you did not prune fuchsias last month and if all danger of frost is past, prune fuchsias promptly by removing last summer's growth, but leave two swelling leaf buds on each pruned branch. Prune hanging baskets back to the edge of the container. Prune the branches of upright standards back to the wires of the form. Prune upright bushes back to about six inches off the ground. Severe pruning helps control fuchsia mites. When active growth starts, pinch off the tips to make the plant fuller. Every single branch should be pinched back, which will result in two branches where there used to be one. Fertilize them with a high-nitrogen fertilizer.

Hints: Be sure to pinch off the seed pods that form as the flowers die. The seed pods signal the plant to stop making more flowers. By removing the seed pods, you are encouraging the plant to produce more blooms. Mist during hot weather.

FUCHSIA RECOMMENDATIONS

Species fuchsias seem resistant to the gall mite, as do small-flowering varieties and certain varieties such as 'Gartenmeister Bonstedt,' 'Voodoo,' and 'Nonpareil.'

Cold winter areas do well with 'Checkerboard,' 'Marinka,' and 'Royal Purple.'

GERANIUMS

See Pelargoniums, page 115.

IN BLOOM IN APRIL

Annuals: Iceland poppy, sweet alyssum, and pansy
Rhizomes: calla and bearded iris
Perennials: cineraria, candytuft, gazania, primrose, and violet
Shrubs: azalea, camellia, and rhododendron
Trees: acacia, various fruit, hawthorn, and tulip
Native plants: woolly blue curls, mountain spiraea, and ceanothus
Wildflowers: California poppies, lupine, and Chinese houses

IN THE NURSERY IN APRIL

Annuals: cosmos, lobelia, marigold, and petunia
Perennials: felicia, geranium, marguerites, Shasta daisies, and yarrow
Bulblike: tuberous begonias, callas, dahlias, gladiolus, and tigridia
Container-grown trees and shrubs
Herbs

IRIS

I am particularly nostalgic about the fragrant, old-fashioned purple bearded iris when they bloom each April because my mother grew them in abundance. She was a firm believer in botanical exchanges, and many neighbors gave her treasured iris from their gardens.

When I became an adult, my mother gave me divisions of some of her iris. Today, many of my iris are known to me only by the name of the neighbor who first gave that variety to my mother. The sturdy, bronze iris with the rust-colored beard was given to my mother by the retired diplomat who lived on the next street. The diplomat had two daughters. One ran away with a real-estate salesman who had been married three times. The other daughter, a tad slow mentally, had a fixation about buses. She would sidle up to my mother and, with a sly grin, ask "What do you think the buses do at night?"

I do not know what the buses did at night or what happened to the diplomat and his two daughters. But I know exactly where some of his iris are. I think of him every April when the sunlight traces the amethyst sheen of the iris falls.

There is a language peculiar to bearded iris. The three up-curving petals are known as standards. The three down-curving petals are known as falls. The beard is a narrow fuzzy area that curves up the throat and down a little onto each fall.

It is easy to become addicted to iris catalogs. I can linger for hours over the large, glossy photographs of the hundreds of iris varieties that are typically listed. The descriptions are even more astonishing than the photographs. Consider, for example, an iris called 'Lemon Brocade': "This waxy, lavishly ruffled exquisite light lemon yellow . . . is a color to enjoy in quietude." Quietude is in short supply in my home so I would have to forego that variety.

The American Iris Society awards the highest honors in irisdom. The very highest award is the Dykes Medal. My favorite iris is the pale coral 'Beverley Sills,' which won the Dykes Medal in 1985. It blends beautifully with the fragrant purple iris from my mother's garden.

The price of an iris, by the way, has little to do with merit. The older the iris, the more abundant the supply and the cheaper it is. A recent hybrid that failed to win any awards but is rare may sell for six times the price of the exquisite 'Beverley Sills.'

Iris growers frequently offer bonuses in their catalogs. One grower sent me a bonus gift of an expensive iris called 'Stormy Stallion.' The catalog description of this plant said that it created "a feeling of élan like a spirited stallion tossing its mane to the wind." The following year 'Stormy Stallion' produced deep purple blooms. I was quite pleased. Apparently, however, 'Stormy Stallion' galloped off into the grower's garden sunset. When I tried to find it in the following year's catalog, it was no longer listed.

Iris Growing Simplified

Botanical name: *Iris germanica.*

Common name: Tall bearded iris.

Site preference: Plant in a location with at least six hours of sunlight each day.

Soil conditions: Iris tolerate every soil except damp soil. If necessary to achieve good drainage, plant them in beds raised slightly above the level of surrounding garden paths.

Water: Newly set plants need water to produce a root system. Once established, however, iris should only be watered during a hot, dry spell. A common mistake is to overwater iris.

Nutrients: Apply a balanced fertilizer in early spring. Be certain to water the fertilizer into the soil or, even better, apply the fertilizer just before a rainstorm.

Problems: Very few—they are drought resistant, pretty much disease free, and forgiving about downright neglect.

Special care: When the iris become crowded, about every four years, dig up the clumps and divide them for replanting. Some gardeners divide every other year, but since iris bloom best in their second to fourth years, it seems better to wait.

Hints: Remember, when planting iris divisions, that the plant expands outward from the fan of green leaves, so point the fan in the direction you want the growth to go.

KIWI VINES

Feed kiwi vines with a high-nitrogen fertilizer—they are heavy feeders.

If your kiwi vines have not carried fruit after growing in place for a few years, take a look at the flowers this spring. Remember that most varieties of kiwi vines require both a male and a female plant to set fruit. It is practically impossible to tell the plants apart except when they bloom. The female flower has an extended appendage called the pistil that rises from the center of the flower; the male flower has a pompon of small, threadlike clusters in the center. Both male and female plants need to flower at the same time for fertilization, which produces fruit, to occur.

LAWN MOWER

As if it is not bad enough to have to remember to get the car tuned, lawn mowers need a tune-up too. To assure easy starts, change the spark plug. Keep the engine from overheating by cleaning the cooling fins. Change the engine oil. To prevent stalling, clean or replace the air filter. Check the condition and tension of the belt and lubricate the wheels and controls. Fill the engine with fresh gas.

LAWNS

If you did not fertilize your lawn last month, fertilize it this month. Take a few minutes to review the watering timetable for your lawn. The California Department of Water Resources has established average ET (evapotranspiration) rates for many Northern California communities. The ET rate is the quantity of water that evaporates from the garden soil plus the quantity of water that transpires from the grass leaves. Based on these ET rates, lawns in different areas need different quantities of water to keep them at their ornamental best without wasting water.

LAWN WATERING GUIDELINES FOR SPRING

For spring the average lawn, watered to a depth of six to eight inches twice a week, will need to have the sprinklers on each time for:

- Between five and twenty-two minutes in the coastal region
- Between thirteen and thirty minutes in the Central Valley
- Between twelve and twenty-six minutes in the high mountains

The lower figures are for larger pipelines. Your lawn will indicate a need for more water by turning from a bright green to a dull blue green. Also you will see footprints in the lawn because the grass does not spring back up.

MULCH

While hoping for rain, prepare for the six-month-long rainless season ahead of us. The garden will look better this summer with proper preparation now. Conserve moisture by applying a three-inch thick mulch around plants. Leave the area immediately around the stem bare to prevent crown rot. Mulch also protects the soil from the baking effects of the sun. Be sure to pull up weeds, which rob plants of moisture.

ORCHID CACTUS

Epiphyllums, popularly known as orchid cactus, start blooming this month. This is a good month to shop for them. They are excellent potted plants in coastal areas. See page 306 for the address of a grower.

PELARGONIUMS

The common geranium, which probably persists on a goodly number of America's back lots alongside rusting car fenders and abandoned tires, has an amazing amount of cheerful grace. Few plants require so little attention in exchange for an abundance of flowers from April to October. See growing instructions on the next page. What we commonly call geraniums are, botanically speaking, pelargoniums, and are, like true geraniums, members of the Geraniacea.

* The most widely grown geranium is *Pelargonium hortorum*, a shrubby perennial about three feet tall and most often used as a bedding plant. The rounded leaves are velvety soft, usually with a distinctive deeper pattern inside the leaf margin. The abundant but modestly sized flowers come in many shades of salmon, rose, pink, red, orange, violet, and white. This hardy plant can be grown from seed as well as from cuttings. 'Mrs. Henry Cox', with its showy tricolored leaves and pert pink flowers, is a good example of these easy-to-grow plants.

* The Lady Washington pelargonium (*Pelargonium x domesicurn*) is the plant most gardeners actually refer to as a pelargonium rather than a geranium. This somewhat sprawling plant has large splashy flowers marked by brilliantly colored blotches. An example is 'Aztec' with its flowers of white blotched with rose and deep maroon.

* Ivy geranium (*Pelargonium peltatum*) is a favorite for window boxes, hanging baskets, or for trailing down the side of a wall. It has polished ivy-shaped leaves growing from graceful, two- to three-foot-long stems. The flowers are double or single, often with stripes or blotches on the upper two petals. A choice variety is 'L'Elegante,' which has striking leaves edged at the margins with creamy white.

* Scented geraniums provide still more varieties. Not showy in flower, they are grown for their enormously varied leaves that can be lacy and crinkly textured. Their scent can resemble fruit, flowers, spices, or other aromatics. They are used in sachets, finger bowls, sauces, frostings, or jellies. Victorian cooks would sometimes line a pan with scented geranium leaves before baking a cake. Truthfully, the effect of cooking with scented geranium leaves always has seemed to me a bit on the delicate side. Fairly easy to obtain are the lemon-scented *Pelargonium crispum*, rose-scented *Pelargonium graveolens*, apple-scented *Pelargonium odoratissimum*, and peppermint-scented *Pelargonium tomentosum*.

Pelargonium Growing Simplified

Botanical name: *Pelargonium.*

Common name: Geranium; pelargonium.

Site preference: Full sun for a minimum of six hours in coastal areas; light shade in hot areas.

Soil conditions: They prefer fairly rich, well-drained soil but will grow under a variety of soil conditions. Potted geraniums do best when somewhat potbound.

Water: They will thrive with normal watering for perennials but prefer to be on the dry side and must not be overwatered. Somewhat drought-resistant once established, most pelargoniums will survive a season or two with little watering. Potted plants require frequent watering.

Nutrients: Fertilize lightly at the beginning of the growing season.

Special care: Pinch off faded flowers to encourage new blooms. Also pinch off growing tips of young plants (or plants that have been severely pruned) to force side branches and to create a bushy plant and an abundance of flowers.

Propagation: Take a tip cutting from a nonblooming stem, dip the cut end in a rooting hormone, and plant it in damp sand or potting soil. Keep the cutting in a shady place until it has rooted.

POTATOES

Pinch off flowers as they appear so the plant's energy goes into the tubers (the potatoes).

RADISHES

The radish seems to be an uncomplicated vegetable. It is easy to imagine that it came into vogue in the era of the shaken cocktail by being served on a silver tray like little pink toes. With slightly more imagination, one could conceive of Russian peasants eating sliced radishes on a hunk of crusty, buttered bread. That would appear to be the extent of the radish's culinary history.

But, in truth, the radish is an ancient vegetable popular in many cultures and often served (dare I say it?) cooked. Before the Egyptians acquired the versatile olive, they grew radishes for radish-seed oil. Herodotus, who had a rather fanciful approach to history, tells us that radishes were fed to the pyramid builders to increase their strength. In Japan, radishes are not only the most widely grown vegetable, but they are also colorfully wrapped and given as a gift.

Lest you believe that is the height of radish lore, consider the rat-tailed radish, which is grown in India not only for its leaves but also for the reddish violet seed pods, which grow to twelve inches in length, taste a lot like the familiar root, and are often pickled.

In Europe, the French and the Germans are fond of what we call spring radishes, which grow several inches long and are eaten within a month after the seed is sown in the garden. Many of our garden varieties are imported from Europe, which is why they have names such as 'French Breakfast,' 'D'Avignon,' and 'Münchener Bier.' The last is the radish traditionally sliced thin and served on black bread during the Oktoberfest.

In Northern California, one of the most honorable radishes is the long white Japanese *daikon* radish, which can reach three feet in length and is often eaten pickled. Koreans have a similar radish that is used in *kim chee*. The Chinese have rose-colored radishes, black radishes, and white, foot-long radishes that may be grated and steamed into a pudding.

If all this inspires you to dabble in radishes, go right ahead. They are among the easiest and quickest to grow of all vegetables. Much of Northern California's coast has an excellent climate for growing radishes as they do not like intense heat. Midsummer is a particularly good time to plant the larger radishes so that they will mature in fall when days are shorter, sunlight weaker, and temperatures lower.

Radish Growing Simplified

Botanical name: *Raphanus sativus.*
Common name: Radish.
Site preference: Full sun.
Soil conditions: Light, rock-free soil.
Water: They need frequent, regular water so that they do not crack or become too hot tasting.
Nutrients: Fertilize lightly, if at all.
Problems: Flea beetles are the biggest pest, but can be discouraged by dusting the tops of the radish with wood ashes. Flea beetles are rare in San Francisco but do appear in warmer areas of the Bay Area.
Special care: Thin the radishes and use the thinnings in salads.
Hints: Plant seeds every few days, tucking them in among other plants for a constant supply of young small radishes.
See page 308 for a source of unusual radish seeds.

ROSES

Both modern and antique roses should be fed this month. Some enthusiastic rose growers apply special fertilizers the first time they feed roses each year. Coastal gardeners and gardeners in the warmer sections of the Central Valley who began feeding their roses last month can apply a regular balanced fertilizer to their roses this month and skip the following paragraphs. For the convenience of gardeners in the colder sections of Northern California who are fertilizing roses for the first time this month (and those who did not get around to fertilizing last month), I am repeating advice given in April. I am fond of a fertilizer suggested by a president emeritus of the American Rose Society: A coffee can full of plain alfalfa pellets (formulated for rabbits and available at pet-food stores) sprinkled around each rose bush. Evidently as alfalfa decomposes it produces an alcohol called triconetal, which is high in nitrogen. Roses seem to thrive on it and I find that it makes a wonderful, weedless mulch.

A friend who grows roses commercially near Petaluma uses granular, water-soluble fertilizers with a high concentration of nitrogen such as 21-0-0 (ammonium sulfate). Shrubs take in nutrients along their drip line, which is where the rain naturally drops off the leaves, so sprinkle the fertilizer there. Be sure to water well. Gardeners in a hurry can simply apply any high-nitrogen fertilizer with a formula like 16-5-5. Rose fanatics will wait a week or two after the nitrogen feeding and then apply half a cup of Epsom salts (magnesium sulfate), available at a drug store, around each rose bush—and again, water well. It is believed to activate plant enzymes that are essential to growth.

ROSES—ANTIQUE VARIETIES

Spring is the blooming season for many antique roses. If you are not yet familiar with antique roses, visit a botanical garden; what you see may surprise you. Some years ago I wandered into a blacksmith's shop in Ferndale, a small Northern California town that takes great pride in its boardwalks, ice-cream parlors, and Victorian houses. The blacksmith worked at his hearth transforming a length of pig iron into a wrought-iron fire poker. I perused, as tourists do, a display of ornamental bric-a-brac.

Among the offerings was a wrought-iron bracket supporting a small glass vial that contained the strangest artificial flower I had ever seen. As large as a saucer and as rumpled as an unmade bed, it seemed on the verge of falling apart. I could not imagine what material it was fashioned of—the dark maroon petals were velvety to the touch, but the edges curled in a crinkly, crepelike fashion.

When I asked the blacksmith what the flower was made of, he gave me a look that said, "Are you kidding me?"

I suspected the blacksmith did not know about such things. I wondered if the artificial flower were antique—it certainly did not resemble any flower that I knew. I could not take my eyes off it.

The blacksmith and I chatted about the old graveyard, and after a while he offered to show me his garden behind the shop. To my amazement, growing just outside the door was a large sprawling bush covered with what I had assumed to be an artificial flower. The leaves quickly identified it as a rose. The blacksmith did not know the name of the rose variety. It was given to him by a customer, and she had grown it from a cutting taken from a bush growing in an old English churchyard.

That was my introduction to antique roses, an imprecise term given to roses grown before the first hybrid tea was named in 1867. Many antique roses look more like camellias or peonies than modern roses. Many antique roses bloom only once a year, a trait that did much to spur the development of continuously blooming modern roses, but when they do bloom, they are smothered in flowers. Because the opportunity to see them in bloom is limited, now is the time to look for a variety that pleases you. Nurseries and botanical gardens are good places to start the search.

SEVERAL ANTIQUE ROSES APPEAR FREQUENTLY ON LISTS OF FAVORITES.

⚙ 'Old Blush' is considered one of the best. It dates back to 1752, when it was brought to Sweden from Calcutta. Probably it is much older as it was previously grown in China, before it was brought to Calcutta. Its pale pink flowers (resembling what is commonly called a cabbage rose) are formed almost continuously from early summer to winter. The sweet scent, the small four-foot size of the bush, and longer blooming period endear it to gardeners.

⚙ 'Austrian Copper' is believed to date to before 1590. It is a sport (spontaneous mutation) of a *Rosa foetida*. The bush grows to five feet and blooms once a year in late spring when it is ablaze with small, brilliant copper-orange and yellow flowers. Branches of 'Austrian Copper ' often revert back to the parent plant, which is pure yellow, so roses of both colors are growing on the same bush. Truly a stunning display.

⚙ 'Reine des Violettes' is a relative newcomer, dating only from 1860. It may be the rose I saw in the blacksmith's garden. It has the same unreal quality. The blooms open a dusky carmine color and later develop a blue violet blush. The seven-foot bush flowers repeatedly and is nearly thornless.

⚙ Even a short list of antique roses is incomplete without mentioning 'Rosa Mundi,' which is the oldest striped rose known. It predates 1581 and is an offspring of the Red Rose of Lancaster, one of the warring factions in the War of Roses. The large pink blossoms are striped with red and are lightly fragrant. The three-foot bush blooms once a year in spring.

All five roses mentioned here have been recommended in the past by the San Francisco Rose Society. Finding them should not be too difficult. When a freeze killed all the historic roses in Empress Josephine's garden at Malmaison outside Paris, the French government went to Roses of Yesterday and Today in Northern California's Watsonville to replace them. See page 306 for a list of rose nurseries.

SLUGS AND SNAILS

Troops of snails and slugs advance on the garden in April. They are voracious eaters and must be stalked persistently. Continue to pursue them. Bait or hand pick them on an overcast, damp morning. See page 98 for more information.

SUMMER BULBS

Plant summer bulbs, corms, rhizomes, and tubers such as agapanthus, tuberous begonias, callas, cannas, dahlias, gladiolus, and tigridia.

Tree Artistry

Controlling the shape of a branch angle on a tree moves beyond basic tree care into the higher realm of tree artistry. When a tree branch is spread to an angle of about sixty degrees from the trunk, it slows the growth of the branch outward from the tip (where it would otherwise race like a competitive horse to overtake the top of the tree) and encourages flower buds to form. The simplest way to promote this angle in a young branch is to use a spreader.

Force a young supple branch to an angle of sixty degrees (not ninety degrees!) and hold it in place with a wooden spreader: a small stick, a short piece of lumber, or a tree pruning is often used. (Rose gardeners often use rose prunings to force rose branches to similar angles.)

I have seen the British, who are maniacal gardeners, use stakes in the ground with guide wires up to the branches to hold them at the proper angle. Very, very young branches may be sometimes spread with a toothpick or clothespin to a full ninety degrees. After a month or so, the toothpick is removed and the branch rights itself to about the proper sixty degrees.

Tree Care

Trees are the backbone of the garden and should be treated with extra care and respect. Give trees a helping hand by removing the grass and the weeds that have responded quickly to spring rain. Research indicates that young trees grow considerably faster when vegetation (particularly grass) is removed from the ground within a radius of between two and four feet around the trunk.

Remember that a tree's active feeding roots grow beneath the drip line of the outer leaves and even beyond the drip line. A large tree is helped by the removal of weeds that are growing a considerable distance from its trunk. Contrary to the popular notion, a tree's roots grow out much further than they grow down.

Tree biology changes with age. When desiring to help a mature tree, remember that it lacks a young tree's ability to respond quickly to change. Avoid big changes. Evidently mature trees, like mature humans, get set in their ways. It is best not to alter the environment of a large tree.

Tree Problems—Sunscald

Sunscald can seriously harm or even kill young trees. Protect the trunks of young trees from the unrelenting gaze of the sun by coating them with diluted white latex tree paint or by covering them with a tree tape or brown burlap. As the tree grows, it will develop enough leafy branches to shade the trunk. One of the problems of sunscald is that the damaged tree bark allows easy entry for borers. If you see the tunnels of tree borers, poke a wire into the tunnels to kill the larvae.

Somewhat amazing, particularly to beginning gardeners, is the discovery that a real trouble-maker for trees is the common ant. The tiny ant is something of a dairy farmer who industriously herds insect "cows," such as aphids, mealybugs, woolly whiteflies, and scales, and milks these sucking insects for their honeydew. The ants are fierce protectors of their cows, even carrying them from tree to tree and protecting them from predators. It is the sucking insects that damage trees, but because they are protected by the ants, the way to get rid of the insect is often to get rid of the ants.

Do not apply an insecticide when you encounter the ants. That is rather like bombing a village to get rid of a houseguest. True, both the ants and the aphids are done in by an insecticide but so are all the beneficial bugs (some of which eat the bad bugs) and even worse, with certain insecticides, so are the bees whose job it is to fly from flower to flower carrying the pollen that results in fruit.

The first line of attack on ants is to wash the tree. Use a soap made for this purpose, such as the one by Safer, or use two tablespoons of dish soap (not dishwasher detergent) in a gallon of water. Spray the tree or sponge off the leaves. This soapy bath discourages aphids as well as ants. It also gets rid of the dust that hides the bad bugs from raids by beneficial bugs.

After the bath, trim off all branches that dip down to the ground to eliminate the ladder that enables ants to climb into the trees. Last, apply a sticky barrier substance, such as Tanglefoot, to the trunk of the tree. The best way to apply the sticky stuff is to spread it onto a piece of loosely woven cloth or an old nylon stocking and wrap that around the tree trunk. Wrap low so that birds, particularly hummingbirds, will not be attracted to it.

Again, I want to caution you against rushing out and spraying chemicals on the tree. It takes several years to get a garden in balance so that there are enough beneficial bugs around to control problem bugs. A hasty chemical spraying of something as large as a tree can massacre a lot of your insect allies in the garden. If you feel you must spray, see page 152 for a homemade remedy.

VEGETABLE GARDENS

See also Tomatoes, page 143; Vegetable Gardens for Children, page 163; and Cucumbers, page 177.

April and May are the best months to plant a summer vegetable garden in most of Northern California.

Sow vegetable seed in place in the garden. Particularly good this month are arugula, beans, carrots, Swiss chard, corn, cucumbers, radishes, and peas. Do not forget herbs such as parsley, mint, and basil.

When the danger of frost has passed, set out seedlings—particularly those of plants, such as tomato, pepper, summer squash, or eggplant, that take a long time to fruit. Remember to rotate vegetable crops so that you do not plant the same crop in the same place year after year. It is best to wait three years before repeating a crop in the same place to avoid a buildup of diseases and insects in the soil. As I indicated in last month's vegetable section, you can speed things up outdoors by growing crops under a row cover, which offers protection from frost and cold. You can use Reemay, a featherlight spun polyester fabric, and place it over the entire bed, to insulate young seedlings from the cold (the manufacturer says down to 28°F). As the plants grow, the fabric rises along with the plant, protecting the young seedling from the weather and many garden pests. It is important to allow room for growth by cutting the fabric larger than the garden bed. I like to secure the fabric to the ground with the wire loops designed for use with drip irrigation. Unfortunately, after a few seasons of use, it will became too torn to be used again and must be disposed of.

More expensive but permanent is the cold frame, a mini greenhouse a foot or two high using an old window frame or a sheet of clear acrylic for the top. This shelter speeds up the growth of seeds in cold or rainy weather. Later, the seedlings are transplanted out into the vegetable garden.

When seeds are sown directly into the garden, remember to thin them when they sprout too closely together by using a pair of scissors to snip off the unwanted seedlings. Pulling the seedlings up usually disturbs the roots of neighboring seedlings.

VEGETABLES: WHAT TO PLANT

The cool coastal areas, where fog visits frequently, do well with leafy greens, lettuces, peas, and potatoes. Growing ripe tomatoes is often a challenge best tackled in full sun backed by a reflective surface such as a white wall to throw off additional heat.

In the warmer, sunnier coastal areas, you can grow almost anything except melons and eggplants. Try short-season tomatoes (those that need the fewest days to mature), snap beans, peppers, and zucchini as well as greens, lettuce, and potatoes.

The Central Valley is the crop-producing area of Northern California and here gardeners have enough heat to get great-tasting tomatoes and melons as well as corn, eggplants, and peppers.

The high mountain areas have a limited growing season so short-season varieties are essential. Some crops, such as beans, the cabbage family, carrots, leafy greens, peas, and radishes, mature faster.

Vegetable Gardening—Organic Method

Gardeners in Northern California have lead the nation in organic gardening. During the mid 1970s, an alternative method known as the French-intensive or biodynamic method was practiced at the model garden at the University of California at Santa Cruz. It borrowed techniques and philosophies from both European and Chinese farming systems. Lately the name has evolved to become Biointensive Mini-Farming (BIMF) because it has been adopted by many small-scale commercial farmers in Northern California's organic gardening movement. These minifarms, by the way, often have less than an acre under cultivation.

The gardens look different from traditional gardens and many have raised beds and paths rather than traditional rows. Nonorganic pesticides and soluble, commercial fertilizers are not used.

The planting beds are dug according to a procedure called double-digging. First a trench about twelve inches deep and between three and six feet across is dug. The soil in the bottom of this trench is loosened with a digging fork to another foot in depth. Then, second, another trench is dug along-side the first. The top layer of soil from the second trench is shoveled into the first trench. Third, another trench is dug alongside the second trench and, yes you guessed it, the process continues along the length of the new planting bed. The soil from the first trench is placed in the last trench dug. These beds and the paths between them become permanent. From then on, in order to avoid compacting the soil, it is important never to walk on the growing beds.

Composting is very important to this system. The planting beds are regularly fertilized with large quantities of compost and other natural fertilizers if needed. Companion planting is often used for pest control. These are very productive gardens. They often yield between two and ten times the crops that more conventional gardens do. As crops are grown very closely together, the method is perfect for gardeners with limited space.

Gardeners interested in this system should look for books by John Jeavons. Other Northern California gardeners who write about organic vegetable gardening are Rosalind Creasy, Jeff Cox, and Pam Peirce. I also like the books on vegetables written by Mimi Luebbermann and Georgeanne Brennan. See the Works Consulted section on page 315 for book titles.

Vegetable Gardening Simplified

1. Select a site that drains well and receives a minimum of six hours sunlight each day.
2. Weed it well.
3. Dig the soil at least one foot deep. Add organic amendments such as compost, leaf mold, peat moss, aged manure, rice hulls, mushroom soil. Add as much as you can; there is no such thing as too much compost in the vegetable garden.
4. Create a watering system. Soaker hoses are good. Irrigation trenches work well with established plants. Overhead sprinklers waste water and promote disease.
5. Sow seeds or transplant nursery plants.
6. Thin close-growing seedlings.
7. Fertilize the plants. Foliar feeding is efficient. Leafy vegetables need high-nitrogen fertilizers, fruitful vegetables such as tomatoes need high-phosphorus fertilizer.

Vegetable Gardens—My Own

A highly productive and ornamental produce garden can be created in a small space. My own small vegetable and fruit garden was created on the south side of my home in a fenced area measuring only thirteen feet by thirty-three feet. Although I grow tiger lilies just outside the fence, I have yet to eat them. This would surprise some people who find my kitchen garden exotic. Here I grow roses, fruits and vegetables that are generally unavailable at the market. The main reason for this garden is gastronomic. The flavor of freshly picked produce is so extraordinary that it has to be counted as one of the joys of gardening.

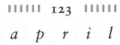

Although the kitchen garden is small, an amazing number of plants manages to grow here. At one end of the garden, a native California grape has escaped the house trellis, marched along the fence, hopped over the gate, and slid down into my neighbor's garden. In the summer, the deer eat the bitter grapes while peering, no doubt longingly, at the roses that are just on the other side of the fence. The deer would eat everything in the kitchen garden, but they love the roses best.

Beyond the roses, trained flat against the house, is a Japanese plum (*Prunus salicina* 'Weeping Santa Rosa') that in two years has grown up two stories. Sometimes, before bathing, I reach out of the upstairs window and pick a soft, fat plum. Luxury is a fresh plum and a hot bath. If this combination seems curious, then you may have forgotten how very juicy a truly ripe plum can be.

In a pot beside the plum tree is a rowdy peppermint, a gangly pineapple sage that is loved most by the hummingbirds, a small culinary bay tree, and four different blueberry bushes. As soon as they ripen, the blueberries are plucked by sharp-eyed children.

To my surprise last year, a passion vine with delicious, fragrant fruit (*Passiflora edulis*) wound its way up the wall behind the blueberries. I used to grow several varieties of passion vines along with a rare pink lemon tree in the spot where the plum tree now grows. They all died in a hard freeze. Most sensibly, the passion vine managed to reseed itself in a protected position behind the blueberries and under the overhanging eave of my office, which looks out onto the garden. The passion vine, I am happy to report, has its own butterfly, the gulf fritillary (*Agraulis vanillae*).

In the middle of this garden is a raised vegetable plot that measures about three feet by ten feet. As I write this there are several varieties of bush beans, peas, scarlet runner beans, three varieties of tomato, two varieties of squash, two types of cucumber, one pepper plant, various garlics including elephant garlic, a red Japanese mustard, many basils with paper cup rings around their stems to keep out sow bugs, a borage (which is one too many), two pumpkins, which will be trained to grow out over the edge of the raised bed, and numerous nasturtiums, radishes, and carrots. To call this an intensive garden might be an understatement, but I do try to harvest quickly.

In addition to the vegetable plot, there is a lettuce garden with a fenced lid that is raised with a rope on a pulley. The fenced top keeps the cats from mistaking it for a litter box. Here we grow salad greens: limestone lettuce, oak-leaf lettuce, 'Rouge d'hiver' lettuce, arugula, 'Curly Cress', Italian parsley, mache, coriander, and Japanese mizuna. Next to the lettuce plot is a strawberry patch with a European grape ('Ruby Seedless') growing on an arbor over the strawberries and the salad greens. The grapes dangle down over my office windows in the summer and in the fall the leaves turn bronze and red. Next to the grape is a 'Improved Meyer' lemon tree, a caper bush, and pots of oregano and lemon thyme.

That brings us around to the apple trees, which are trained on espaliers. A 'Cox's Orange Pippin' keeps company with a 'Pink Pearl.' My favorite apple, 'Thompkins King,' which I could not obtain on semidwarf rootstock, is espaliered behind the roses and will be allowed to grow up over the fence and frustrate the deer no end.

Behind the espaliered apples and trained along the fence are two kiwi vines, one female (*Actinidia deliciosa* 'Hayward') and one male (*Actinidia deliciosa* 'Vincent'). As I write this in May, the female has about four hundred blossoms and the male only one. If the bees do not find that one blossom, it will be another year with no kiwi fruit. There is also a pineapple guava (*Feijoa sellowiana*) for which I will soon find a mate. Although pineapple guavas are self-fertile, they will give more fruit with cross-fertilization.

I have just added a narrow, bottomless container, one foot wide and six feet long, along the north fence, where I will transplant the Alpine strawberries and Japanese parsley and a climbing rose which can clamber up the fence to the sun. Whenever someone asks why I bother to grow these things, I tell them that my family loves the freshly picked produce. Privately I remember a Chinese proverb: "That which I earn is for family—that which I eat is for myself alone."

Vegetable Garden Pests

Insects are less of a problem if you start preparing the soil a few weeks ahead of the time you plant. Begin by removing the old mulch and other garden debris. Probably you will find a lot of hungry little pillbugs (those tiny bugs that roll up into a ball when touched) milling about wondering where their meal went. Hopefully, they (along with hungry snails, slugs, and earwigs) should move on to greener pastures before you sow seeds or put in a few transplants. Tiny pillbugs can devour seedlings and transplants overnight.

A nifty way to foil pill bugs and other seedling-eating pests is to deny access to the marauders by planting the seedling or seed with a bottomless paper cup around it.

WEEDS

In April many weeds are still small and the smart gardener will pounce upon a weed whenever one is encountered. Weeds compete with garden plants for moisture, sun, nutrients, and space. Whatever you do, be sure to weed before those weeds set seed. We said it last month, and we repeat it again: Heed the gardener's warning, "One year's seeding makes seven years' weeding."

WISTERIA

Wisteria are choice vines for Northern California because they are easy to grow, cold hardy, and drought tolerant once established. While they are in bloom this month and in May, select a favorite variety.

The popular Chinese wisteria (*Wisteria sinensis*) has very showy, blue violet, grapelike clusters of flowers all at one time on bare vine branches.

Japanese wisteria (*Wisteria floribunda*) has a longer blooming period and longer clusters that open from the top down as the leaves appear. Japanese wisteria is best trained on an arbor or fence to show off the pendulous clusters of fragrant flowers. The variety 'Longissima' has clusters of pale violet bloom between eighteen inches and three feet long.

Wisteria Growing Simplified

Botanical name: *Wisteria*.

Common name: Wisteria.

Site preference: Plant Japanese wisteria in full sun; Chinese wisteria will bloom in either sun or shade.

Soil conditions: Wisteria will adapt to many soils, but they do need well-drained soil.

Water: When established, wisteria are drought tolerant but they will do better with water during the dry summer months.

Nutrients: Apply a balanced fertilizer before blooming, scattering it on the soil around young wisteria vines. Older vines usually bloom better without fertilizer.

Problems: Wisteria are very vigorous vines. Either train them to grow away from the house, or plan on pruning them diligently every year. They are notorious for pushing up shingles and toppling gutters.

If wisteria do not bloom, withhold nitrogen fertilizer; also watch to see if birds are pecking at the young buds in spring. As a last resort, spear a few of the roots with the blade of a shovel, a treatment that sometimes shocks the poor wisteria into bloom.

Special care: Every summer cut back the long streamers, saving only those you wish to train along an arbor or other supporting device. Every winter, shorten the flower-bearing spurs to two or three buds; the buds that form flowers are nice and plump.

Hints: Wisteria can be pruned into many different shapes from the familiar vine sprawling up a wall to a small tree fastened to a sturdy stake. A wisteria trained as a small tree should be pinched back frequently to maintain a treelike shape.

... **M** a y ...

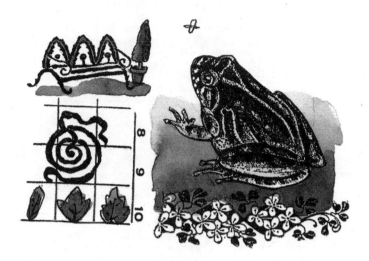

◄●◄ *May Features* ●►►

May is one of the most pleasant months outdoors in Northern California. Gardens are in full bloom and the weather is usually balmy and sunny. Naturally the gardener, who recognizes a blessing when it appears, wishes to spend lots of time in the garden. Almost any excuse will do; suddenly the gardener remembers that there are dead fronds that must be removed from the fern garden. Bending there in the dappled green shade with the sweet, rich smell of damp humus wafting up, the gardener may hear a horned lark break out into song. Such moments of near perfection are often encountered in the garden in May.

If gardening tasks have been attended to regularly, the gardener may want to do nothing more than watch plants grow in May. However, if the vegetable garden has not been prepared, it is best to hurry to do so. Many vegetables take months to mature and should be planted promptly. Irrigation basins and trenches should be made while the ground is still soft from spring rains and mulch should be spread to protect tender roots from the long, dry summer.

KEY GARDEN TASKS

All Gardeners

Plant frost-tender plants such as citrus and bougainvillea (in cold winter areas plant in containers to be brought indoors in the fall).

⊛ Weed while the weeds are young and the soil is still damp enough to make pulling the weeds easy. Do not let the weeds form seed heads. Heed the gardener's warning: "One year's seeding makes seven years' weeding."

⊛ Add young, seedhead-free weeds to the compost pile. Remember to keep the pile as damp as a wrung-out sponge for faster composting.

⊛ Continue to watch out for snails and earwigs, both of which devour seedlings.

⊛ Use a strong spray from the hose to wash away aphids. If an aphid colony does persist, it will take a few days before predators arrive so be patient.

⊛ Wrap fruit tree trunks with a sticky tape to control ants, but remember to wrap low so that birds, particularly hummingbirds, will not be attracted.

▲ ▼ ▲

Coastal Gardeners

In addition to the tasks listed for all gardeners, prune spring-blooming plants as they finish blooming.

⊛ Take cuttings for new plants from azaleas, carnations, chrysanthemums, geraniums, and succulents.

⊛ If you did not fertilize last month, fertilize citrus, trees, and shrubs.

⊛ Fertilize the lawn.

⊛ Fertilize all flowering plants that are about to bloom.

⊛ Fertilize azaleas, camellias, and rhododendrons when they finish blooming. Fertilize roses.

⊛ Prune rhododendrons after flowering. Pinch out the old buds and shape by pruning away as much as one-third of the plant. Do it promptly before the plant creates next year's flowering buds.

⊛ Plant out summer bulbs such as callas, cannas, dahlias, gladiolus, lilies, tigridia, and tuberous begonias.

⊛ Set out summer-flowering plants.

⊛ Plant the vegetable garden promptly. Thin vegetable seedlings that were sown too close together by snipping them with scissors.

⊛ Mulch.

▲ ▼ ▲

Central Valley Gardeners

In addition to the tasks listed for all gardeners, prepare for the coming hot, dry season by applying a mulch. The rice growers in the Sacramento Valley remove the fibrous hulls from the grains. Rice hulls are an excellent, inexpensive soil amendment. Contact a rice growers' cooperative to find the nearest local source.

⊛ Prune spring-blooming plants as they finish blooming. To keep old lilacs vigorous, prune a few of the lilac stems to the ground each year, and prune suckers off grafted varieties of lilacs.

⊛ Continue to take cuttings for new plants from azaleas, carnations, chrysanthemums, geraniums, and succulents.

⊛ Fertilize lawns, roses, and all flowering plants about to bloom. Fertilize azaleas, camellias, and rhododendrons when they finish blooming. If you did not fertilize them last month, fertilize citrus, trees, and shrubs.

Plant out summer bulbs such as callas, cannas, dahlias, gladiolus, lilies, tigridia, and tuberous begonias.

Set out summer-flowering plants.

Watch out for snails and earwigs. Use a strong spray from the hose to wash away aphids.

Plant the vegetable garden and thin vegetable seedlings that were sown too close together by snipping them with scissors.

▲ ▼ ▲

High Mountain Gardeners

In addition to the tasks listed for all gardeners, prune spring-flowering plants as they finish blooming.

Set out summer-flowering annuals and perennials. Also set out summer-flowering bulbs such as cannas, dahlias, gladiolus, and tuberous begonia.

Plant the vegetable garden promptly using nursery transplants. Choose varieties that require the shortest amount of time to ripen. Thin vegetable seedlings that were sown too close together by snipping them with scissors.

Fertilize lawns, roses, and all flowering plants that are about to bloom. If you did not fertilize last month, fertilize trees and shrubs.

Watch out for cutworms and earwigs, both of which devour seedlings. Use a strong spray from the hose to wash away aphids.

AZALEAS

As soon as azaleas have finished blooming, fertilize them with an acid-type fertilizer. Many growers believe that it is a mistake to fertilize azaleas regularly. Twice a year is enough: once after they have bloomed and once again in the fall. Prune the outer layer of growth to an attractive shape; the dormant buds will respond by smothering the plant with flowers next year.

BALCONY AND ENTRYWAY GARDENS

Continue to transplant summer-flowering plants into pots. Cosmos, fuchsias, geraniums, gerberas, impatiens, marguerites, petunias, tuberous begonias, and zinnias are dazzling bloomers. Pinch back fuchsias and petunias to create more flowers and fuller plants. Established plants should be fertilized now.

BLUEBERRIES

Apply an acid-type fertilizer to the blueberry bushes.

CAMELLIAS

After they have finished blooming, fertilize camellias with an acid-type fertilizer. Prune them by finding the bump on each branch where the new growth grew out of the old. Cut back to this point and you will have more flowers next year. You can even cut back into the older, gray growth but flowers will probably be delayed there until the year after next. Mulch, preferably with pine needles or oak leaves.

CLEMATIS

May is an excellent month to look for clematis at the nursery. Many of them are grown on the East Coast and shipped west late in the spring. Some bloom now; others are summer or fall bloomers.

> Like many other plants, the right location is critical. Three rules must be followed to grow thriving clematis vines.
> *1.* They must grow in rich, well–drained, preferably slightly acid soil.
> *2.* Their roots must be planted in the shade and kept cool. Often gardeners place a large flat rock over the soil that covers the root ball to keep it cool and dark. Clematis grow out of the cool ground to climb for the sun.
> *3.* Clematis should have something to grow up into or onto. Any of the following is fine: a tree, arbor, pergola, fence, garden shed, or even a large shrub.

CLEMATIS — TOP CHOICES

◉ *Clematis armandii*, also know as the evergreen clematis, is covered with fragrant white bloom each spring. It grows in all but the coldest areas of Northern California, and it will survive in a shady spot in the Central Valley, but is at its best along the coast. Slow to start, once it gets going, it will cover a fence.

◉ *Clematis jackmanii* is a vigorous, fast-growing variety known for its large blue purple summer flowers. In cold winter areas it will freeze back to the ground.

◉ *Clematis montana* is perhaps the hardiest and easiest of the popular clematis. In spring it is covered with so many white (turning to pink) blooms that the leaves are hidden.

◉ *Clematis* 'Nelly Moser' is one of the most popular of the large-flowered hybrids. It deserves its success. The huge, pink-striped blooms are showstoppers. It is easy to grow.

COSMOS

Some flowers are so easy to grow that gardeners, who have their pride, disdain to grow them. Cosmos comes to mind. For the price of a seed packet you can have a whole garden full of cosmos and a lot of happy butterflies. Planted in a sunny spot and given only minimal water, cosmos will bloom all summer and well into fall. Then the flowers will shrivel up, set seed, and come back next spring. It is ridiculously easy.

Some cosmos are native to the southwestern section of the United States. Others came from nearby Mexico and South America. In 1788 members of an expedition sent to Mexico by Charles III, the king of Spain, identified and catalogued many native plants, including cosmos. Spanish priests grew cosmos in their mission gardens in Mexico. The priests gave the flower the name *cosmos*, a Greek word meaning harmony or "ordered universe."

I imagine that a glimpse of colorful cosmos waving in a sunny spot along an adobe wall would have brought a moment's inner harmony into a difficult mission life. This momentary repose, after all, is one of the primary reasons for gardening. But Spanish priests aside, let us not forget that flowers are basically a sexual display designed to lure insects, butterflies, and birds to them in order to spread pollen and thereby propagate the species. Cosmos is the Marilyn Monroe of flower stardom—friendly, open, and seductively alluring. Everybody likes cosmos.

TWO SPECIES OF COSMOS ARE COMMONLY GROWN:

⊛ *Cosmos bipinnatus* produces bushy plants with airy, fernlike foliage. The four-foot Sensation strain has large flowers and is sold in single or mixed colors of white, pink, rose, and crimson. Sea Shell comes in similar colors but each petal is rolled in an unusual flute shape.

⊛ *Cosmos sulphureus* has small leaves and flowers in bright sunny colors of yellow, orange, gold, and scarlet. The Klondyke strain as you might expect has bright colors. 'Sunny Red' is an award-winning cultivar producing compact dwarf plants that stand the Central Valley heat better than most cosmos will.

Cosmos Growing Simplified

Botanical name: *Cosmos.*

Common name: Cosmos.

Site preference: Full sun; grown in part shade, they will produce fewer blooms.

Soil conditions: Rich soil is not necessary. In fact, poor soil has the advantage that the plants do not grow as tall. Adequate drainage is important.

Water: Keep seedlings moist. In areas with water rationing, watch for wilting foliage and then water. Avoid overhead water, which encourages disease-producing organisms.

Nutrients: Feed plants a month to six weeks after planting with a flower-encouraging fertilizer such as 5-10-5.

Problems: Red spider mites and aphids may damage the plants; spray with weak soapy water with a little salad oil added. Tall cosmos plants may need to be staked.

Hints: Cosmos is ridiculously easy to start from seed. When all dangers of frost are past, sow outdoors where they will grow. Firm the seed into the soil and water gently.

May brings an abundance of blooms to Northern California. There are several techniques that will result in longer-lasting bouquets.

The act of cutting flowers usually causes a callus to form over the cut that impedes the intake of water through the stem. Take a bucket one-third full of water into the garden when cutting flowers and immediately plunge the cut stems into the bucket. Try to cut flowers early in the morning before the dew has dried. During the heat of the day, flowers tend to wilt. Foggy or rainy days provide enough moisture in the air so that flowers may be cut at any time.

Most flowers are best cut just before full bloom. Tight flower buds may never open. Flowers already in full bloom may drop their petals soon after being arranged. Use a sharp pair of scissors or a knife. Make an angular cut across the stem to help the flower take in water. Woody stems, such as those of azalea or lilac, should be cut straight across and then split.

Inside the house, strip away foliage that would decay and foul the vase water. Under running water, recut the stems at an angle. Set the flowers in a deep container of water, mist the tops, then place the container in a cool, dark place for several hours. Darkness helps the pores (stomata) to close, which reduces water loss.

Some flower arrangers scrape the stems of flowers with a kitchen knife to help them absorb water. Certain flowers do better with special treatment—see the following advice for specific flowers. Arrange flowers in a clean container with fresh water. You may add a commercial floral preservative.

An easy, all-purpose, homemade preservative consists of two parts boiling water to one part lemon-lime soda—not diet soda; the flowers can use the sugar. Add a little water each day. See the Rose section this month, page 142, for two recipes for rose preservatives.

CUT FLOWERS—TECHNIQUES

⚘ Azaleas, lilacs, and wisterias—Split the woody stems for an inch or two up from the cut before soaking them. Some flower arrangers smash the stems rather than split them.

⚘ Chrysanthemums—Drip a little candle wax at the base of large-bloomed flowers such as chrysanthemums to keep the bottom petals intact.

⚘ Dahlias and delphiniums—Turn upside down, fill the hollow stems with water, and plug the stems with cotton or melted wax before soaking them. Alternatively, the stems can be seared with flame.

⚘ Hydrangeas and violets—Immerse entirely for an hour or two (these flowers can absorb water through their petals) and then place the stems in a container of water.

⚘ Roses—Cut a rose as the second petal unfurls. Always cut the stem just above a five-leaf branch so that the plant will continue to bloom.

⚘ Poppies—Cut the night before you think it will open. Sear the cut end of the stem in a flame or seal the cut end by dipping it into boiling water for half a minute. Flowers with oozing or milky sap (such as poppies) do better if you seal their stems. A drop of wax in the center of the open flower will keep it open.

⚘ Zinnia—Sear the stems in flame and then soak them.

CUTTINGS

May is an excellent month to take softwood cuttings from the new spring growth of azaleas, carnations, chrysanthemum, dianthus, fuchsias, and geraniums.

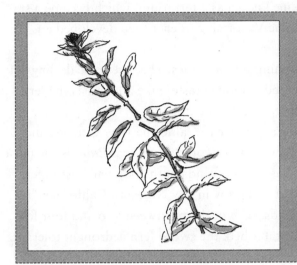

1. Water the plant the day before.

2. Cut about four inches from the tip of a nonblooming branch.

3. Strip the lower leaves off the cutting and dip the cut end in a rooting hormone. (The rooting hormone helps but is not essential.)

4. Bury the bottom one–third of the cutting in damp sand or damp vermiculite.

5. Water from the bottom only by setting the container, with the cutting, in a pan of water.

CYMBIDIUMS

Fertilize every two weeks with a high-nitrogen, water-soluble fertilizer formulated for orchids.

DELPHINIUMS

Nothing is more spectacular for summer bloom than tall blue delphiniums. Contrary to their reputation, they are actually easy to grow in Northern California as long as you stake them and keep them out of the wind. Buy a few (two or three pack a visual wallop) and set them in a sunny, cultivated bed that is watered in the summer. Fertilize and water delphiniums regularly, avoiding overhead watering, which weighs down the flowering heads and promotes mildew. To keep them flowering, cut off faded flower spikes. Later, when the foliage yellows, cut the remaining stalk down to the crown. After two or three years, most delphiniums lose vigor and die.

FERNS

Plants are different from gardeners in one important aspect. They make their own food. If the gardener were sealed in a glass case along with his favorite fern and then placed in a mildly sunny spot, the gardener would perish. But not the fern. It took a while before a gardener, one Dr. Ward, could use this to his advantage.

Dr. Nathaniel Ward had a passion for caterpillars. In 1827, he placed one in a jar to pupate. When he looked in the jar some time later a tiny fern had sprung from a spot of mold in the jar. Dr.

Ward observed that a natural cycle of condensation and respiration occurred in the jar. The fern survived in the jar for four years until the lid rusted and the polluted London air did the fern in.

Dr. Ward was no fool. He developed a large-scale version of the jar. The Wardian case, as it was known, improved the chances of survival for exotic plants that were being shipped from one corner of the world to another. He also developed what became known as a terrarium, which became a staple of Victorian England as well as the United States. The Victorian gardener then developed an obsession with ferns.

Hundreds of varieties of ferns were grown in terrariums and ferneries. They were the darlings of the plant world; their frothy fronds were thought to embody refined taste. Like all manias the fern craze ended and many exotic fern cultivars fell into obscurity, if not extinction.

Fortunately for us, some of the most beautiful ferns are native to California river canyons and redwood forests. The attractive and widely adaptable sword fern (*Polystichum munitum*) is the most commonly encountered fern of the redwood forest. It has the cut fronds of the popular Boston fern houseplant but, for all its beauty, it is a sturdy plant that will grow in any Northern California climate. Old plants can have as many as one hundred fronds, each of them between two and four feet long. Once the tough fibrous roots have become well established, the sword fern is drought tolerant. It is a perfect choice for shady spots and can even be grown as a large-scale ground cover. A choicer and rarer member of this genus is the smaller *Polystichum dudleyi*.

Fern Growing Simplified

Botanical names: Varied.

Common name: Ferns.

Site preference: Shade or semishade.

Soil conditions: Soil should be rich in organic material and, for most varieties, moist. Add pine needles or oak leaves as a mulch.

Water: Summer water is needed, except for a few well–established varieties.

Nutrients: Use a general, balanced fertilizer.

Problems: Some varieties are susceptible to frost.

Special care: Cut off dried brown fronds after the new fronds have unfurled. Some ferns go dormant in the fall and winter and all their dried fronds may be removed.

Hints: Some varieties need protection from slugs and snails.

A favorite of landscape architects is another native, the dramatic giant chain fern (*Woodwardia fimbriata*), which can grow up to seven feet tall although it is usually about four feet tall in home gardens.

Less frost tolerant than the native sword fern is the commonly sold southern sword fern (*Nephrolepis cordifolia*). This sword fern resembles and is in the same genus as the Boston fern (*Nephrolepis exalta* 'Bostoniensis'). This is a very adaptable fern, which is why it is so widely available. For gardeners wanting a decidedly tropical look, the Tasmanian tree fern (*Dicksonia antarctica*) is a popular choice. This slow-growing fern eventually reaches fifteen feet with a ten-foot spread. Faster growing is the lighter green Australian tree fern (*Cyathea cooperi*).

FERTILIZE

If you fertilized in March, give a second application to lawns, landscape plants, and established annuals and perennials. Azaleas, camellias, and rhododendrons prefer acid-type fertilizer after blooming. Citrus prefer citrus fertilizer with iron. If you applied fertilizer in April, wait four weeks before feeding again. If you have not fertilized yet, start now. The type of fertilizer is not of critical importance. Despite a plant's preference, an all-purpose fertilizer, high in nitrogen, can be applied to almost everything.

Also fertilize indoor plants.

FLOWERS

Sow seeds of summer flowers such as cosmos, marigold, and zinnia, which are all easy to grow from seed. Also set out bedding plants. Nurseries are now well stocked with summer-blooming annuals and perennials.

FUCHSIAS

If you have been tip-pinching fuchsias for the last two months, you are now finished with this task. If you pruned your fuchsias last month and have only begun to tip-pinch, tip-pinch them again now. Feed with a balanced fertilizer and keep fuchsias well watered. Remember to remove the old blooms and the swollen seed pods in order to keep the fuchsias blooming.

FRUIT TREES

Continue to thin fruits when they are as big as a dime. This produces larger fruit and results in less weight damage to limbs. Be sure to thin Japanese plums (this includes the popular 'Santa Rosa') so that the fruit is between four and six inches apart or it will be too small.

HOUSEPLANTS

Although gardeners tend to water all their houseplants on the same day once every week or two, houseplants actually have widely varying needs for water. If watering houseplants is a chore you would like to minimize, consider growing the following plants:

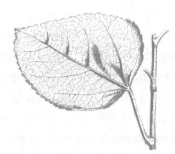

- Heart-leaf philodendron (*Philodendron scandens*)
- Snake plant (*Sansevieria trifasciata* 'Laurentii')
- Parlor palm (*Chamaedorea elegans*)
- Kangaroo vine (*Cissus antarctica* 'Minima')
- Jade plant (*Crassula argentea*)
- Weeping fig (*Ficus benjamina*)
- Prayer plant (*Maranta leuconeura*)
- Wandering Jew (*Zebrina pendula*)

IRIS

Tall bearded iris are in bloom now. They are particularly well suited to Northern California. You may want to visit a local iris nursery now or order a catalog now as iris are shipped for a limited time only from July to September. See page 304 for iris growers and page 113 for instructions on growing iris.

LAWNS

To water a lawn efficiently, watch your sprinkling method to see when runoff occurs. Adjust the timing to prevent runoff. Often this means running your sprinklers for only ten minutes at a time.

Aerate your lawn to increase water penetration by removing core-type plugs of lawn about every six inches; nurseries carry a simple tool designed for this purpose. A properly aerated lawn readily absorbs water with little runoff. Be sure to remove the plugs of earth from the lawn. Rake coarse sand into the holes to keep them from collapsing.

Dethatching also increases water penetration. Thatch is a layer of dead grass and weeds that collects in the lawn. To determine the extent of the thatch, simply pull up a small section of lawn. Any more than half an inch of thatch will deter water movement into the lawn. Dethatching rakes and dethatching attachments for power lawn mowers are available.

As a preventative measure, treat your lawn with predatory nematodes to battle underground insect pests. Nematodes are sold in a semidormant state and are activated by water. They are an organic control for fleas in the pupae stage. Fleas are common in mild weather areas.

The lemon tree has a contrary nature. When in bloom its sweet fragrance is almost intoxicating. Even the leaves when crushed yield a sweet citrus scent that perfumeries imitate in aftershave. Yet the fruit itself is so far from sweet that it cannot be eaten out of hand but must be squeezed and used sparingly.

The growing habits of lemon trees are no less contrary. They are reliable producers of fruit in coastal climates that do not have enough prolonged heat to grow other citrus such as oranges and grapefruits. Yet, with one notable exception, they are comparatively less hardy than most other citrus and none will survive temperatures much lower than 20° F.

The lemon tree likes plenty of water but not plenty of rain. It is positively despondent in monsoon areas because so much overhead water leaves it vulnerable to disease. Neither does it care for a wide fluctuation of temperature. Like the gardener it is susceptible to sunburn. What the lemon tree really prefers is a cool coastal climate in an area of low rainfall, which is why many lemons are grown in favored areas of Northern California and why they are grown commercially in Sicily and Southern California.

Goethe had it right. "Know you the land where lemon-trees bloom? . . . a soft wind hovers from the sky, the myrtle is still and the laurel stands tall—do you know it well? There, there, I would go, O my beloved, with thee!"

Lemon trees are romantic trees to live amongst but even better, given the right selection, they are fairly easy to care for. The first choice for much of Northern California is the 'Improved Meyer,' which is markedly different from the grocery store lemon. The 'Improved Meyer' lemon is almost round with a thin, yellow skin and a juicy, almost sweet flavor. The fruit appears practically continuously and profusely. Of all the lemons, 'Improved Meyer' is the most cold resistant.

The standard lemon of the supermarkets is 'Eureka.' A better choice for Northern California gardens is 'Lisbon,' which is more vigorous and has almost identical fruit. 'Ponderosa' bears huge round lemons with a tart lemon flavor. There are novelty varieties with variegated leaves such as 'Sungold.' I once grew a wonderfully fragrant, pink lemon that had creamy white and green leaves—unfortunately a severe cold snap killed it.

Lemon Tree Growing Simplified

Botanical name: *Citrus limon.*

Common name: Lemon tree.

Site preference: Grow in full sun. In areas of high heat lemon trees will tolerate some shade.

Soil conditions: Lemon trees must have well-drained soil. In areas where soil does not drain quickly, plant in a container.

Water: Water frequently, but never keep the soil soggy because lemons need air in the soil. Container trees will always need frequent watering, but trees that have grown in the ground for three or four years will survive with watering every other week in the dry season.

(continued)

Nutrients: Because lemons need a high-nitrogen fertilizer and often require iron, magnesium, manganese, and zinc, it is best to use a fertilizer especially formulated for citrus.

Problems: Wash away ants, aphids, mealybugs, or spider mites with a strong blast of water. Repeat for several days in a row.

Special care: Provide frost protection for young lemon trees whenever temperatures sink below 26°F. Paint the trunk with a diluted white or brown latex paint to prevent sunburned bark.

Hints: Mulch, but keep the mulch six inches away from the trunk to prevent diseases. Prune away dead or crossed branches.

MOSQUITOES

Rain and warm weather in April often conspire to give us a batch of newly hatched mosquitos in May. To keep down the population, make sure to overturn empty pots or other containers that collect standing water. Some of the biggest breeding sites throughout the world are abandoned tires. For other measures, see page 202.

To keep mosquitos at bay consider planting a new, genetically engineered geranium hybrid (*Pelargonium crispum* 'Citronella') that is said to repel them. The citronella plant has a strong but pleasant lemon scent that mosquitos avoid. It eventually reaches a height of five feet. Unfortunately it will not survive frost.

OAKS

In ancient Greece, groves of old trees were so sacred that both the Spartans and the Athenians would spare them in battle. Our beautiful old oak trees need the care of gardeners to spare them as gardens are created around their spreading roots. Two rules are most important: Never change the level of soil around an existing oak, and never water within a four-foot radius around the trunk of an existing oak.

Oak Growing Simplified

Botanical Name: *Quercus*.

Common name: Oak.

Site preference: Full sun.

Soil conditions: Oaks are not fussy about soil, although they prefer it well-drained. Some oaks, such as our native scrub oak (*Quercus dumosa*), thrive in very lean soil with nothing but rainwater once established.

Water: Oaks trees planted in a garden setting will tolerate normal garden conditions and grow rapidly once established. Old oak trees, in place before the house or garden, should be watered only at the drip line where rain water would naturally drip off the outermost leaves. Many oaks are drought tolerant.

Nutrients: Fertilize established oaks at their drip line, using a low nitrogen formula such as 5-10-10.

Companion plants: Fallen oak leaves provide an acidic soil that is perfect for growing acid loving plants such as azaleas, camellias, and rhododendron. But it is best not to plant those plants, which will need watering in summer, around an established oak unaccustomed to summer water. Use drought-tolerant natives such as ceanothus and manzanitas around the outer edges of established oaks.

Problems: An abundance of rain in spring often leads to an abundance of oakworm moth caterpillars. These caterpillars have large oval brown heads and lengthwise black and yellow stripes. Sometimes the caterpillars are so numerous that when their feces fall to the ground it sounds like rain. The sight of so many insects in one tree is very disconcerting, although oak trees seldom, if ever, die from the ravages of oakworms. Later the caterpillars enter a cocoon stage and then metamorphose into moths that flutter around the trees during the late afternoon.

Some gardeners believe that oakworms so severely damage the oak trees that they become more susceptible to disease. Gardeners who wish to spray for oakworm should use an organic biological spray of *Bacillus thuringiensis*; see page 35.

Amillaria mellea is a root fungus that exists in many soils that once grew oaks. It is identified by the presence of a white fungus, which is usually discovered when the bark near the soil is lifted; an arborist may be able to save the tree although the fungus is difficult to eradicate.

Oak wilt, another menace to oak trees, is not currently a problem in California, although it could become one. This insidious disease kills thousands of oaks annually in Minnesota. To protect our California oak trees, do not prune them in May or June. A recent study by a research pathologist at the University of Minnesota shows that the overland spread of this devastating fungal disease occurs because insects carry the spores to trees wounded in May and June.

POTATOES

If you planted potatoes in early spring, continue to harvest them when the tops begin to flower. For a fall harvest, plant potatoes from mid-May through mid-June. Here are the basic instructions: Cut seed potatoes (certified disease-free seed potatoes are available from some nurseries, farm supply houses, and mail-order houses) into chunks with at least two eyes per chunk. Plant seed potatoes (sprouting eyes up) not more than four inches deep. When the emerging shoots reach about five inches, cover all but the top inch with more soil. Continue to hill up (cover with soil, dead leaves, or straw) whenever the shoots reach about ten inches. Potatoes should be protected from light, which turns their skins a mildly toxic green.

For more information on potato growing, see page 96.

PRUNING

Prune uneven or unshapely growth on hedges, shrubs, and vines. Cut out deadwood wherever you find it. Prune winter- and spring-flowering plants when they finish blooming.

After the plants have finished flowering, pinch out the old buds and shape the bushes by pruning away as much as one-third of the plant. Do this promptly before the plant creates next year's flowering buds.

ROSES

Pick off faded blossoms and always cut to a five-leafed stem. Fertilize when most of the current buds have bloomed and blast off aphids with a strong spray of water. Water early, prune to open the plant to good air circulation, and pick up and discard any diseased leaves. Feed both modern and antique roses with a balanced fertilizer such as 10-10-10, 15-15-15, or 20-20-20. From now on rosebushes need equal quantities of nitrogen, phosphorous, and potassium. Rose fanatics will also apply half a cup of Epsom salts to each bush during the third week of May. Of course, water everything well.

Rose Bouquet Preservative

Gardeners who want to admire their bouquets of freshly picked roses longer than usual will be happy to learn of research done at the University of Arkansas Department of Horticulture and Forestry. The researchers tested local garden club recipes for preservatives. Two outlasted both commercial products and plain tap water.

This, the best recipe, extended the vase life of flowers to nine days. Mix:
- 1 tablespoon sugar
- 1 teaspoon vinegar
- 1 325-milligram aspirin
- 3 cups (24 ounces) water

The second-best recipe extended the vase life of flowers to 8.3 days. Mix:
- 1 tablespoon sugar
- 1 teaspoon vinegar
- 1/2 tablespoon household bleach
- 3 cups (24 ounces) water

Continue to pursue slugs and snails. There is more news from the front on the constant battle against snails. The Department of Zoology at the University of Gorakhpur in India reports that an infusion of garlic and water was more toxic to snails than were several synthetic chemicals commonly used to control them. How the snails were to be lured into the garlic broth was not disclosed. For those with a culinary passion for snails, the possibilities are tantalizing. See page 98 for more on eradicating snails and slugs.

TOMATOES

I have often thought that every vegetable garden should have a small table and two chairs where the gardener could sit with a friend at dusk. Between them they would share a bottle of wine, a loaf of crusty bread, a crumbly cheese such as feta or goat cheese, and whatever they could reach out and pluck. Imagine the soft, crimson red tomatoes still warmed by the sun. Juicy. Sweet. Conversation would seem superfluous—so might the friend.

Of all the crops grown in the garden, the favorite is the tomato—at least in America where eighty-five percent of the estimated twenty-nine million vegetable gardeners grow tomatoes. The reason is simple: taste.

There is an immense difference between the flavor of a homegrown variety and the flavor of a supermarket variety. Commercial varieties are bred for disease resistance and durability before flavor. Commercial tomatoes are also picked in a green stage, well before they ripen, and then refrigerated. Cold affects the enzymes that control tomato flavor. (Gardeners take heed: when tomatoes are stored at the standard refrigerator temperature of 40°F, the flavor is wrecked in a mere two days; so avoid refrigeration.) Many commercial tomatoes are colored (not ripened) by being placed while still green in an atmosphere of ethylene gas. Apples and bananas also give off ethylene gas; the problem is not the gas itself. The offense is in the deception. When we see a red tomato, we think that it is sweet and ripe.

There are many garden varieties of tomatoes; all of them are tastier than the supermarket varieties. Oddly, taste is not the only factor in choosing a tomato. Another important consideration is the length of time that a variety will take to ripen in your climate. A fully ripe tomato is a tasty tomato.

The tomato is a semitropical plant that gardeners grow as an annual. In the Andean mountains where it originated, the tomatoes were smaller than our cherry tomatoes— so small in fact that they were ignored by the Incas. The birds, who did not ignore them, probably carried the seeds to Central America, where the tomato was cultivated for its decorative appearance by the pre-Mayan Indians and later eaten by the Aztecs, who named it *tomatl* or *xtomatl*. Spanish conquistadors brought the tomato to Europe; colonists brought it to the United States.

Europeans and Americans do not garden in the tropics, so many varieties of tomatoes have been bred to ripen quickly. Tomatoes are also bred for disease-resistance and are labeled for resistance to the following diseases: V (verticillium wilt); F and FF (fusarium wilt); N (nematodes); T (tobacco mosaic virus); and A (alternaria leaf spot). There are varieties suitable for areas with cool or short summers such as 'Early Girl' VFF improved hybrid, which requires fifty-two days. There are varieties bred for hot summer areas such as 'Heatwave' VFFNTA hybrid and 'Solar Set' VFF hybrid, which yield best when the daytime temperature is between 90° and 96°F. My favorites are 'Better Boy' VFN hybrid, which bears huge crops of fine tasting tomatoes, and 'Sweet 100' hybrid, which yields small cherry tomatoes so sweet that children hover over them and eat them like candy. I also like the French 'Dona' and Italian heirloom 'Costoluto Genovese,' both of which have the hearty flavor I prefer in tomatoes.

There always seems to be someone around to annoy the gardener by insisting that botanically the tomato is not a vegetable but a fruit. I am happy to pass on to other gardeners who may be similarly irritated by such pedants that, at least in the United States, the tomato is legally a vegetable. The Supreme Court ruled in 1893 that, because the tomato was used as a vegetable, it must be considered one for trade purposes.

> ### *Tomato Growing Simplified*
>
> **Botanical name:** *Lycopersicon lycopersicum.*
> **Common name:** Tomato.
> **Site preference:** Tomatoes need between six and ten hours of sun daily.
> **Soil conditions:** Tomatoes prefer rich, well-drained soil.
> **Water:** Water regularly and consistently.
> **Nutrients:** Work fertilizer into the soil before planting. When the tomatoes are as big as plums, fertilize every four weeks.
> **Problems:** Tomato diseases are usually only a problem in areas where tomatoes are grown commercially. Pray for sun because tomatoes need six hours of sunlight and night temperatures above 50°F in order for the pollen tube to form in the flower.
> **Special care:** When setting out transplants, bury them deeply, covering part of the stem. Then wrap the stem with newspaper or place a collar made from a styrofoam or paper cup around the transplant to protect it from cutworms. Support the vine with stakes or wire cages.
> **Hints:** When a vine makes many blossoms at the same time, pinch off about one-third of them so that, when the remaining blossoms set fruit, they will be larger and ripen sooner.

VEGETABLES

Do not delay in planting your vegetable garden. Many crops take several months to mature. Sow seeds of basil, bush bean, carrot, chard, corn, cucumber, melon (in areas where there is enough summer heat to ripen melons), pumpkin, radish, snap beans, and squash.

Buy and plant seedlings of eggplant, pepper, and tomato, which take months to mature to fruition. Also plant seed potatoes for a fall crop.

Almost any vegetable plant can be grown in a container, so even gardeners limited to a small balcony can enjoy picking their own fresh produce. Herbs are perfectly suited to growing in pots.

See also Organic Vegetable Gardening, page 122, Potatoes, page 96, Radishes, page 116, Beans, page 164, Cucumbers, page 177, and Vegetable Gardens for Children, page 163.

Vegetable Patch Thinning

Remember to thin out overabundant young seedlings to get the best crop. Some vegetable seedlings, particularly those of leafy greens and lettuces, can be gently dug up with something thin such as a table knife or a screwdriver, and transplanted elsewhere in the garden. Other crops, particularly root crops such as carrots, cannot be transplanted without ruining the vegetable.

Do your thinning with a pair of scissors. Carefully cut out plants to be thinned (assuming that they cannot be transplanted), because digging or pulling seedlings up unnecessarily damages the roots of the seedlings growing nearby.

Read the back of the seed packet to see how closely crops can be grown. A well-prepared vegetable plot, with lots of organic compost, can sustain crops planted closer than is typically recommended. The larger-sized vegetables that need lots of room to grow should, however, be carefully thinned or the roots will compete for valuable nutrients and result in a less successful crop.

◉ *Vegetables Needing Lots of Room*
Corn
Cucumbers
Melons
Squash
Tomatoes
Zucchini

◉ *Vegetables to Plant Closer Together*
Beans
Beets
Broccoli
Cabbage
Cauliflower
Eggplant
Leafy greens
Lettuce
Peppers

◉ *Vegetables to Plant Close Together*
Carrots
Radishes

WATER

Gardens and gardeners both face between four and six rainless months ahead. Now is the time to build basins around plants—many well-established plants will survive the dry season with only one or two deep soakings. Consider installing a drip system or switching from old sprinklers to the newer low-volume sprinklers. Mulch heavily to reduce evaporation and to protect roots from the baking heat of the sun. To prevent rot, be sure to keep the mulch away from the stem or the trunk of plants.

WEEDING

Weeding is still an important task, so continue all month. Weeds steal both water and nutrients needed by cultivated plants.

WILD AND RUTHLESS GRASSES

Most of the cattle ranches that once covered the sweeping valleys of Northern California are long since gone, but the grasses remain to plague both gardeners and fire departments. During the mission and rancho years, overgrazing in coastal areas thinned the native bunchgrasses and made the area ripe for a full-scale takeover by noxious European grass species during the late 1800s. Now we have to contend with unwanted stands of oat grass, soft chess, ripgut, nit grass, and silver hairgrass. Uproot these invaders, being certain to haul away their seedheads. Grasses will soon dry to a buff brown, and, although lovely to behold when backlit by the sun, they pose a danger during the fire season.

...June...

Summer flowers in bloom now:

►•◄ *June Features* ►•◄

June begins the traditional summer months. In Northern California the weather dance peculiar to this part of the country also begins in June. As the Central Valley heats up, it inhales the cooler ocean air, pulling it through mountain gaps. On its way overhead, this cooler air creates a sun-shielding layer of high fog that gives our coastal areas their cool, overcast summers. Some summers are, however, almost fog free.

In the fog-free summers, we can all grow corn and tomatoes. But in most summers (and none of us can predict the weather ahead of time) coastal gardeners have to plant their vegetable gardens early, selecting varieties known to ripen quickly. Flower gardens too are affected by the fog. Powdery mildew blankets the roses on warm foggy days. Central Valley gardeners have to contend with the heat and worry more about destructive larvae than about fog. Mulching is particularly important in the Central Valley. High mountain gardeners should look for container-grown plants rather than seedlings for their limited gardening season.

Even more constant in Northern California than the fog is that mass of cool, heavy air sitting about a thousand miles offshore. Known as the Pacific High, it almost always blocks rain storms from entering Northern California in summer. So the number-one task of all Northern California gardeners is to see their plants through our rainless summer. Keeping the weeds pulled not only helps to conserve moisture for cultivated plants but helps curtail that other summer wonder—fire.

KEY GARDEN TASKS

All Gardeners

❋ Weed. Do not let the weeds form seedheads. Be sure to knock down tall dry grasses because they create a serious fire hazard.

❋ Add young, seedhead-free weeds to the compost pile. Remember to keep the pile as damp as a wrung-out sponge for faster composting. Turn the pile occasionally.

❋ Watch out for snails and earwigs, both of which devour seedlings.

❋ Use a strong spray from the hose to wash away aphids.

❋ Wrap fruit tree trunks with a sticky tape to control ants. Wrap low so that birds, particularly hummingbirds, will not be attracted. Fruit will be ripening soon and the ants will go after the fruit.

❋ Water plants as needed.

▲ ▼ ▲

Coastal Gardeners

❋ In addition to the tasks listed for all gardeners, fertilize plants if you see signs of pale, lackluster growth. Yellow leaves with green veins often indicate an iron deficiency, which can be corrected with chelated iron.

❋ Fertilize the lawn.

❋ Fertilize all flowering plants that are about to bloom.

❋ Fertilize roses.

❋ Pinch off dead flowers, particularly off fuchsias. Make sure that you get the entire flower head, including the swollen ovaries where seeds form. This will encourage new flowers as the plant rushes to reproduce itself.

❋ Transplant summer-flowering plants into the bedding plot. Stake tall, sprawling flowers such as delphiniums and foxgloves.

❋ Plant the vegetable garden promptly. Thin vegetable seedlings that were sown too close together by snipping them with scissors. Harvest vegetables as they ripen; picking them early in the day.

❋ Mulch.

▲ ▼ ▲

Central Valley Gardeners

❋ In addition to the tasks listed for all gardeners, insulate the garden soil from hot, dry weather by applying a two-inch-thick mulch.

❋ Fertilize plants if you see signs of pale, lackluster growth. Yellow leaves with green veins often indicate an iron deficiency, which can be corrected with chelated iron.

❋ Fertilize the lawn. Fertilize all flowering plants about to bloom. Fertilize roses.

❋ Pinch off dead flowers, particularly off lilacs and other late-spring flowering shrubs. Make sure you get the entire flower head when deadheading annuals—including the swollen ovaries where seeds form. This will encourage new flowers as the plant rushes to reproduce itself.

❋ Transplant summer-flowering plants into the bedding plot. Hot weather is hard on newly transplanted plants. Shade them for a few days with the temporary shelter of an umbrella or wooden shake. Stake tall sprawling flowers such as delphiniums and dahlias.

❋ Continue to plant the vegetable garden. Thin vegetable seedlings that were sown too close together by snipping them with scissors. Harvest vegetables as they ripen; picking them early in the day.

⚇ Be very attentive to your watering system to make sure that it is in good working order. Soak all newly transplanted plants deeply.

▲ ▼ ▲

High Mountain Gardeners

⚇ In addition to the tasks listed for all gardeners, continue to prune spring-blooming plants as they finish blooming. To keep old lilacs vigorous, prune a few of the lilac stems to the ground each year and be sure to prune suckers off grafted varieties of lilacs.

⚇ Set out summer-flowering plants.

⚇ Plant the vegetable garden promptly, using nursery transplants. Use varieties that require the shortest amount of time to ripen. Thin vegetable seedlings that were sown too close together by snipping them with scissors.

⚇ Fertilize lawns, roses, and all flowering plants about to bloom. If you did not fertilize them last month, fertilize trees and shrubs.

⚇ Consider planting several varieties of drought-tolerant ceanothus, which are excellent plants for preventing soil erosion on steep mountain slopes. Both of those mentioned below are in bloom in June.

⚇ Snowbush (*Ceanothus cordulatus*) forms a small four-foot shrub with pale, smooth bark, gray-green leaves, and the white flowers, from late spring through early summer, that lend this shrub its common name.

⚇ Tobacco brush (*Ceanothus velutinus*) has brown bark, striking, glossy green leaves and clusters of white flowers from May through August. It forms a handsome four-foot to six-foot screen.

APHIDS

The warming weather produces lots of tender young plant shoots, which in turn encourage hordes of aphids to appear and reproduce themselves. Female aphids can give birth to other female aphids through an asexual process called parthenogenesis. Those young aphids mature in a mere seven to ten days and then give birth to one hundred more little aphids over the following ten days. It is easy to see how aphids can seemingly appear from nowhere.

Unfortunately aphids suck the nutrient-rich sap from plants and weaken the plant. Given enough aphids, the leaves can become terribly curled and disfigured. Worse, some aphids carry viruses that can actually kill trees.

It is wisest not to get too worked up over aphids. This is not the time (as if there is any time) to bring out a heavy arsenal of chemicals. A strong spray of water from the hose usually does in these soft-bodied creatures. Hose them off for several days in a row.

If water only does not work, move on to water and insecticidal soap, which will kill aphids. Alternatively buy and release lady bugs. In a pesticide-free garden, lady bugs usually appear of their own accord to feast on those delectable soft bodies. Parasitic wasps (buy them at a nursery supply store) also kill aphids.

You may need to get rid of ants, which actually protect the aphids. The relationship between ants and aphids is described on page 121. Briefly, ants herd aphids to milk them of the honeydew they secrete. Honeydew not only draws ants but also it promotes a black fungus called sooty mold—a very descriptive name.

Aphid and Ant Spray

This is a recipe, passed from gardener to gardener, that seems to work. Use it selectively so that beneficial insects are not harmed. Mix:

- 1 tablespoon vegetable oil
- 1 tablespoon dishwashing soap (not detergent)
- 1/2 teaspoon eucalyptus oil (available in health, drug, and soap shops)
- 1 gallon water

Try it on a few leaves. Then, if it does not burn the leaves, spray it on the entire plant.

BALCONY AND ENTRYWAY GARDENS

Continue to transplant summer-flowering plants into pots. Cosmos, fuchsias, geraniums, gerberas, impatiens, marguerites, petunias, tuberous begonias, and zinnias are all good choices. Established plants should be fertilized with a bloom-promoting formula, such as 0-10-10. Gardeners with more space may want to try one larger flowering plant in a pot such as a showy hydrangea (*Hydrangea macrophylla*) or one of the newer shrub roses, such as 'Bonica'.

CAMELLIAS

Fertilize camellias with an acid-type fertilizer after they have finished blooming. Prune them to a more attractive shape. Find the bump on each branch where the new growth grew out of the old and cut back to this point to have more flowers next year. Yes, you can even cut back into the older, gray growth but flowers will probably be delayed there until the year after next. Mulch, preferably with pine needles or oak leaves.

CARNIVOROUS PLANTS

Summer excursions offer opportunities to become acquainted with new plants. Northern California abounds in botanical gardens and nurseries specializing in unusual plants. In the hopes of encouraging the reader, I offer the following story. One June vacation, I encountered one of Northern California's most endearing carnivorous plants alongside Highway 101 in Oregon's Darlingtonia Wayside. It might be described as a cross between a plant and an animal, the *Darlingtonia californica*, commonly known as the cobra plant or California pitcher plant.

Rising up off the forest floor, cobra plants with their broad, cupped hoods and forked tongues seemed poised to strike. Although in a primordial setting, these plants are actually highly evolved plants able to trap and to digest living organisms.

Woe to the fly lured by the sweet nectar on the cobra plant's tongue. The nectar is laced with a narcotic that compels the fly to search for more nectar. Once it crawls into the cobra plant's hood, escape is nearly impossible. The helpless insect slips down the narrowing pitcherlike neck and into digestive enzymes strong enough to digest a frog.

Naturally my gardener's heart coveted such a wily plant. Shortly thereafter, I found myself on another journey up the Northern California coast to California Carnivores in Forestville where there are no fewer than four hundred varieties of carnivorous beauties.

Once one gets past the horror of a flesh-eating plant, one notices that these are plants of impressive shape and intriguing colors. The sundews (*Drosera*) are covered with burgundy-colored hairs holding drops of a clear, sticky glue that glisten with prismatic elegance. The very quality that gives them such magical grace is the substance that holds their prey captive. In some drosera the entire leaf folds to trap an insect. Charles Darwin once wrote that he cared "more about Drosera than the origin of all the species in the world." Fortunately, the Cape sundew (*Drosera capensis*) is easy to grow on a windowsill or outdoors in our mild climate.

Still, I could not get over the beguiling cobra plant, so I also bought a carnivorous plant of similar stature—a *Sarracenia flava*. Sarracenia, commonly called pitcher plants, once grew in bogs and fens from Virginia to Texas. Their nectar contains a paralytic agent, coniine, which intoxicates the hapless insect and hastens its fall into the pitcher of digestive enzymes.

Sarracenia are easy to grow. Simply set their container in a saucer that is kept constantly full of water. They need bright light, either indoors or out. Surprisingly, these exotic plants need a chilly dormant period, so in coastal areas set their container outdoors from Thanksgiving to Valentine's Day; in cooler mountain and valley areas, place in an unheated room.

CITRUS

Citrus trees do not require much pruning. They are, however, given to bearing so many heavy fruits that the branch breaks. This is particularly true of lemon trees, which bear fruit at the ends of thin branches. When you see an overburdened branch, cut it back between one-third and one-half, then pinch the new growth back several times during the summer growing season.

CYMBIDIUMS

Fertilize every two weeks with high-nitrogen liquid fertilizer formulated for orchids.

FERTILIZE

Fertilize summer-blooming annuals and perennials.

FLOWERS THAT ARE EASY TO GROW

There are three flowering plants that are so easy to care for that, after getting them established, there is very little the gardener must do, except for watering, to keep them in bloom year after year. The only disadvantage to growing them is that they are grown everywhere—parking lots, shopping malls, and median strips.

⚜ Agapanthus (*Agapanthus orientalis*, also sold as *Agapanthus africanus* and *Agapanthus umbellatus*) is a dependable plant for all Northern California gardens except for those in high mountain regions with severe winter cold. The agapanthus, also known as the lily-of-the-Nile, forms a handsome, circular clump of broad straplike leaves. For several months in summer it forms tall stems bearing a showy ball of blue or white flowers at the top. A dwarf variety, 'Peter Pan,' tends to bloom much of the year. There are no real drawbacks to agapanthus. Snails tend to congregate under the leaves but are easily dealt with.

⚜ The fortnight lily (*Dietes vegeta*, also known as *Dietes iridioides* and *Moraea iridioides*) does not survive the cold of either high mountain areas or the Sierra foothill areas, but it will grow almost everywhere else in Northern California. It forms a stiff, circular clump of pointed narrow strap-shaped leaves that fulfill a landscape role even when it is not in bloom. Flowers, rather like the open, flat Japanese iris, form for a day or two during much of spring, summer, and fall. Pinch off the spent flower to prolong the bloom period. However, do not cut off the long, willowy branch that bears the flowers; these bloom year after year. It is quite drought tolerant.

⚜ Indian hawthorn (*Rhaphiolepis indica*) is a trim shrub with a lot of virtues. Among them are flowers in late fall through spring, bronze-shaded new leaves, and small blue berries. There are many varieties, and they range in height from a compact two-foot 'Ballerina' to a tall fifteen-foot 'Majestic Beauty.' Shape by pruning the plant to the desired form and height.

FLOWERS THAT THRIVE IN HEAT

Hot weather can wilt flowering plants. Fortunately several flowering beauties take the heat in stride.

⚜ The canna lily (*Canna* x *generalis*) actually prefers heat and provides a tropical aura with bright orchid-like blooms.

⚜ Cosmos, see page 132, also endures heat without any noticeable strain.

⚜ Petunias (*Petunia hybrida*) not only thrive in heat but also tolerate occasional neglect; look for F1 hybrids to obtain the most vigorous plants.

⚜ Zinnia (*Zinnia elegans* or *Zinnia grandiflora*) prefer the Central Valley to the coast. A large variety of strains offer many choices in flower form and color.

FLOWERS WITH OLD FASHIONED CHARM

⚜ Hollyhocks (*Alcea rosea*) are easy to grow. Planted along a fence or at the back of a flower bed, these tall spires of bloom are a friendly sight. The old varieties of hollyhock are nine feet tall; newer varieties are between two feet and six feet tall and come in both single and double flower forms.

⚜ Feverfew (*Chrysanthemum parthenium*), once the favorite of Victorian gardeners, ranges from one to three feet tall and come in shades of white and yellow. The old white variety is so well adapted to Northern California that it self-sows as freely as a weed and persists year after year with little help from the gardener.

FIRE

Clear all dry brush and volunteer grasses at least thirty feet from your home. Remove or prune to thin out native chaparral growth on hillsides. However, leave native trees and large shrubs because their roots anchor the soil on hillsides. Irrigate them occasionally in the summer (keeping water six feet away from an oak's trunk) to help maintain the moisture level and to prevent leaves from drying too much.

FRUIT TREES

Continue to thin tiny fruit now to about four inches between remaining fruit to help trees bear larger, tastier fruit. A fruit tree may drop many immature fruits now, a phenomenon known as June drop, although it sometimes occurs at other times; this is simply nature's way of thinning fruit on trees that set more fruit than they can ripen.

> ❀ Be sure to pick up the fallen fruit as it may be infested with bugs or disease and controlling the spread of fruit tree ailments is one of the chief defenses of the gardener.
> ❀ Remove suckers (spindly branches sprouting from the ground near the trunk).
> ❀ Whitewash trunks to protect them from sunburn and to control borers.

FRUIT TREES—PHEROMONE

Pheromone has been a buzz word in the perfume trade, but it is actually more seductive in the garden. A pheromone is a chemical secreted by an animal that serves to communicate to another of the same species and elicit a specific behavioral response. It may not work as desired with the human species, but insects fall for it readily. In a pheromone trap, the scent of the female insect scent lures the male insect into a sticky glue.

The lures, which are insect specific, are placed either in a delta trap (a small triangular tent for row crops) or a wing trap (a flying diamond shape suspended from trees). Pheromones are usually used to monitor the presence of insects by enabling the gardener to count the number of insects trapped over a given period of time in order to kill the insects with other means). In small gardens they can be used to diminish the insect population. Trapping the males before breeding tends to cut down significantly on the next generation of insects. These biolures are insect specific for codling moths, apple maggots, cabbage loppers, grain moths, oriental fruit moths, corn earworms, and other insects.

FUCHSIAS

Feed fuchsias with a balanced fertilizer and keep them well watered. Remove the old blooms and the swollen seed pods in order to keep the plants blooming.

HERBS

Do not fertilize herbs. Fertilized herbs grow lush, full, and wonderfully green at the expense of flavor—better to have a scrawnier herb and intensified flavor.

HYDRANGEAS

Hydrangeas are surprisingly varied; there are several species that will survive anywhere in Northern California. Their leaves are varied too. There is a hydrangea with an oak-shaped leaf (*Hydrangea quercifolia*). A plant breeder, William Flemer III, noticed that one of his plants had a profusion of unusually upright, creamy white blooms that looked like large lilac flowers. He took out a patent on this beauty, which has won many horticultural awards, and began propagating *Hydrangea quercifolia* 'Snow Queen.'

It may surprise gardeners to learn that, in 1930, the United States was the first country to let plant breeders patent their creations and collect royalties. Some breeders maintain that no one should own genetic material.

I favor the Lacecap hydrangea, which resembles a whole bouquet captured in a single bloom. Another favorite is the climbing hydrangea (*Hydrangea anomala petiolaris*), which produces fragrant white blooms. In Great Britain, climbing hydrangeas are often planted to sprawl through trees. Both the climbing and the oakleaf hydrangea will grown anywhere in Northern California.

Hydrangeas have an unusual sensitivity to aluminum ions in the soil. When the soil pH drops to 5.5 or lower, this acid condition allows the aluminum ions to turn hydrangea blossoms blue. Gardeners who insist on blue hydrangeas can add aluminum sulfate to the soil.

Hydrangea Growing Simplified

Botanical name: *Hydrangea.*

Common name: Hydrangea.

Site preference: Part-shade inland to full sun along the coast; generally full sun should be avoided when the plants are in full flower in order to provide the longest bloom. They are hardier than generally believed—many will take temperatures of –4° to –13°F.

Soil conditions: Native to moist, fertile woodlands, they need a rich, well-composted soil that drains well.

Water: They need lots of water during our long, dry summer and fall.

Nutrients: Feed with a balanced fertilizer in spring and mulch in spring to keep the roots cool in summer. For blue flowers, feed with aluminum sulfate before the flowers form. For redder flowers, feed with superphosphate.

Problems: Because hydrangeas are heavily dependent on summer water, be sure to group them with other water-loving plants.

Special care: Prune carefully. Many cultivars are of *Hydrangea macrophylla* and bloom heaviest on last year's growth—prune out only the weakest growth and gently remove the dried flower heads each spring. Vigorous species such as *Hydrangea arborescens* and *Hydrangea paniculata*, which bloom on the current year's growth, can be cut back to several buds per stem (swollen bumps under the thin bark skin) in late winter or early spring—this will result in huge blooms. Left unpruned, there will be more but smaller blooms. When in doubt, prune only stems that have already bloomed.

Hints: Old hydrangeas may be rejuvenated by cutting back each stem close to the ground. When the new growth comes bursting out in thick profusion, be sure to thin it out, leaving only the most vigorous shoots.

IN BLOOM IN JUNE

- Annuals: ageratum, lobelia, petunia, sweet alyssum, and sweet William
- Perennials: daylily, carnation, felicia, geranium, and marguerite
- Bulblike: gladiolus, Japanese iris, and lily
- Shrubs: fuchsia, hibiscus, hydrangea, and rose
- Vines: bougainvillea, clematis, and star jasmine
- Natives: clarkia, columbine, Donner (California) buckwheat, mariposa lily, Matilija poppy, and Western azalea

IN THE NURSERY IN JUNE

- Annuals: impatiens, marigold, and petunia
- Perennials: agapanthus, daylily, geranium, and marguerite
- Shrubs: fuchsia, hibiscus, and hydrangea
- Summer vegetables

KIWI VINES

Prune back those vigorous arms of growth to four to five buds. Those swollen places along the stem called buds will then be forced to grow into a dense growth that will bear large clusters of kiwis. Be sure to water the vines. Although the plants are fairly drought tolerant, they need the water for the fruit.

LAWNS

To conserve water, mow your lawn higher: one inch for Bermuda, two and one-half inches for bluegrass, and three inches for tall fescue. But do not let your grass grow to more than twice the recommended mowing height before cutting it.

Lawn Watering in Summer

Take a few minutes to review your watering timetable for your lawn. The California Department of Water Resources has established average ET (evapotranspiration) rates for many Northern California communities. The ET rate is the quantity of water that evaporates from the garden soil plus the quantity of water that transpires from the grass leaves. Based on these ET rates, lawns in different areas need different quantities of water to keep them at their ornamental best without wasting water.

LAWN WATERING GUIDELINES FOR SUMMER

For summer the average lawn, watered to a depth of six to eight inches twice a week, will need to have the sprinklers on each time for:

- Between six and thirty-eight minutes in the coastal region
- Between twenty-three and forty-eight minutes in the Central Valley
- Between seventeen and forty-six minutes in the high mountains

The lower figures are for larger pipelines. Your lawn will indicate a need for more water by turning from a bright green to a dull blue green. Also you will see footprints in the lawn because the grass does not spring back up.

LEMON TREES

Lemon trees tend to set fruit at the tips of skinny branches that often break under the weight of this fruit. Correct this tendency by pinching back the side branches by half during the summer months.

NASTURTIUMS

Nasturtium flowers are particularly lovely in June when you can eat them in a summer salad. I never really appreciated them as a decorative until I visited Boston and entered the Isabella Stewart Gardner Museum to gaze at a few Italian oil paintings. With a Botticelli on my right and a Bellini on my left, I fell under the spell of a live nasturtium.

The flowering vine trailed over a marble balustrade and cascaded down into the interior courtyard. It swayed ever so gently above the potted palms and blooming azaleas. Who would have thought to decorate an elaborate Venetian-style palazzo with a humble nasturtium?

Isabella Gardner, of course. Her will stipulated that everything remain exactly as she left it. The esteem with which she regarded the nasturtium might surprise a few Northern California gardeners who consider the vine as little more than a weed.

But ever since a few nasturtium seeds made their way with sailors from Peru to Europe sometime in the sixteenth century, the nasturtium has graced more than one palace. Le Nôtre, the lofty landscape architect of Louis XIV, even used nasturtiums in the formal flower beds popular during the seventeenth century.

By the eighteenth century nasturtiums had become a favorite of European gardens. Later, the Victorians used nasturtium flowers in their tussie-mussies—fragrant, handheld bouquets—a use that might surprise a few gardening friends who maintain that the nasturtium scent itself is offensive. They have their case. The popular name, nasturtium, is a combination of the Latin words *nasus* (nose) and *tortum* (twist). The flowers are sweet smelling, but the leaves contain a mustard oil that releases a potent and somewhat disagreeable scent.

The mustard oil in the leaves led to another popular name, Indian cress, which the English used to describe the edible nature of the flowering vine. Both the leaves and the flowers are used in salads, where they contribute a peppery flavor much like that of watercress. Nasturtiums have been eaten almost as much as they have been admired. Sailors used to take barrels of pickled nasturtium seeds (they resemble capers) along on voyages to ward off scurvy. They would have done better to have pickled the leaves, which are high in vitamin C.

Gardeners today can select from several varieties of nasturtiums. There are climbers, trailers, and compact types. Some nasturtium flowers have a single layer of petals; others have double layers of petals. Typically nasturtium blossoms are in bright shades of orange, scarlet, and yellow. There are also varieties with variegated leaves.

Nasturtiums are very easy to grow from seed. Because the large seeds are easy to poke into the ground one at a time, they are suitable for children's gardens. It is best to grow them in place from seed as they do not like to be transplanted. They sprout in seven to ten days and grow quickly.

In the coastal areas of Northern California, nasturtiums flower freely from spring through fall and even into winter if the weather is still warm. Nasturtiums tend to set seed and reappear year after year with little help from the gardener except for weekly water during the dry season. In fact they are so easy to grow that many accomplished gardeners foolishly disdain them.

Nasturtium Growing Simplified

Botanical name: *Tropaeolum majus.*
Common name: Nasturtium.
Site preference: Sun or part shade.
Soil conditions: Any soil, particularly lean, well-drained soil.
Water: Needs water in the dry season.
Nutrients: Do not fertilize. Fertilizer will promote lush leaves at the expense of bloom.
Hints: Best grown from seeds sown directly into the desired site.

OAKS

Oak wilt is not currently a problem in California, although it could become one. To protect our California oak trees, do not prune oak trees in May or June because the overland spread of this devastating fungal disease is carried overland by insects to trees wounded in May and June.

ORCHID CACTUS

Epiphyllums, popularly known as orchid cactus, will probably finish blooming this month. They should then have a rest period of between two and four weeks. During this time, keep the plants slightly moist, but do not fertilize them.

PARTY TIME IN THE GARDEN

It is easy to panic when hordes of guests are about to descend on the garden, but there are a few tricks that professionals use to give an immediate boost. The first trick is reduce the clutter. Clear away weeds and sulking plants. Trim away sprawling growth. A carefully placed bench adds instant interest to an otherwise dull area. Paint also works wonders. Take a look at the mailbox, garden gates, fences, arbors—sometimes a strong color is very effective against a backdrop of green. Imagine a bright red gate on a fence overgrown with ivy.

POWDERY MILDEW

According to several reports in horticultural journals, a spray of baking soda and horticultural oil mixed with water offered better protection from powdery mildew than any of a number of tested commercial sprays. Here is one home-brewed recipe.

- 2 tablespoons baking soda (sodium bicarbonate, to control black spot)
- 1 tablespoon horticultural oil (to control fungus)
- 1 gallon water

Mix everything together. The addition of a little spreader-sticker, such as Tween 20, helps too. Spray on both the upper and lower surfaces of leaves.

There are other ways to combat powdery mildew:

- Allow plenty of room around the plant to provide good air circulation.
- Always water early in the day.
- Spray the plant with an antitranspirant (available from garden supply stores), which will form a film around the leaves and so lessen mildew.

POTATOES

If you planted potatoes in early spring, harvest them when the tops begin to flower. Continue to plant potatoes until mid-June for a fall harvest. For more information on potato growing see page 96.

PRIMROSES

By June, primroses have finished their spring display of flowers. If you cut back their leaves (to do that, hold them up like rabbit ears) by between one-third and one-half, they will probably flower again in midsummer.

ROSES

Continue to feed both modern and antique roses with a balanced fertilizer such as 10-10-10, 15-15-15, or 20-20-20. From now on rosebushes need equal amounts of nitrogen, phosphorous, and potassium. Rose fanatics will also apply half a cup of Epsom salts to each bush during the third week of June. Of course, continue to water everything well.

In the coastal areas, the combination of evening fog and warm weather (a typical early June pattern) often causes a layer of powdery mildew to form. To lessen mildew, see page 161.

SHADE AND FLOWERING PLANTS

In June, the gardener seeking the comfort of a shady garden spot may well wish there were flowers growing there. The good news is that there are flowering plants that do well in the shade. The following perennials are a few favorites.

⚬ Bleeding heart (*Dicentra*) has airy, fernlike foliage and a slender stem that bears a stunning row of heart-shaped, deep pink flowers. Look for the cultivar 'Luxuriant', which blooms from spring through summer.

⚬ Corsican hellebore (*Helleborus lividus corsicus*, also known *Helleborus argutifolius*) is a long-lived plant with distinctive leaves with sharply toothed edges. It bears clusters of nodding, pale green flowers as early as winter, and they persist well into spring.

⚬ False spiraea (*Astilbe*) shows off airy plumes of bloom from late spring until well into summer. It is partial to rich soil and fair amounts of water. It is short lived in areas of high summer heat.

⚬ Japanese anemone (*Anemone hybrida*) is an old-fashioned white flower on graceful two- to four-foot stems. The plant blooms from late summer until well into fall. The leaves resemble maple leaves. It does better in part sun along the foggy coast, but inland it does best in full shade.

STRAWBERRIES

Watch out for snails, slugs, and sowbugs in the strawberry patch. Make sure that strawberries are well watered to keep them producing fruit. Although I am generally against plastic in the garden, it is heaven-sent for the strawberry patch. It keeps the berries clean and the soil warm and moist.

VEGETABLES

There is still time to put in a summer vegetable garden. From seed, you can grow bean, carrot, chard, pumpkin, radish, snap bean, and summer squash. From nursery transplants you can grow corn, cucumber, eggplant, melon (in areas with enough summer heat to ripen melons), pepper, and tomato. For a fall crop, cut up and sow pieces of seed potatoes. But do not delay any longer. Many plants require several months to mature.

Warning: Gardeners should be aware that there is a slight risk of transferring pathogens such as salmonella, bacteria, such as E. coli, and parasites, such as tapeworms and roundworms, from manure to the vegetable garden. Individuals who are particularly susceptible—pregnant women, toddlers, and those with chronic diseases such as cancer, diabetes, or AIDS—should avoid eating uncooked vegetables from manured gardens. To reduce the risk of contamination, gardeners should apply manure only in the fall (or put it in the compost heap in fall) so that the pathogens will break down before the garden is planted in spring. Wash raw vegetables well before eating. It is not advisable to use cat, dog, or pig manure in the vegetable garden or even in the compost pile because of the risk of infectious parasites.

See also organic vegetable gardening, page 122, Potatoes, page 96, Radishes, page 116, Tomatoes, page 143, Beans page 164, Cucumbers, page 177.

VEGETABLES—COMPANION PLANTING

Gardening has its mysteries and one of them is that some plants do well when planted in the company of other plants. Sometimes the cause is obvious, at other times the cause is mysterious, but the observation is true. Here are a few pointers.

❁ Interplant vegetables with flowering plants because the bright flowers draw insects and birds that then feast on the vegetable pests.

❁ Plant radishes and onions between other vegetables. Not only will they grow in small spaces, but also they emit an odor that is repugnant to many insects.

❁ Do not plant members of the nightshade family (eggplants, potatoes, and tomatoes) together because they share common pests that would then thrive in the garden patch.

❁ Plant marigolds in the vegetable garden because insects dislike their scent. The roots of French marigold (*Tagetes patula*) emit a substance that repels nematodes.

❁ Sweet basil (*Ocimum basilicum*) repels aphids, mosquitoes, and mites. Planted with tomatoes it is said to repel tomato worms.

❁ Nasturtiums deter whiteflies and squash bugs. Aphids, alas, adore nasturtiums.

Gardeners in search of something unusual for the vegetable garden should consider a few flowering plants.

⊛ It may be a bit difficult to find your first borage plant (*Borago officinalis*), but once you plant it, you will have borage plants forever (whether you want them or not!) It self-seeds prolifically. Borage grows into a two-foot mound covered with heavenly blue, star-shaped flowers. The cucumber-flavored blossoms and small leaves may be tossed in salads or used to garnish soups or deserts. The cool blue flower is perfect for freezing in ice cubes for summer drinks.

⊛ Edible chrysanthemum or shungiku (*Chrysanthemum coronarium*) produces delicate yellow flowers but is grown for the edible green leaves, which are cooked. The aromatic leaves taste just as you would imagine a chrysanthemum would, and there is no mistaking the flavor for anything else. The first time I sampled them in a *sukiyaki* in Tokyo, I looked to see if part of the flower arrangement had fallen into the kimono-clad waitress's skillet. The flavor grows on you; you may find yourself craving it—at least occasionally.

VEGETABLE GARDENS FOR CHILDREN

Magic places do not need to be created for children; children create magic wherever they are. Creating special places for children in the garden can, however, lure them out of the petunia bed and save an adult temper. Sharing gardening activities with children can be beneficial to both adult and child. After all, we adults are hard pressed to find a suitable excuse to build a bean-pole tepee or to grow a cucumber in a bottle.

A bean-pole tepee is constructed out of between six and eight bamboo poles, or pieces of narrow scrap lumber (each between six and ten feet long), pushed securely into the ground in a six-foot circle and tied together at the top. The tepee may be covered with any bean vine (not bush beans). One of the showy, scarlet-flowering runner beans, such as 'Red Knight,' 'Enorma,' or 'Prize Winner,' makes a spectacular display. These are true, edible, landscaping plants growing thirteen feet high and covered with huge crimson blossoms. Their nectar often attracts hummingbirds. The fat meaty beans can grow up to twelve inches long and can be cooked fresh or dried for using later.

Carrots are a favorite with children because they are easy to grow, and they love to pull them up, rinse them off, and eat them on the spot. The problem with carrots is that the seeds are so tiny that they are difficult to space when planting. The solution is to use a seed tape on which the seeds are already spaced in the proper position for planting. Carrots take about two months from seed to eating.

A large cucumber grown in a narrow-necked bottle is something like having a model ship in a bottle—both are wonders to show incredulous friends. To achieve this marvel, slip a growing baby cucumber into a narrow-necked bottle. The secret is to select a cucumber in a shady spot or to make a parasol for the cucumber while it is growing in the bottle because, if the bottle is exposed to the sun, it will heat up and kill the cucumber. When the cucumber is large, snip it (and the bottle) off the vine.

Pumpkins are always a hit with children. To grow a really large pumpkin, you must start with a variety known to create immense pumpkins. 'Atlantic Giant,' which has been grown into an enormous 429-pound pumpkin, is currently the choice of pumpkin-growing contestants in North America. When growing pumpkins, it is fun to scratch an initial or two in the skin of a young pumpkin (gently score the skin with the tip of a knife) and then watch the initials grow with the pumpkin.

Radishes grow quickly, a quality that makes them popular with everyone. Many radishes are ready to harvest within a month after seeding. My favorite as a child was the long, thin white 'Icicle' radish. Now I am partial to the 'French Breakfast' radish because it is so handsome—an oblong cylinder as thick as my thumb brilliantly colored with crimson red on top and creamy white at the bottom. In hot areas, wait until the weather cools to grow great-tasting radishes.

Bean Growing Simplified

Botanical name: *Phaseolus coccineus*.

Common name: Scarlet runner bean.

Site preference: Full sun, warm sheltered position.

Soil conditions: Rich soil.

Water: Water the soil before planting and then not again until the beans have sprouted. Once the beans have sprouted, keep the soil well watered.

Nutrients: Feed beans with a balanced fertilizer when plants start to grow and again when pods form.

Problems: Unfortunately, scarlet runner beans do not form pods in really hot weather. If the temperature rises above 90°F in your area, plant another variety or enjoy the flowers and wait until the weather finally cools in the fall to enjoy the crop.

Special care: A beneficial and harmless bacteria called nitrogen legume inoculant (available from some nurseries, particularly the organically oriented) greatly increases the yield of all beans. Dust the seeds with the inoculant before planting them or add it to the planting hole.

Hints: Harvest beans before they become mature as they tend to become tough.

Few plant groups are more undervalued by American gardeners than vines. We plan our gardens horizontally rather than vertically, missing the opportunity of enjoying growing plants that grow up through other plants and cover vertical structures. June is a fine month to stroll the garden and see where a vine or two might be added. (As if a gardener needed an excuse for another plant!)

For summer shade and winter sun, cover an arbor or trellis with a deciduous vine such as a wisteria or a grape. Some grapes have such magnificent red leaves in the fall that they should be grown for autumn color and have the grapes considered a bonus. Flowering vines add color when grown through evergreen trees. The English have been growing large-flowered clematis vines through trees for decades—a technique that would be equally successful here. To soften a fence or cover an ungainly structure consider a honeysuckle or a trumpet vine.

The following are a few favorites, including clematis (see also page 132) and wisteria (see also page 125) which have been covered in previous months.

◉ Boston ivy (*Parthenocissus tricuspidata*) is (as you might expect from someone from Boston) the polite and proper ivy. Its naughty cousin, English ivy, tears the shingles right off of a house, but Boston ivy clings delicately with tiny little disks that will not harm either wood or stone. The best feature of a Boston ivy is the splendid fall color. It will grow anywhere in Northern California.

◉ The Cécile Brunner climbing rose, sometimes called the Sweetheart Rose, is not technically a vine, but someone ought to tell that to 'Cécile Brunner.' This climbing rose will easily overtake many vines as she winds her way twenty feet up into a tree. Cécile Brunner produces a profusion of fragrant, tiny, pale pink roses in early summer and continues to bloom intermittingly the rest of the summer. This extraordinarily hearty rose will thrive in most of Northern California.

◉ Japanese honeysuckle (*Lonicera japonica*) is an evergreen vine that may be deciduous in very cold areas. It has sweet, fragrant, small white flowers in late spring and summer and is grown for their fragrance. It is so vigorous that the variety known as Hall's honeysuckle is used as a ground cover in areas with erosion problems. It should be pruned in both spring and fall to keep it manageable.

◉ The trumpet vine (*Campsis radicans*) grows in even the coldest areas. This fast-growing vine can reach up to forty feet on the side of a house. Pretty, trumpet-shaped orange flowers appear in the fall. Plant with care; it is almost too vigorous.

◉ *Clematis armandii* is smothered with fragrant white bloom each spring. Unlike most clematis, it is evergreen, and although it is slow to start, once it gets going, it will cover a fence. It grows in all but the coldest areas of Northern California but is at its best along the coast.

◉ *Clematis jackmanii* is known for its large blue-purple summer flowers and vigorous, rapid growth. In cold winter areas it will freeze back to the ground, but in spring it will stage a powerful comeback.

◉ *Clematis montana* is covered with so many white (turning to pink) blooms in spring that the leaves are hidden. It is also hardy and easy to grow.

◉ *Clematis* 'Nelly Moser' is also very dependable and easy to grow. It is a favorite of gardeners because the huge, pink-striped blooms are showstoppers.

⊛ Chinese wisteria (*Wisteria sinensis*) has blue violet, grapelike clusters of fragrant flowers all at one time on bare vine branches. Although most Chinese wisteria are blue or violet, there is a white variety called Alba. It is drought tolerant once established and will grow anywhere in Northern California. Unlike Japanese wisteria which needs full sun, Chinese wisteria will bloom in part shade.

⊛ Japanese wisteria (*Wisteria floribunda*) has slender, longer flower clusters that open from the top down as the leaves appear and a longer blooming period. Train Japanese wisteria along an arbor or a fence to show off the pendulous clusters of flowers.

WATERING

A California summer for Northern California gardeners typically means no rain until next October. The chief task of the gardener is to get plants through this rainless period. Here are a few ideas.

⊛ Save both water and time by grouping plants with high water requirements in a specific area.

⊛ Create water basins for large plants and furrows for garden crops or, even better, install a drip system.

⊛ Conserve moisture (and discourage weeds) by applying a two-inch-deep mulch. Small or medium wood chips are good for borders. Shredded bark is wonderful for keeping down weeds, but it knits so tightly together that it sheds water, so it is best placed outside the watering basin.

WATER-HOLDING POLYMERS

Water-holding polymers, sold under several trade names, absorb and hold water in nuggets that resemble little chunks of gelatin. Mixed with soil, these soft nuggets make water available to plant roots when the soil is dry. They simplify watering chores because they lengthen the time plants can go between waterings. They are useful both indoors and outdoors.

WEEDING

Weeds steal valuable water and nutrients from cultivated plants, so be sure to eliminate them.

If your wisteria vine did not bloom this spring, welcome to the chorus. Wisteria are notoriously slow to bloom, usually taking three or four years and sometimes even seven years to bloom.

There are some tricks that might be used to encourage next year's bloom. Remember that wisteria will make masses of vegetative growth instead of blooms until something signals it to bloom, which is a plant's way of reproducing. So do not fertilize wisteria. Fertilizer, particularly one high in nitrogen, encourages vegetative growth. The exception is a fertilizer containing only phosphate that will help blooms to form. Landscape gardeners sometimes shock wisteria vines into blooming by using a spade to prune the roots about two feet away from the trunk. Not all gardeners believe such shock treatment is wise; other gardeners swear by it.

After a wisteria has been growing in place for a year, prune out the weaker side shoots growing along the stronger main stem. This will make a more attractive vine and more flowers next year. Every summer cut back the long streamers, saving only those that you wish to train along an arbor or other supporting device.

SPREKELIA FORMOSISSIMA

... July ...

Summer bulbs in bloom?

In July the fog is cycling back and forth along the coast so the coastal gardener never can predict when, or if, the tomatoes will ripen. In the Central Valley, the north winds are sweeping down in such hot blasts that it is often too hot for transplanting seedlings. In the high mountains, the days are warm enough to call it summer, but the evenings are apt to bring chill. Despite these challenges, gardeners love to garden in July.

Wherever the gardener is in Northern California, the chief task is always the same this month: Tend to the watering. Make sure plants do not dry out too much. Pay particular attention to potted plants, which tend to dry out, causing the soil to shrink away from the sides of the pot.

All Gardeners

◉ Weed. Do not let the weeds form seedheads.

◉ Add young, seedhead-free weeds to the compost pile. Remember to keep the pile as damp as a wrung-out sponge for faster composting.

◉ Watch out for snails and earwigs, both of which devour seedlings.

◉ Plant bulbs that bloom in autumn.

◉ Use a strong spray from the hose to wash away aphids.

◉ With fruit crops ripening this month, watch out for ants. Wrap fruit tree trunks with a sticky tape to control ants (wrap low so that birds, particularly hummingbirds, will not be attracted) and if necessary, spray (see Ant and Aphid Spray, page 152).

◉ Water plants as needed.

▲ ▼ ▲

Coastal Gardeners

In addition to the tasks listed for all gardeners, fertilize plants if you see signs of pale, lackluster growth. Yellow leaves with green veins often indicate an iron deficiency, which can be corrected with chelated iron.

◉ Fertilize the lawn.

◉ Fertilize all flowering plants that are about to bloom. Fertilize camellias. Fertilize roses, except most antique roses.

◉ Pinch off dead flowers, particularly off fuchsias. Make sure you get the entire flower head, particularly the swollen ovaries where seeds form. This will encourage new flowers to form

as the plant rushes to reproduce itself.

◉ Transplant summer-flowering plants into the bedding plot, and stake tall sprawling flowers such as delphiniums and foxgloves.

◉ Thin vegetable seedlings that were sown too close together by snipping them with scissors. Harvest vegetables as they ripen. Pick them early in the day.

◉ Mulch.

▲ ▼ ▲

Central Valley Gardeners

In addition to the tasks listed for all gardeners, insulate the garden soil from the hot, dry weather by applying a two-inch-thick mulch.

◉ Fertilize plants if you see signs of pale, lackluster growth. Fertilize the lawn. Fertilize all flowering plants that are about to bloom. Fertilize camellias. Fertilize roses, except most antique roses. In really hot areas, roses will probably stop flowering until the weather cools.

◉ Pinch off dead flowers. Make sure you get the entire flower head when deadheading annuals—particularly the swollen ovaries where seeds form.

◉ Transplant summer-flowering plants, such as cosmos, petunias, and zinnias that will endure heat, into the bedding plot. See additional suggestions on page 107. Hot weather is hard on newly transplanted plants. Shade them for a few days with the temporary shelter of an umbrella or wooden shake. Stake tall sprawling flowers such as dahlias.

◉ Continue to plant the vegetable garden. Thin vegetable seedlings that were sown too close together. Harvest vegetables as they ripen. Pick them early in the day.

◎ Soak all newly transplanted plants. Prune berry vines when you have finished harvesting.

▲ ▼ ▲

High Mountain Gardeners

In addition to the tasks listed for all gardeners, set out summer-flowering plants.

◎ Plant the vegetable garden promptly using nursery transplants. Use varieties that require the shortest amount of time to ripen. Thin vegetable seedlings that were sown too close together by snipping them with scissors.

◎ Fertilize lawns, roses and all flowering plants about to bloom. If you did not fertilize last month, fertilize trees and shrubs.

ANGEL'S TRUMPET

In July the angel trumpet casts its spell, and gardeners who see them for the first time are likely to ask, "What in the world is that? Is it real?" Of all the plants that captivate the gardener in summer none is more dramatic than angel's trumpet (*Brugmansia versicolor*). They are the crown jewels in a treasury of ornamental plants. Towering over other blooming plants, they seductively dangle foot-long trumpet-shaped flowers that look like fragile bells of saffron yellow ('Charles Grimaldi') or creamy pink ('Frosty Pink'). Everyone that passes by them during the day is sure to stop to stare in awe at the plant.

Yet long after the gardener has deserted the flowerbeds, when dusk has blanketed the garden in shadow, the brugmansias perk up to perfect their showy display. Slowly the immense blooms swell as the delicate flares arch out like a trumpet. Instead of a lush melody, from deep within each flower's throat a heavy musky scent emerges—an intoxicating fragrance meant to lure the insects of the night.

The brugmansia is a deadly enchantress. Every part is poisonous, but most particularly the seeds and the leaves. The plant contains a strong alkaloidal drug that has often been used as a narcotic. Ingestion is dangerous and causes nausea, hallucination, coma, and even death. In ancient Colombia, a kissing cousin of brugmansia called datura was used to drug the wives and slaves of deceased rulers before they were buried alive in their master's tomb. All the brugmansias were formerly classified as daturas and the names are frequently confused. But currently the daturas include only the herbaceous or subshrubby species with erect rather than pendulous flowers. Many brugmansias and daturas originated in South America, where they were used as sacred hallucinogens in tribal initiation rites. Even today you will find the angel trumpet's lingering beauty gracing South American graveyards.

One weedy species native to the United States, *Datura stramonum,* was made into a type of salad and eaten by British soldiers sent to quell the rebellion in Jamestown, Virginia, in 1676. The troops behaved bizarrely for days. Ever since that famous incident, the plant has been known as jimson weed.

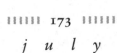

> ### *Brugmansia Growing Simplified*
>
> **Botanical name:** *Brugmansia versicolor*; also known as *Datura versicolor*.
> **Common name:** Angel's trumpet.
> **Site preference:** Warm sheltered spot in sun or part shade along the coast. It can also be grown as a container plant and moved to a warm, sheltered spot during the winter.
> **Soil conditions:** Rich soil.
> **Water:** Ample water.
> **Nutrients:** Fertilize with an all-purpose or a bloom-promoting fertilizer frequently.
> **Problems:** It is damaged by frost.
> **Special care:** Cut back severely in winter. In areas where a light frost is possible, prune it back in spring when the danger of frost has passed.
> **Hints:** Rooting cuttings to make new plants is ridiculously easy. Simply place the cuttings in a bucket of water over the winter. The cuttings will sprout many thin white roots that will become elongated over the winter and be ready to plant in potting soil in spring.

Despite its deadly reputation, brugmansia is commonly grown in the mild weather areas of Northern California; in colder areas, it can be grown as a potted plant and moved inside in the winter. It is particularly fine by moonlight when the ghostly flowers haunt the night.

ANTS

Ants cause trouble in the garden by herding insects such as aphids to obtain the honeydew these insects create. Watch out for these troublemakers and discourage them promptly. Washing off dusty leaves discourages both ants and aphids. See Ant and Aphid Spray, page 152.

AZALEAS

Check the azaleas to make sure that they are well mulched, preferably with an acid-forming mulch such as oak leaves or pine needles. If their leaves are turning yellow while the veins are still green, feed them with a chelating product containing iron, manganese, and zinc.

BALCONY AND ENTRYWAY GARDENS

Continue to transplant summer-flowering plants into pots. Cosmos, petunias, and zinnias are excellent for hot, sunny spots and impatiens, fuchsias, and tuberous begonias are good for shady spots. Established plants should be fertilized with a bloom promoting formula such as 0-10-10. Be sure to keep potted plants well watered.

BEE STINGS

The bees are one of the primary pollinators of many plants, so we would not really want to banish them from our gardens despite the anguish the mere sight of one often engenders. According to the Garlic Seed Foundation, bee stings may be relieved by rubbing a cut garlic clove on the sting.

BERRIES

Prune berry vines when you have finished harvesting the fruit. Everbearers may still yield more berries.

> ❀ Old blackberry and old boysenberry canes (those that have just finished fruiting) are cut off at the base, and the new canes are then tied down to the trellis. Coastal gardeners and mountain gardeners may want to wait until August as there may be more berries.
>
> ❀ Old raspberry canes are cut off at the base as soon as they begin to die. Protect the new green canes that will bear fruit in the future.
>
> ❀ Everbearing raspberry vines can be trimmed at the top, which has already given fruit; the bottom of each cane will give more fruit.

BULBS

Autumn-blooming bulbs appear in the nursery this month and in August. Plant them now and they will bloom in the fall. If you wait until September, they probably will not bloom until next year. Look for autumn-blooming crocus and spider lilies. For more information see Autumn Bulbs, page 196.

CAMELLIAS

Fertilize camellias with an acid-type fertilizer if you have not fertilized them within a month. If you did fertilize them recently, wait four to six weeks and then fertilize. The general rule for feeding camellias is to fertilize them three times after they finish blooming, spacing the feedings from four to six weeks apart. This should be the last time you need to fertilize camellias this year. Mulch camellias, preferably with pine needles or oak leaves, so that the soil does not dry out too much over their shallow roots.

CHEMICALS IN THE GARDEN

In July the garden is likely to have a few pests as well as blackspot, mildew, and rust. To spray or not to spray, that is the question. Every gardener I know who has perfect rose plants sprays for blackspot, mildew, rust, aphids, and earwigs at regular intervals throughout the summer. If you have been reading along in this guide, you already know that I generally do not believe in spraying pesticides or fungicides.

Consequently, my roses are viciously attacked each year by black spot and occasionally have a touch of mildew. Fortunately these problems do not affect the flowering. The bouquets are plentiful, although I will admit to picking earwigs out of the blooms occasionally and to peeling off a few damaged petals. What I do have in my imperfect cut-flower garden is plenty of butterflies, and confidence that pesticides have not entered the vegetable garden.

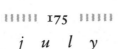

Over the years, I have learned to choose roses with a high resistance to disease. I also minimize problems by watering early in the day. I often spray them vigorously with water in the morning to discourage aphids. In the fall, I collect all the fallen leaves and discard them to avoid encouraging overwintering spores. I have learned to accept that plants can live with disfigured leaves just as the gardener lives with yearly invasions of colds and flus. A little black spot seems a small price to pay for the hovering grace of a brilliant butterfly.

CHEMICAL USE – PRECAUTIONS

If you do decide to use to use chemicals, be cautious. Wear long-sleeved, high-necked clothing, use goggles and gloves, and be aware that a simple laundering does not remove chemicals from clothing. According to a textile and clothing specialist, multiple washings are required to draw out the chemicals.

All chemically soiled clothing should be handled with gloves and washed separately and as soon as possible. Use hot wash water and plenty of it. Afterward rinse out the washing machine.

◉ If the chemical label reads "CAUTION" (which indicates slight toxicity), soiled clothing should be washed at least once and up to three times.

◉ If the chemical label reads "WARNING" (which indicates moderate toxicity), the clothing should be washed more than three times.

◉ If the chemical label reads "DANGER POISON," the clothing should be discarded.

◉ Do not add bleach if clothing is soiled with an ammonia fertilizer because a fatal chlorine gas could be created.

◉ Plan ahead and apply a fabric starch on work clothes before using chemicals. Pesticide residues will adhere to the starch and be washed out with it in the laundry.

CHILIES

Everyone knows that hot chili peppers grow in hot climates, right? Wrong. Peppers are native to the high Andes mountains, where evenings are cool, and they grow best where days are warm (70° to 80°F) and nights are cool (60° to 70°F).

The hotness of the pepper increases as the chili ripens from green to red. A few hot peppers go through a yellow stage before turning red. The hotness in chili peppers derives from the capsaicin, which is concentrated in the seeds.

Chili peppers grow better in ordinary soil and with ample water. Too much nitrogen fertilizer will produce more leaves than fruit. Do not touch pepper plants after handling tobacco or your plants may get the dreaded tobacco mosaic virus.

Northern California is the home of some of the most magnificent conifers on this planet. Unfortunately they are susceptible to several insect invaders. One of the worse culprits is the bark beetle. Beetles can carry an even worse danger—a fungus known as pitch cancer. The danger of the fungus is so grave that entomologists have warned Northern California gardeners to think twice before planting pines, particularly the Monterey pine (*Pinus radiata*), which is not only the most popular landscape tree in California, but also the most widely grown pine in the world.

Pitch cancer was discovered in Santa Cruz in 1986 and since then has moved south to San Diego and north into the Bay Area. In some areas the disease has spread rapidly. In less than two years, twenty-five percent of the Monterey pines in Carmel at Pebble Beach became infected. Other varieties of pine and other species of conifer are also susceptible. A beetle is suspected of carrying the disease from tree to tree. The disease begins at the trunk and causes the tree to exude resin. To inspect for beetles, look for holes drilled into the tree trunk. There will usually be boring dust (frass) and sometimes pitch in the beetle holes.

CONIFER GUIDELINES

The following measures may prevent conifer problems.

◉ Do not prune conifers during warm weather as this seems to promote beetle attacks and puts stress on the trees. Wait until the cool fall season before trimming them.

◉ Do not plant conifers in soggy or poorly drained areas. They do like deep irrigation during the summer but not standing water or soggy roots, conditions that promote fungus.

◉ If a conifer is obviously infested and dying, have it removed promptly. If you save the wood from an infested tree for firewood, remove the bark, dispose of it, and stack the logs away from other conifers to avoid contaminating them.

CUCUMBERS

Considering that cucumbers have been consumed since 9750 B.C., they are surprisingly controversial. Samuel Johnson, several centuries ago, believed that "a cucumber should be well sliced, and dressed with pepper and vinegar, and then thrown out, as good for nothing." He is not alone in his opinion.

More than one acquaintance refuses to dine on cucumbers. "Indigestion," they claim. What they really mean is gas that ups itself indiscreetly. Burps and belches have been the lot of those who eat cucumbers. Nonetheless, cucumbers are among the favorite vegetables grown by modern gardeners.

The cucumber's gastronomic trek has been a curious one. An ancient Egyptian recipe recommends that a hole be poked in the end of the cucumber and the insides stirred with a stick. Then the hole is plugged and the cucumber buried for several days. When dug up, the pulp is said to have been converted to an agreeable liquid. Frankly, it will take a braver woman than I am to try this recipe.

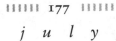

Columbus brought cucumber seeds with him to America and grew them in an experimental garden in 1493. By 1539, de Soto declared that cucumbers grown in Florida were superior to those grown in Spain. In the 1600s, physicians cooled feverish patients by placing them on a bed of cucumbers—not as wacky as it might seem as the cucumber is ninety-six percent water. In the 1800s, colonialists grew eight varieties of cucumbers in their gardens. Believe it or not, they fried them and ate them for breakfast.

Still, the cucumber's grandest moment was yet to come. In 1870, one H. J. Heinz of Pittsburg began bottling pickles. Of course, pickles had been cured in a brine before. But now they were available to anyone—a welcome addition to a bland diet of meat and potatoes. They were an instant success.

Heinz would be amazed by many of today's cucumbers, which are marketed as burpless. Cucurbitacins, which account for the burp and the bitterness associated with cucumbers, have been genetically bred out of certain varieties. Environmental stress such as insufficient water or high temperatures increases the bitterness in cucumbers. The newer burpless cucumbers remain savory even under stress.

Henry Heinz, who coined the slogan "Heinz 57 Varieties," would also be impressed with the varieties of cucumbers available. Some catalogs offer as many as forty-five varieties.

Cucumbers are divided into two categories—pickling cucumbers and slicing cucumbers. Some varieties can be used for both. For example, the lemon cucumber can be pickled when immature and eaten fresh when mature. One popular variety is not really a cucumber. The Armenian cucumber is actually an elongated cantaloupe, a close cousin. Cucumbers, along with squash, melons, pumpkins and gourds, are members of the Cucurbitaceae family.

Cucumbers can also be categorized by their sex lives. Gynoecious cucumber seeds produce only female flowers and are sold with a few seeds for pollinator plants in the same packet. Monoecious cucumber seeds produce both male and female flowers. Only female flowers produce fruit. The female flower is receptive to pollination for only one day. If the weather is cold and the honeybees (which are the chief pollinators of cucumbers) stay in the hive, that's it; no cucumber from that flower.

There are also gynoecious cucumbers (female flowers only) that are parthenocarpic, which means that no male flowers are necessary to set fruit. The problem is that, if these flowers are, by chance, pollinated, the resulting cucumbers tend to be misshapen, which may explain why some cucumbers end up looking like boomerangs.

CYMBIDIUMS

Fertilize every two weeks with a low-nitrogen liquid fertilizer formulated for orchids. Except for those grown along the coast, they should be in filtered sun.

DROUGHT

Northern California experiences cycles of drought. To mitigate the effects of drought consider the following techniques.

DROUGHT AND THE GARDEN

❁ Weed. Be sure to keep weeds pulled because they steal valuable moisture from the plants you wish to grow.

❁ Mulch. Cover the ground around plants with a mulch such as ground bark, small rocks, or compost to keep water from evaporating rapidly and to discourage weeds. Be sure and keep the mulch away from the trunks of trees and shrubs, particularly those of native plants, because the damp mulch could cause the trunk to rot.

❁ Water early in the morning when the air is still. Watering at night is also effective in that less water is lost to evaporation, but it promotes plant diseases.

❁ Use drip irrigation; soaker hoses also use less water.

❁ Use and monitor an automatic sprinkler system.

DROUGHT AND THE LAWN

Do you really want a lawn? Mowed grass uses a lot of water. A strip of lawn measuring twenty feet by twenty feet uses about two thousand, five hundred gallons. That may be one-fourth of your water bill each month.

- Mow your lawn higher.
- Reduce the use of fertilizer, which will slow the growth of the grass.
- Aerate the lawn with a tool that pokes holes in the lawn to increase water penetration; these tools are available in both power and step-on models.
- Sharpen the lawn mower blades; grass shredded by dull blades uses more water.

DROUGHT AND TREES

Trees are the backbone of the garden, so use your water first to save the trees; other plants can be replaced more quickly.

- Weed, particularly around the drip line of each tree where the rain would naturally drip off the outer leaves of the trees.
- Build basins around small trees, remembering that the active growth roots are located beneath the drip line of the tree.
- Mulch, but keep the mulch pulled away from the trunk.
- Water deeply during the summer, using a soaker hose or a deep root irrigator. Remember that a water-stressed tree becomes vulnerable to diseases and attacks from insects.

DROUGHT AND THE FLOWER GARDEN

- Limit the planting area.
- Choose less thirsty varieties such as cosmos, marigolds, petunias, and verbena.
- Mulch heavily.

DROUGHT AND THE VEGETABLE GARDEN

Avoid rootbound transplants; the smaller the transplant, the better the root system will develop in your garden.

- Build watering basins around large plants such as melons, tomatoes, and squashes.
- Space plants closely together.
- Plant early ripening varieties.

FERTILIZE

July is a month to fertilize everything that is in bloom or budding, particularly fuchsias, begonias, and roses. If the soil is dry, water well before fertilizing.

FLOWERS

Throughout the summer pick off faded flowers to encourage plants to make more blooms. If flowers are allowed to remain, they set seed, which cuts back flower production. Shear back overgrown, straggly, brownish lobelia, felicia, petunias, and sweet alyssum. Soon you will have new growth and more flowers.

Tip-pinch chrysanthemums to make them bushy.

The nurseries are full of summer flowers; you can expect months of continued bloom from ageratum, felicia, marigold, and petunia. Impatiens will brighten partially shady spots for months.

FRUIT TREES

Pick up and dispose of fallen fruit and vegetables to avoid spreading fungus spores such as brown rot and to thwart the invasion of pests such as worms, slugs, and white flies. Prop up the limbs of fruit trees that are carrying a heavy burden of fruit, or the weight may break the limb.

FUCHSIAS

Feed with a balanced fertilizer and keep fuchsias well watered. Remember to keep removing the old blooms and the swollen seed pods in order to keep the fuchsias blooming.

HEAT-LOVING PLANTS

Oleanders and crape myrtles flower profusely even during the hottest weather in the Central Valley. Naturally this trait has not gone unnoticed; nurseries carry these plants in a wide variety of flower colors and different heights. It is particularly wise to chose a crape myrtle while it is in bloom because the colors of the flowers are intense and electric. Both are in bloom this month so it is an excellent time to pick out plants with suitably colored flowers.

Crape myrtles *(Lagerstroemia indica)* grow from between six and thirty feet tall depending upon the variety. They can be pruned into a shrub or trained as a tree so that their attractive bark (smooth gray bark exfoliates to reveal another smooth, pink-toned bark beneath) is revealed. Some varieties have pretty fall foliage, but they are all grown for their spectacular clusters of flowers from July well into fall. They are so dramatic that coastal gardeners often plant them, and just as often they regret that decision as crape myrtles are prone to mildew. The Indian Tribes varieties (*Lagerstoemia indica x fauriei* hybrids introduced by the U.S. National Arboretum) resist mildew and are considered to have larger trusses of flowers and excellent fall foliage.

Oleanders (*Nerium oleander*) grow from between six and twelve feet high. They are usually grown as large shrubs but can be trained into small trees. They flower in shades of white, yellow, pink, salmon, and red all summer and well into fall. Because the leaves and flowers are toxic, they should not be planted around young children or livestock. 'Mrs. Roeding' is of a more refined habit than most oleanders; she has elegant foliage and double flowers and grows to a modest six feet.

In Bloom in July

- Annuals: impatiens, lobelia, petunia, and zinnia
- Perennials: agapanthus, fuchsia, and Shasta daisy
- Summer bulbs: daylily, dahlia, gladiolus, tuberous begonia, and lily
- Shrubs: hibiscus, gardenia, star jasmine, and oleander
- Natives: perennial penstemons, and scarlet mimulus
- Trees: crape myrtle and silk trees

In the Nursery in July

- Summer annuals and perennials in bloom
- Container-grown summer bulbs: daylily and tuberous begonia
- Hibiscus, gardenia, and star jasmine
- Crape myrtle

INVASIVE PLANTS

Gardeners are a contrary lot. What pleases one gardener, another may consider a weed, or worse, a noxious invasive plant that should be forbidden by law. In case you think I exaggerate, there are gardening groups that have tried to get certain plants outlawed. Our agricultural economy in California has required that plants imported into California be strictly controlled. Passing through the agricultural station at one of California's international airports is often tougher than passing through customs.

Invasive plants have a means of reproducing themselves either through self-seeding or through root systems that spread rapidly. Once they get started they, in theory, are difficult to control. The issue is particularly thorny with native plant gardeners who find that imported plants are overwhelming native species.

INVASIVE PLANTS—THE AWFUL

These are plants that most horticulturists agree should not be planted or tolerated in Northern California.

🌼 Yellow star thistle *(Centaurea solstitialis)* has overtaken thousands of acres in California. It is toxic to horses because it accumulates in their bodies.

🌼 Scotch broom *(Cytisus scoparius)* produces sprays of yellow bloom in spring. It is very hardy and self-seeds like crazy.

🌼 Jubata grass *(Cortaderia jubata)* often incorrectly called pampas grass, is an extremely invasive cousin of pampas grass *(Cortaderia selloana)*. It has exotic plumes that shed lightweight seeds that may be carried in the wind for miles. It is difficult to dig up as the sharp-edged grass leaves cut delicate skin.

INVASIVE PLANTS—BOTH ADORED AND CURSED

These are plants that are favored by many gardeners because they are beautiful and easy to grow. Given the right conditions and an inattentive gardener, they can also become difficult to control.

🌼 Bamboo (running types only)
🌼 Cape weed *(Arctotheca calendula)*
🌼 Forget-me-not *(Myosotis sylvatica)*
🌼 Ice plant *(Carpobrotus edulis)*
🌼 Ivy *(Hedera)*
🌼 Japanese anemone *(Anemone japonica)*
🌼 Mexican evening primrose *(Oenothera berlandieri)*
🌼 Fleabane *(Erigeron karvinskianus)*

IRIS

Bearded iris are divided during their semidormant period, which begins a few weeks after bloom and continues until new growth begins in the fall. Experts in Northern California iris growing societies translate this into mid-July through mid-September. It is important to divide iris every four years or they pretty much stop blooming.

Iris—Division

1. The thick brown iris stem growing along the soil's surface is called a rhizome. With a spading fork or shovel, carefully lift up the rhizome, keeping as much of the root attached as possible.

2. Wash the soil away from the roots and rhizome.

3. Trim the fan of green leaves to about six inches long.

With a knife, cut off the healthy outer rhizomes with the fans of leaves attached. Throw away the old, dead, center portion without any leaves attached. Remove any disfigured leaves, rotted portions, and old bloom stalks. Dust the exposed cut surfaces with a fungicide, or set the exposed sections in the sun for several hours.

4. Plant the rhizomes with the tops just below the surface of the soil. Irises grow in the direction of the fan of leaves. Plant three iris rhizomes to a clump with the fan pointing out from the center. On a hillside, plant so that the rhizomes are pointing downhill and the leaves are on the uphill side. Water well and then allow the top of the rhizomes to dry before watering again.

1.

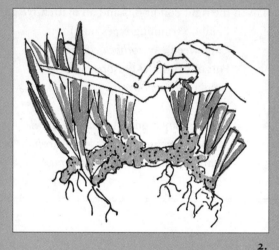

2.

3.

4.

p a r t   t w o

KIWI VINES

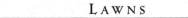

Continue to prune back those vigorous arms of growth to four or five buds. Those swollen places along the stem called buds will then develop into a dense growth that will bear large clusters of kiwis. Be sure to water the kiwis. Although they are fairly drought tolerant, they need the water for the fruit.

LAWNS

Keep lawns well watered and examine the outer edges of the lawn, which may not get enough water, particularly if they are in contact with a hot nonporous surface such as cement or pavement.

LILIES

Apart from their remarkable beauty, lilies are known for their fragrance. Colette (the pen name of the French writer Sidonie Gabrielle Colette, 1873–1954) described a lily as "lord of all it surveyed by virtue of its scent." She relates that the fragrance was such that her mother would occasionally call out to her, "Close the garden gate a little, the lilies are making the drawing room uninhabitable!" Colette would carry armloads of these lilies to church where "the uncompromising scent of the lilies made the air dense and disconcerted the hymn singing. Some of the congregation hurriedly left the building, while others let their heads droop and slumbered, transported by a strange drowsiness."

Colette does not say which lily grew in her mother's kitchen garden but most likely it was the fragrant white madonna lily that has been grown in Europe for over two thousand years. In the nineteenth century Europeans developed a passion for new lily varieties and plant hunters went to great lengths to collect them. Fortunately for Northern California gardeners, many lilies do well here, particularly the dependable California leopard lily (*Lilium pardalinum*), which is said to grow without summer water. (Native lily bulbs, by the way, are propagated by native plant societies and sold at their annual fall sales.)

Ornamental lilies are often divided into four categories, three for hybrids, and the fourth for species.

❁ Asiatic hybrids are relatively easy to grow. They bloom in June and July. Lily enthusiasts tell me that the easiest and most prolific of all lilies may be the vibrant orange Asiatic lily called 'Enchantment'.

❁ Aurelian hybrids, or trumpet lilies, are usually taller than Asiatic lilies. They bloom in July and August and retain their color better if planted where they receive only morning sun.

❁ Oriental hybrids are considered the most spectacular and exotic of all because of their large flowers. Blooming in August and September, they provide a fitting grand finale to the lily season. 'Stargazer' is that large vivid, crimson-and-white lily sold in the millions by florists. It is a fragrant choice for growing in containers.

❁ The tiger lily (*Lilium lancifolium*), which has petals that curve back dramatically toward the stem, is an example of a species lily. They are apparently called tiger lilies because of the spots that dot the petals. This, of course, does not make much sense as tigers have stripes. They are said to have "escaped" in the eastern United States, which is, I think, appropriate for tigers. The lilies bloom from late July to late August.

Lily Growing Simplified

Botanical Name: *Lilium*.

Common name: Lily.

Site preference: Sun or partial shade; morning sun is preferred. Plants seem to do best when the roots are shaded and the flowering tops are in the sun.

Soil conditions: Good drainage is essential; deep, organically enriched soil will yield the best lilies. Peat moss or leaf mold are excellent additions.

Water: Water regularly as lilies never really go dormant as tulips and daffodils do. Conserve moisture and cool the roots with a three-inch-deep mulch.

Nutrients: When the shoots come up, feed with a complete fertilizer.

Problems: Protect from gophers by lining the bottom and sides of the lily bed with wire screening. Spray the plants with water occasionally to control aphids, which spread diseases.

Special care: Plant the bulbs soon after receiving them; set them three times as deep as their vertical diameter, and water.

Hints: When cutting flowers for arrangements, leave two-thirds of the stem and leaves on the plant to provide nutrients for next year's flowers. And do be certain to cut off the stamen from the center of the bloom or the pollen may fall off and stain the tablecloth or your nose or anything else it contacts!

MAGNOLIA GRANDIFLORA

With its huge, fragrant, and very elegant white flowers and glossy green leaves, the *Magnolia grandiflora* is the best-loved magnolia in Northern California. It blooms from summer until well into fall, and will grow successfully everywhere in Northern California except the high mountain areas. Because it can take up to fifteen years before blooming if grown from seed, always select a plant grown from grafts or cuttings, which can cut the waiting time down to two to three years. Many varieties of *Magnolia grandiflora* are available, and this is a good month to look around and see what appeals to you.

MAGNOLIA GRANDIFLORA — SUPERB VARIETIES

● In cold areas 'Edith Bogue' is an excellent choice. This variety has withstood cold down to –24° F. Avoid sites with strong winds when planting it.

● 'Majestic Beauty' has extremely lush green foliage and very large white flowers.

● For containers a good choice would be 'Little Gem,' which grows slowly to a modest fifteen or twenty feet.

● If you are smitten with a rust-colored velvet underside to the glossy green leaf, than 'Samuel Sommer' is the variety for you. Its flowers are exceptional too.

ORCHID CACTUS

Fertilize orchid cactus (epiphyllums) with a balanced fertilizer such as 10-10-10. Spray the foliage with water-soluble fertilizer as well as pouring the fertilizer into the soil as the orchid cactus readily absorbs fertilizer through the stems.

POISON OAK

Fireworks are not the only thing exploding in July. In backyards throughout Northern California, poison oak is now turning a lovely shade of red and the skin of hapless gardeners is exploding with itchy pustules. There are now several products on the market that the gardener can apply before being exposed to poison oak. These lotions provide a temporary barrier to the toxic urushiols in the plant. There is also a product called Tecnu that washes the toxic urushiols away if it is used within eight hours of exposure.

POTTED PLANTS

If you forget to water potted plants during warm weather, the soil may shrink away from the edge of the pot. When you resume watering, the water fails to penetrate the dried root ball and instead cascades over the hard soil surface and down the shrunken edges. There are two solutions: Submerge the pot in water, weigh it down, and do not remove it until all the bubbling stops; or buy a soil-wetting agent that you add to water to make it penetrate dry soil.

RHODODENDRONS

Remember that rhododendrons, camellias, and azaleas need sufficient water now to set buds for next year's bloom.

ROSES

There are still lots of blooms ahead for the modern roses so continue to feed them with a balanced fertilizer—all three numbers on the fertilizer package should be about the same, for instance 10-10-10, 13-15-12, or even 20-20-20. Rose fanatics will also feed them again two weeks from now with fish emulsion at the rate of one teaspoon per gallon; use several gallons of the mixture for each rose bush.

Generally, do not fertilize antique roses any more this year—their season is drawing to a close. Follow the pruning directions on these pages for alba, centifolia, damask, gallica, and moss roses.

Roses—Pruning a Gallica Rose

Gallica roses are pruned each summer when they have finished blooming. Cut back the side shoots by about two-thirds of the length. On older plants, cut some of the older main shoots (but not more than one-fourth of them) all the way to the ground so that they will produce new flowering shoots. Remove any unhealthy, weak, or dead growth.

Roses—Pruning Alba, Centifolia, Damask, and Moss Roses

Alba, centifolia, damask, and moss roses are pruned after they have finished blooming. Begin by cutting back old woody canes by about one-third of their total length: one-third off, two-thirds left.

Then prune back the side shoots growing out of the main shoots to about one-third of their former length: two-thirds off, one-third left.

Watch the new growth as it develops over the summer. Several months from now prune back any growth that is much longer than the rest so that the bush looks balanced.

TOMATOES

Tomato gardeners take note; here are a few tricks of the trade. If you want large ripe tomatoes, thin the blossoms on what are known as determinate tomato varieties. Determinate varieties such as 'Roma' and 'Tiny Tim' tend to be bushy and do not require staking. Thinning the fruit by one half, just as apples are thinned, produces bigger, riper fruit.

At this stage in the tomato season, do not let the soil dry out too much or you may find the leaves curling and the blossom ends of the fruit turning black and rotting.

It is not a great idea to prune away any of the protective tomato foliage. The green shoulders of the first tomatoes of the season come from lack of sufficient shade from the leaves.

TREES

Occasionally the gardener is inspired by good weather to climb into a tree and saw the top off. Topping, also known as turning a tree into a hat rack, is frowned upon by tree experts and many professional arborists refuse to do it. If you wish to reduce the size of a tree, you should prune it selectively instead of hacking the top off or amputating large branches to ugly stubs. Initially the hack job may be cheaper, but two years later the ugly stubs will have sprouted a mass of truly unruly growth. After about six years, the hacked tree is usually far bushier than the carefully pruned tree. Having a tree pruned properly results in a beautiful tree and ultimately saves money because its size is more easily controlled.

VACATIONS

Summertime is vacation time. Automatic irrigation systems have solved the problem of outdoor watering for many homeowners. But there is still the problem of indoor plants, which tend to dry out quickly with increased temperatures and dry summer air.

No matter how fond we are of our houseplants, we seldom take them on vacation. I like to imagine checking into a hotel with a philodendron. I would look the desk clerk right in the eye and demand a room with a southern exposure. Then with an airy wave of my hand, I would send the bell boy out for bottled water. One cannot be too careful, you know.

For plants heartlessly left alone at home, there are many self-watering pots that will support them for two or three weeks without additional water. There are also commercial wicking systems available for watering potted plants. Buy water wicks (which are made of fiberglass or nylon) or make some out of old nylon stockings. Push the wick one-third of the way down into the pot. Set a large reservoir of water above the pot and place the other end of the wick in the water. This system works by a combination of gravity and capillary action. It is not aesthetically elegant, but it does make it easy for someone to oversee the system by adding water to the reservoir.

Simpler is the capillary mat, which waters plants through the drainage holes in their pots. Unfortunately this system does not work well with pots with rocks in the bottom or with anything that keeps the soil too far from the mat.

VEGETABLES

There is still time to plant a second crop in your vegetable garden. Plant beets, bush beans, carrots, radishes, and turnips.

Postpone planting transplants of winter vegetables as the really hot weather is probably still ahead of us in September. You can, however, sow seeds of winter vegetables such as cabbages, bok choy, broccoli, and kale, and transplant the seedlings into your garden when the summer vegetables finish producing.

Gardeners in the Central Valley may need to hand pollinate melons and squashes when high temperatures inhibit the fruit from setting. The simplest way is to pick a male flower (you can see the difference between male and female flowers: females have swollen bases) and pull off the petals before shaking it over a female flower. Alternatively, take a small watercolor brush and transfer the male's pollen to the stigma in the center of the female flower.

See also Chilies, page 176, and Tomatoes, page 143.

VEGETABLES—HARVESTING

Summer vegetables are at their best now. Here are a few hints for harvesting them for best flavor. Of course, all vegetables taste better if eaten the day they are picked.

   ● Beets are superior when they are smaller than Ping-Pong balls.

   ● Carrots should be pulled when you are ready to eat them. As soon as they are as large as a finger, they are large enough to eat. Pull gently so that other plants growing nearby do not have their roots disturbed.

   ● Cucumbers need to be picked regularly to keep them productive.

   ● Eggplants should look glossy and smooth skinned. Do not let them mature too much; younger is better.

   ● Green beans should be picked when small for succulent texture and the best flavor. The immature beans should fill the pod but not be large and bumpy. Do not pick green beans when they are damp with dew or you may unwittingly spread diseases.

(continued)

◉ Melons need watching if they are to be picked at their best flavor. Pay particular attention to the stem area so you can observe changes there. Cantaloupes are usually at their best when a crack begins to form between the stem and the fruit so that the fruit is pulled free by its own weight. Watermelons will begin to dry out along the stem when the fruit is ripe.

◉ Peppers should be picked to keep more peppers coming. It is fine to leave a few peppers on the vine to turn red, but only a few.

◉ Radishes should be picked young as they have the unpleasant habit of splitting as they grow older.

◉ Squashes should be picked when small for succulent texture and best flavor. Your fingernail should easily pierce the tender young skin. Squash blossoms can be stuffed and cooked—a particularly good idea when a crop such as zucchini seems about to overrun the garden. Winter squash should be picked only when the skin feels hard, but it is best to leave them unpicked until you are ready to use them as they will sweeten on the vine.

◉ Tomatoes should mature on the vine for best flavor. Let them turn really red.

WATERING

Summertime is drought time, so see that plants are watered. In particular young trees and young shrubs, which will grow to become the backbone of a garden, need deep watering to produce strong, drought-resistant roots. Use a trowel to dig down into the earth, and gauge its dryness.

When the gardener waters a potted plant that has dried out what often happen is the water cascades down the sides of the pot without wetting the soil at all. If you disturb the soil, you will see that it is still as dry as before you began watering. There are two solutions. One is to put the entire pot in a larger container of water. After a lot of bubbling and belching, the pot (probably floating) will settle down and the soil will become soaked. For pots too large to soak, the solution is to buy a wetting agent, which actually makes water wetter.

WISTERIA

Cut back the long streamers, saving only those that you wish to train along an arbor or other supporting device. Wisterias are very vigorous plants; train them to grow away from the house along a fence or an arbor.

...august...

⊶⊸◉ *August Features* ◉⊷⊶

August is a month of contradictions in Northern California. In the Central Valley areas it is true summer. Days are hot enough here to encourage the gardener to seek shade. A hammock and glass of lemonade are welcomed. Harvesting the vegetable garden is a daily pleasure, and giving away the bountiful supply can become something of a chore. It is too hot in the Central Valley to set out new plants; they would bake in the heat. High mountain gardeners are also experiencing summer, at least during the day. Cool nights set limits on certain crops in the high mountains, but these are definitely pleasant gardening days. Yet, in most years, the coastal areas will have to wait until September before their summer weather arrives. Under the cover of fog, planting still continues in August. The gardener waits patiently, knowing the weather tends to cycle fog, then sun, then fog, then sun.

All Gardeners

Continue to weed. Unfortunately as long as it's the growing season, it is also the weeding season. Add young, seedhead-free weeds and excess summer growth to the compost pile. Remember to keep the pile as damp as a wrung-out sponge for faster composting.

❀ Keep after the snails.

❀ Use a strong spray from the hose to wash away aphids.

❀ Pick up fallen fruit and vegetables (particularly if they are planted near the house) to discourage ants from forming colonies near your dwelling.

❀ Water plants as needed.

▲ ▼ ▲

Coastal Gardeners

In addition to the tasks listed for all gardeners, fertilize plants if you see signs of pale, lackluster growth. Yellow leaves with green veins often indicate an iron deficiency that can be corrected with a chelated iron.

❀ Fertilize the lawn.
Fertilize all flowering plants that are about to bloom.
Fertilize roses, except most antique roses.

❀ Pinch off dead flowers, particularly off fuchsias. Make sure you get the entire flower head, including the swollen ovaries where seeds form. This will encourage new flowers as the plant rushes to reproduce itself.

❀ Sow seeds of fall- and winter-flowering plants, such as calendula, Iceland poppy, pansy, prim-

rose, and stock, into the bedding plot. Stake tall sprawling flowers.

❀ Harvest vegetables as they ripen. Pick them early in the day. Tie sprawling tomato vines to supports. Plant the fall vegetable garden with beets, broccoli, cabbage, carrots, and cauliflower. Thin vegetable seedlings that were sown too close together by snipping them with scissors.

❀ Mulch.

▲ ▼ ▲

Central Valley Gardeners

In addition to the tasks listed for all gardeners, insulate the garden soil from the hot, dry weather by applying a two-inch-thick mulch.

❀ Fertilize plants if you see signs of pale, lackluster growth. Yellow leaves with green veins often indicate an iron deficiency that can be corrected with a chelated iron.
Fertilize the lawn.
Fertilize all flowering plants about to bloom.
Fertilize roses, except most antique roses.

❀ Pinch off dead flowers. In particular pick off spent blooms from crape myrtles to bring on extra flowers in the fall. Make sure you get the entire flower head—particularly the swollen ovaries where seeds form.

❀ Hold off transplanting fall- and winter-flowering plants into the bedding plot. Hot weather is hard on newly transplanted plants. If you do transplant, shade them for a few days with the temporary shelter of an umbrella or wooden shake. Stake tall sprawling flowers.

❀ Harvest vegetables as they ripen. Pick them early in the day.

❀ Continue to monitor your watering system. Soak all newly transplanted plants.

High Mountain Gardeners

In addition to the tasks listed for all gardeners, dig and divide overgrown perennials. Replant them promptly so that their roots have time to become established before the cold season begins.

◉ Set out fall-flowering plants.

◉ Harvest the vegetable garden. Continue to thin vegetable seedlings that were sown too close together by snipping them with scissors.

◉ Fertilize lawns and all flowering plants about to bloom.

◉ Do not snip off the spent blooms from rugosa roses as they will form bright red fruits that make a fine seasonal display.

◉ Withhold fertilizer from woody plants so they have time to harden before the cold season begins.

◉ Plant spring flowering bulbs as soon as they come on the market.

AMARYLLIS BELLADONNA

Should you have a naked lady in your garden? Yes, if you like surprises. The *Amaryllis belladonna* (also known as a naked lady) is a large, graceful, pink-flowering bulb that emerges immodestly without any leaves each August.

Buy one or more in bloom now. When the bloom has finished, plant the bulb so that the top is just beneath the soil's surface. Robust straplike leaves will appear in fall and winter, and then before any sign at all of a flower, the whole plant will die back to the ground as if it had given up.

In August, like a magic trick, the reddish brown flower stalk begins pushing through the soil until it has reached a height of several feet. Then the large flowers unfold to perfume the air.

Naked ladies do not like to be disturbed (naturally), so choose the site wisely. Transplanted bulbs may refuse to bloom for several years. They are drought resistant and long lived.

ARCHITECTURAL PLANTS

Architectural plants possess such striking form that they can stand alone as the center of attention; often they are also so large or so bold that they had better stand alone because other plants would look wimpy if planted beside them.

> ◉ The magnificent foliage of acanthus (*Acanthus mollis* and *Acanthus spinosus*) was extensively copied in classical Greek and neoclassical ornamentation so the shape may seem familiar. This fast-growing plant has deeply lobed leaves about two feet long and tall spikes of tubular, delicately tinted flowers in spring or early summer. It grows best in light shade in the hotter Central Valley areas or in full sun in coastal areas. The only problem this plant seems to have is that slugs and snails love it dearly. The roots are somewhat invasive so this is not a plant for the bedding garden. This is a plant for drama and beauty in a spot where other plants would be lost.
>
> ◉ Gunnera (*Gunnera manicata* and *Gunnera tinctoria*, also known as *Gunnera chilensis*) is an amazing plant with leaves up to five feet across. English gardeners often plant gunnera at the edge of a pond or
>
> *(continued)*

bog, where they look primordial. They love water and need to be watered frequently during the summer. August is a good month to plant them as the roots should become established before cold weather appears. To protect the plant, the leaves are cut off late in the fall and the stub is covered with a mound of mulch. In spring the plant should be uncovered and fertilized. Despite the extra care needed, gunnera is a plant worth growing. One gunnera in a pot makes a bold statement. Its only flaw is that it has prickles that protect the amazing leaves.

Unfortunately neither plant is suited to the colder high mountain areas.

AUTUMN BULBS

Autumn-blooming bulbs are in the nursery this month. If you plant the bulbs now they will bloom this autumn. If you wait until next month, they may not bloom until the following autumn.

◉ Autumn-flowering crocus (*Crocus speciosus*) has showy, deep violet-blue flowers on short, five-inch stalks. *Crocus sativus* has a similar appearance and the added merit of possessing an orange red stigma, which is harvested and sold as saffron.

◉ Meadow saffron (*Colchicum autumnale*) has poisonous corms despite its food-oriented common name. Look for the varieties 'The Giant', which has pale mauve petals, and 'Waterlily', which has a double layer of violet-colored petals.

◉ Spider lilies (*Lycoris*) are the most spectacular of the autumn bulbs. Their straplike leaves appear each spring and then die down to the ground before the stalks rise up one-and-a-half to two feet high to bear large, spiderlike blooms. Plant them four inches deep in light shade or full sun. Do not disturb them once they are planted. When planted in pots, they do best with their roots crowded, so use a small pot rather than a large one.

◉ *Lycoris squamigera* (also known as *Amaryllis hallii*) does well in all areas of Northern California. It has trumpet-shaped flowers in pastel shades of lilac or rose pink. In the coldest areas, plant the bulbs a few inches deeper than the normal four inches.

◉ *Lycoris radiata* with orange red flowers is the best known spider lily. It is also relatively easy to grow.

BALCONY AND ENTRYWAY GARDENS

Continue to fertilize summer-flowering potted plants, such as cosmos, fuchsias, geraniums, gerberas, impatiens, marguerites, petunias, tuberous begonias, and zinnias, with a bloom promoting formula such as 0-10-10. Be sure to keep potted plants well watered. Start pots of fall-blooming favorites such as calendulas, chrysanthemums, and nemesia.

Gardeners wanting a plant that blooms over a very long season should consider a choice new cultivar of the popular daylily 'Stella d' Oro.' Called 'Black-Eyed Stella,' this little plant actually has yellow flowers with red eyes in the center. It is well suited to Northern California.

BERRIES

Berry vines are pruned after you have finished harvesting the fruit.

> ◉ Old blackberry and old boysenberry canes (they have just finished fruiting) are cut off at the base, and the new canes are then tied down to the trellis.
>
> ◉ Old raspberry canes are cut off at the base as soon as they begin to wither and die. Protect the new green canes that will bear future fruit.
>
> ◉ Hold off on pruning everbearers, as they may still yield more berries. Everbearing raspberry vines can be trimmed at the top (which has already given fruit); the bottom of each cane will give more fruit.

BIRDS AND BUTTERFLIES

If the gardener has refrained from using pesticides, by August the garden usually is full of life: butterflies, birds, and spiders. Herewith, for your enjoyment in August, is a short explanation about these charmers. Songbirds may provide the most engaging concerts for the gardener's ear, but the performing artistry of hummingbirds and butterflies is more apt to catch the gardener's eye. Both butterflies and hummingbirds stage their aerial acrobatics in search of flower nectar. Hummingbirds require considerable quantities of nectar to sustain their high energy levels. If the gardener had a hummingbird's metabolism, our three daily meals would have to include a total of 1,140 hamburgers. Hummingbirds seek trumpet-shaped or tubular blossoms, which are well suited to their long slender bills. Butterflies' tastes are more mysterious. We know they prefer flowers with a heavy perfume, but why they prefer buddleia blossoms to rose buds is still unclear.

Birds and butterflies may be the star performers of the garden, but the most theatrical backdrops are spun by spiders. Their wondrous webs mark the vacant spaces in a garden with auras of mystery and danger. The spiders themselves, may the Fates be praised, prefer to lurk out of sight.

When we speak of our gardens, we are likely to mention our plants, but these guest performers contribute significantly to the experience of the garden. What a pity, then, to leave these pleasures to chance. With a few simple alterations, we can lure birds, butterflies, and (dare I say it?) spiders into the garden.

> ### BIRDS AND BUTTERFLIES—ATTRACTING
>
> To attract birds and butterflies it is necessary to eliminate or cut back on pesticides. Not only are all these small creatures insect eaters, but also they are damaged by pesticides. Remember that the caterpillar who eats leaves may turn into a lithe butterfly. It is all part of the life cycle of the garden.
>
> *(continued)*

By simply eliminating pesticides, you will encourage spiders. To attract butterflies requires the right plants. Butterflies are very particular. The lovely black and yellow anise swallowtail may draw nectar from zinnias and then move on to a fennel to lay her yellow eggs. When an egg hatches, the emerging caterpillar will dine on the remaining yolk and then finish off his unhatched siblings before nibbling on the fennel itself. Eventually the fat little green and yellow caterpillar will attach himself to the fennel and form a chrysalis resembling a stick from which will emerge another anise swallowtail.

BUTTERFLY FAVORITES
Plants favored by butterflies include asters, butterfly bushes, cosmos, fernleaf yarrow, lavenders, milkweed, mint, petunia, rosemary, thistles, and zinnia. Passion vines are quickly inhabited by gulf fritillary butterflies who only feed on passion vines.

BIRDS—ATTRACTING

From a bird's point of view, an attractive garden provides food, breeding sites, and protection. Shallow water is also loved by birds who need it for drinking and bathing all year. Birds like places to perch so trees, particularly trees bearing fruits, berries, seeds, or nuts, are favored. You can always provide a bird feeding station if you are prepared to witness bird slaughter close at hand. A survey by the Cornell Laboratory of Ornithology indicates that the advantages of a feeder to the bird population outweigh the disadvantages. Nonetheless, predation at bird feeders is on the increase. Hawks are more skillful than cats and just as apt to lurk around a feed station. Hawks are less than delicate in their killing and have been known to drag a bird over to the bird bath and drown it.

BIRD FAVORITES
Natural food sources for birds include trees such as apple, birch, cedar, cherry, hawthorn, holly, maple, oak, plum, pine, spruce, and sweet gum. Birds are also partial to large vines such as grape, honeysuckle, and Virginia creeper.

Hummingbirds can be fed in special feeders on a mixture of one part sugar to four parts water, boiled and cooled. To attract hummingbirds, plant trumpet vine, fuchsia, gladiolus, columbine, nasturtium, petunia, hollyhock, and morning glory.

CHLOROSIS

Chlorosis is an abnormal yellowing of leaves that is due to a partial or a complete loss of chlorophyll. Chlorotic areas usually turn brown and the leaves often fall off the plant. It is a typical midsummer problem in Northern California and is caused by a deficiency of iron or zinc. If the younger leaves of a plant turn yellow, or if the veins of the leaves remain green while the leaves turn yellow, apply a chelated iron either by spraying the leaves or by spreading it over the soil.

There are other causes of yellow leaves. When all the leaves on a plant turn yellow, the light may be much too bright or the temperatures too high. When only the older leaves turn yellow, the plant may need nitrogen fertilizer. Cold water can cause yellow spots or yellow sections or even a mosaic pattern on leaves.

CHRYSANTHEMUMS

Stake and tie chrysanthemums as they grow tall. For really large flowers, pinch off all but one bud per stem.

CYMBIDIUMS

Fertilize every two weeks with a low-nitrogen, high-phosphorus liquid fertilizer formulated for orchids. You will notice the formulation changes this month to promote bloom instead of green growth.

FERTILIZE

Fertilize azaleas, camellias, hydrangeas, and rhododendron with an acid type fertilizer. Fertilize all plants now in bloom with an all-purpose fertilizer. Chrysanthemums should be fertilized until the buds show color.

FIRE PREVENTION

Summertime is fire time in Northern California. The first priority is to clear all the dry grass and dead shrubs at least thirty feet from the house. Remember, fire is a naturally occurring phenomenon in California—our climate and topography conspire to promote summer fires. The gardener's timely actions could save both home and family. For more information, see page 240.

Gardeners should be careful about piling wood chips from a backyard chipper or a commercial source. Piles of wood or leaf debris can generate internal temperatures hot enough to catch fire weeks or even months after they were piled. Limit the height of wood chip or leaf piles to less than two feet to minimize the heat built up.

FLOWER DEADHEADING

The August garden is usually in bloom. To keep those blooms coming, remove mature flowers and any developing seed pods. When seeds develop, plants stop blooming because their efforts at reproducing are completed. By removing mature flowers and seed pods, you force the plant to continue to bloom in order to set seed. Cosmos, coreopsis, marigolds, and zinnias are particularly helped by this technique, which is called deadheading.

FLOWERS—WINTER ANNUALS

Sow seeds of winter-blooming flowers such as sweet alyssum, calendula, pansies, and violas.
Larkspur (*Consolida ambigua*) does particularly well when seed is sown in place because it does not like to be transplanted. Chill larkspur seed in the refrigerator one week before planting it to help propagation.

A splendid combination grown from seed are tall 'Pocket' snapdragons, Giant Imperial stocks, and Giant Imperial larkspur. All three are fine for cutting and are long lasting in the flower bed.

FRUIT TREES

Prop up fruit-heavy tree branches so that they will not break from the weight. Pick up fallen fruit so that it will not attract insects.

Rake up all fallen leaves to prevent disease and discourage insects. Remove injured or diseased limbs, but wait until the dormant season to prune.

FUCHSIAS

Feed fuchsias with a balanced fertilizer and keep them well watered. Remember to remove the old blooms and the swollen seed pods in order to keep the fuchsias blooming. This is a good time to take cuttings to propagate new plants.

HEAT

To minimize the effects of warm weather on the gardener, wear loose-fitting clothing in light colors. Light colors reflect the sun away from the body. Natural fibers promote air circulation. A hat can also make a big difference. Do not forget to drink lots of fluids.

HERBAL INFUSIONS FROM THE GARDEN

Iced tea and lemonade are traditional summer treats during a heat wave. August is the perfect month for brewing a beverage from the garden. Although we seldom think of drinking something from the garden, only plain water surpasses a plant leaf infused with water as the beverage of choice. The most famous plant leaf drink is, of course, tea.

In a curious way, tea also led to other herbal infusions in America. On December 16, 1773, on a cold and rainy night, one hundred and fifty Sons of Liberty dumped 342 chests of Ceylon and Darjeeling tea into the Boston Bay. After that infamous Boston Tea Party, the patriotic colonists needed an alternative drink. So they plucked herbs from their gardens and infused them in hot water. This was not too difficult as most of the population were subsistence farmers and more than fifty herbs were grown in colonial America. These liberty teas, as they were known, were most frequently made from mint, rosemary, sage, and lemon balm.

After the Revolutionary War in 1776, Americans could dispense with King George and buy their teas directly from China. So Americans returned to their old tea-drinking ways and the garden herbs went back into the cooking pot. Except for mint, American gardeners have not bothered much with plants that might be made into a drink until recently. Now that herbal teas are popular, it seems natural for the gardener to include in the garden plants for drinking.

For cool summer drinks, brew the herbal infusion stronger than normal and then pour it over ice. My favorite summer infusion, what the French call a *tisane*, is a combination of lemon verbena leaves and peppermint leaves brewed for ten minutes and served over ice with borage flowers or jasmine flowers floated on top. Nothing could be simpler to make. Clip off a six-inch length of verbena and an equal length of peppermint. Stick the stems in a glass and pour in the hot water. When it is strong enough (this will take between ten and twenty minutes) pull the stems out with the leaves still attached.

Herbal Favorites

❀ Chamomile (*Matricaria recutita*) is a low-growing decorative plant that flourishes in light, sandy soil under full sun to part shade. The flowers, which appear in the summer, are used for drinks.

❀ Fennel is a tall, wild-looking herb that resembles dill. It is easy to grow in full sun and average soil. The licorice-flavored leaves are used in an infusion.

❀ Silk flower (*Abelmoschus moscheutos*) is a four-foot shrub commonly grown for its showy tropical flowers, which resemble hibiscus. It grows well in sheltered, sunny spots with rich, moist soil, but it is killed by a heavy frost. The tart, lemon-flavored flowers are used for ruby-colored infusions.

❀ Lemon verbena (*Aloysia triphylla*) is a tall, leggy shrub that grows up to five feet tall, preferably in rich moist soil and full sunshine. It dies back to the ground each winter but comes back in spring. The leaves make a subtle lemon-flavored infusion.

❀ Mint (*Mentha*) is almost too easy to grow in rich, moist soil in full sun to partial shade. Many gardeners prefer to grow it in pots for fear it will take over the garden.

In Bloom in August

❀ Annuals: ageratum, impatiens, marigold, sweet alyssum, and petunia
❀ Perennials: aster, begonia, campanula, geranium, and phlox
❀ Bulblike plants: dahlia, tuberous begonia, and gladiolus
❀ Shrubs: fuchsia, hydrangea, lavender, and rose
❀ Vines: bougainvillea, clematis, jasmine, and passion vine
❀ Crape myrtle
❀ Native plants: wild buckwheats, late penstemon, evening primrose, scarlet larkspur, and Milo Baker's lupine

IRIS

It is important to divide bearded iris every two to four years or they pretty much stop blooming. They are divided in Northern California during their semidormant period, which begins a few weeks after bloom and continues until new growth in the fall; this translates into mid-July through mid-September. For illustrated instructions on dividing Iris, see page 183.

For illustrated instructions on dividing Iris, see page 183.

> ### IN THE NURSERY IN AUGUST
>
> ❀ South African bulbs: clivia, freesia, ixia, and watsonia
> ❀ Madonna lily bulbs
> ❀ Bearded iris
> ❀ Winter vegetable transplants

KIWI VINES

Continue to water kiwi vines and to prune back those vigorous arms of growth to four to five buds.

LAWNS

Continue to water and mow lawns. You may notice dry, brown spots in your lawn caused by a variety of reasons such as shallow soil, uneven water, dog urine, too much fertilizer, or insects. Whatever the reason, often the dry grass begins to repel water, which makes the situation worse. Try breaking up the thatch (dead grass) in the area and poking one or more deep holes through the dry spot. You can also use a wetting agent, which helps the water penetrate dry soil.

MOSQUITO CONTROL

If mosquitoes are spoiling the evening stroll in the garden, then fight back.

❀ Trap female mosquitoes by adding a dose of soap to buckets full of water. When the female attempts to lay eggs in the soapy water she will not be able to escape.

❀ Gardeners with ponds should stock them with mosquito-loving fish such as *gambusia* or minnows.

❀ While barbecuing, add branches of rosemary or sage to drive the invaders away.

❀ Encourage mosquito predators such as birds, frogs, lizards, dragonflies, and praying mantises.

❀ And, above all, empty all possible breeding sites such as watering cans, wading pools, and decorative pots. Fill in holes in trees or stumps that collect water from sprinklers. Empty the pet's water bowl every day. Check the birdbath for mosquito larvae twice a week. A mere two cups of water will support five hundred mosquito larvae.

❀ If you should be so lucky as to live in an area with bats, by all means, supply a bat house near your home. Bat houses are currently popular, but it is difficult to lure a bat into residence unless you have a pond or other water source nearby. One bat can consume four thousand mosquitoes a night.

MOSQUITO REPELLENTS

I am sorry to report that the organic repellents do not appear to be as effective against mosquitos as are the commercial varieties available from any drugstore. According to a report published by the North Carolina State University Cooperative Extension Service in 1994, entomologists recommend commercial repellents sprayed or rubbed on the skin. Citronella oil does repel insects but not as well as drugstore repellents do. According to the report, electronic zappers or devices that supposedly repel mosquitoes with sound were not very effective.

NIGHT BLOOMERS

The languid nights of August may leave the gardener wishing for night-blooming plants. Many fragrant, light-colored, flowering plants produce a glorious scent, not for the gardener but for the benefit of hovering moths that pollinate the flowers.

🌼 Some gardeners consider the most fragrant of plants to be the night-blooming jessamine (*Cestrum nocturnum*). As the botanical name indicates, this is not a true jasmine. It is a tropical plant, and typical of plants that have to compete for attention in a jungle, this plant's most striking feature is its powerful fragrance. It is so powerful that it is often recommended that the gardener plant it away from the house or the fragrance may overwhelm the would-be sleeper. Being of a tropical origin, it is hardy only in the milder-winter climates of Northern California.

🌼 The moonflower (*Ipomoea alba*) is an old-fashioned annual that produces luminous white flowers with a heavy fragrance. One trick to growing it is to cut it back after blooming to promote another wave of bloom.

🌼 *Nicotiana alata* 'Grandiflora' is a dependable summer source of fragrant night bloom in the bedding garden of annuals and perennials. It combines well with the taller four o'clocks, which have fragrant blooms that last well into the evening, if not the entire night.

🌼 You would not want to overlook the magnificent magnolia for exceptional night bloom and fragrance. Look for *Magnolia fraseri* and *Magnolia sieboldii*. Both varieties may need to be specially ordered from the nursery.

🌼 Angel's trumpets, see page 173, particularly the fast-growing *Brugmansia candida*, all have fragrant night bloom.

🌼 Several varieties of orchid cactus (*epiphyllum*), which are potted plants suited for growing along the coast, produce fragrant blooms at night.

ORCHID CACTUS

Continue to fertilize orchid cactus (*epiphyllums*) with a balanced fertilizer such as 10-10-10. Spray the foliage with a water-soluble fertilizer as well as pouring the fertilizer onto the soil as orchid cactus readily absorb fertilizer through the stems.

In the heat of August, a gardener's thoughts are apt to turn to palm trees—those symbols of the cool oasis. Currently there are more than two hundred varieties of palms that will grow in Northern California and many are frost tolerant. There are even palms growing in the foothills of the Sierra Nevada that have survived snow storms. The one palm native to California lines many Central Valley streets including Sacramento.

The California fan palm is a relic from a time predating the Ice Age when luxuriant growth and interconnecting lakes covered the California desert. The lakes dried up and so did most of the rain, leaving behind a few seeps and pools of water that continue to support small groves of palms.

The Californian fan palm is considered so beautiful that it now dots the streets of the Riviera, Algeria, and even Hawaii, where it is referred to as the hula palm because of the petticoat of dried brown fronds beneath the crown. It grows fairly fast for a palm, reaching about eight feet at ten years and twenty-five feet at forty years. Enthusiasts of the California fan palm believe that it is criminal to cut away the dry brown fronds and deprive the palm of its skirt. Once the palm has reached a notable height (it grows to sixty feet at maturity), the lowest dry fronds may be cut away to reveal an interesting crosshatch pattern on the trunk.

The California fan palm produces fruiting stalks, which hang down between the fronds. When the small but sweet dates drop down to the desert floor, they are eagerly gobbled up by coyotes. The very best way to grow the California fan palm from seed is to gather the seeds from coyote droppings. Close to one-hundred-percent germination can be expected from seeds that have passed through a coyote's digestive system.

Dates have been cultivated since Biblical times, and they "date" back to Paleolithic times. Because dates are grown commercially in the United States only in California's Coachella Valley and a place or two in Arizona, date palms (*Phoenix dactylifera*) in gardens would seem as rare as oases. Actually date palms thrive in both desert and seaside settings and are used to landscape golf courses in perpetually sunny places such as Palm Springs. Fruit production depends upon long, hot, dry summers, copious irrigation, and no summer rain or even moisture in the air, which would rot the fruit.

Date palm fronds are killed by temperatures dropping to 20°F, but the tree itself will survive down to −5°F. Date palms will grow in areas where they will not set fruit. The Promenade des Anglais in Nice is lined with date palms bearing large clusters of fruit that never ripen.

One of the most reliable palms in Northern California is the Canary Island date palm (*Phoenix canariensis*),which grows to about forty-five feet in thirty-five years. Eventually its trunk will reach an impressive five feet in diameter. It will survive temperatures down to −12°F.

Another popular palm is the elegant, graceful queen palm (*Syagrus romanzoffianum*), which grows rather quickly for a palm, up to twenty-four inches a year. Although it is planted in the Central Valley, it grows better along the coast.

A remarkable aspect of most palms is their ability to be transplanted without setback, which is one reason for the black market in palms. More than a few unfortunate gardeners have discovered that a sizeable palm was surreptitiously removed during the night. For the address of a palm nursery, see page 306.

For the address of a palm nursery, see page 306.

Fan Palm Growing Simplified

Botanical name: *Washingtonia filifera.*
Common name: California fan palm.
Site preference: Full sun, or partial shade when young.
Soil conditions: Well-drained soil is essential.
Water: Palms prefer frequent water but will survive drought conditions when established.
Nutrients: Fertilize during the hottest months.
Problems: Hardy to about 18°F. Like many other palms, it will survive several short periods of frost better than a long frost that penetrates the trunk. The way to make an older, well-established palm tree frost tolerant in the Central Valley is to withhold water during the summer; a dry palm can survive a freeze much more easily than a moist one.

PLANTING

As we approach the hottest months of the year in most of Northern California, gardeners should postpone planting new plants in the garden. Heat can be debilitating to tender new plants. Plan now and plant later.

It is better to wait until October, when the weather cools and rain is expected, to set out new landscaping plants. If you do set out new plants, be sure to provide them with temporary shade for the first few critical days.

RACCOONS

As fruit and vegetables ripen in August, raccoons sometimes move in for the harvest. They are fairly tidy guests and usually devour what they take on the spot, leaving the rest of the harvest in good shape for two-legged *Homo sapiens*. Trouble occurs when they invite themselves into the garage or kitchen through the pet door. A easy solution is to leave a radio playing near the pet door.

This will often work in the garden also. As smart as they are, raccoons are still baffled by the sound of the human voice when no human is in sight. If raccoons persist in coming in through a cat door, another solution is to place the door up high enough to require the cat to jump up to a ledge to enter. Cats jump; raccoons climb. With their bulky, heavy bodies, raccoons have difficulty jumping any higher than their shoulders.

Do you have a favorite camellia or azalea, a wisteria, or a passion vine growing in your garden? Want another one?

With patience, the gardener can obtain a new rooted plant from the old one by staking down a low-growing branch.

1. Either fill a pot with damp potting soil and place it under a branch that will easily reach it, or gently till the soil directly beneath a low-growing branch.

2. Make a slanting cut in this branch between seven and ten inches below the tip—if you can make this wound close to a node (a small, raised bump), so much the better. Dust a little rooting compound (a mixture of rooting hormones and fungicides) into the cut and tuck a pebble into the cut so that it cannot close up. Remove any leaves from the portion to be buried.

3. Pin the cut section into the damp soil in the pot or down to the garden soil. The wire hoops that hold down drip systems are excellent for this purpose. The tip of the branch is tied upright to a small vertical stake.

4. Keep the soil damp until the branch is well rooted in the pot, then cut it away from the parent plant.

See Air Layering, page 289, for another method of layering using peat moss.

ROSES

Generally, do not fertilize antique roses any more this year—their season is drawing to a close. Continue feeding the modern roses with a balanced fertilizer—all three numbers on the fertilizer package should be about the same such as 10-10-10, 13-15-12, or even 20-20-20. Rose fanatics will also feed their roses again two weeks from now, with fish emulsion at the rate of one teaspoon per gallon and using several gallons of the mixture on each rose bush.

A late-summer excursion into the countryside will often reveal roadside produce stands with a bucket of sunflowers offered for sale alongside the tomatoes. Sunflowers have become popular cut flowers. This should not be too surprising as the sunflower has a long history in the United States. It was cultivated by North American Indians along Lake Huron. The Indians used ground sunflower seeds for flour and oil from the seeds for cooking, paints, and hair dressing.

American settlers also ate the seeds and used the leaves and stalks as fodder. Fibers from the stalks were woven into a fabric. Leaves could be smoked like tobacco. Apparently some part of the sunflower could be used for almost anything. The seed husks were ground for a drink similar to coffee. The flower petals produced a permanent yellow dye. The oil from the seeds was used in both cooking and making soap. It is no wonder that the sunflower had many admirers, or that it was so popular in the prairie states that it was voted the state flower of Kansas.

The sunflower not only looks like the sun, but also the young flower heads have the beguiling habit of following the sun's arc across the sky. Sunflowers are easy to grow when planted in a sunny spot and watered during the summer. There are many varieties available.

For extra large flowers, both 'Russian Giant' and 'Mammoth' produce the huge heads (between nine and twenty-four inches across) that win ribbons at county fairs. These are sizeable plants growing between eight and twelve feet tall. For charm there are cultivars such as 'Teddy Bear,' which has fluffy dwarf blooms, or 'Sunspot,' which grows only eighteen inches tall. Sunflower blooms come in deep crimson, brownish bronze, and creamy yellow as well as the familiar bright yellow.

Sunflower Growing Simplified

Botanical name: *Helianthus annus*.

Common name: Sunflower.

Site preference: Full sun.

Soil conditions: Any soil, but rich soil is best for large flowers.

Water: To produce large flowers, water well.

Nutrients: Fertilize with a balanced fertilizer once or twice during the growing season.

Problems: The aggressive sunflower limits the growth of nearby plants, so space them wisely and plant them so that they do not shade other flowering plants.

Special care: Sunflowers have a long growing season (at least 120 days), so sow seed or set out plants as soon as the danger of frost has passed. Thin seedlings to eighteen inches apart as these are large, robust plants.

Hints: Plant the large varieties for the best seed production. As the seeds develop, the giant seed heads will droop with the weight. Cut off the flower heads and let them dry for several weeks in a well-ventilated place. Leave some flower heads for the birds to peck at.

SWEET PEAS

It is possible in most coastal areas of Northern California to grow a new crop of sweet peas from seed and have flowers by December. Sow seeds now of early-flowering varieties. When the days begin to shorten with the change of seasons, the sweet peas will begin blooming.

TREES

This is a time of stress for some trees in California. Monitor your garden trees closely and give them a good soaking.

VEGETABLES

August is prime time in the vegetable garden. If the zucchini or other squash are falling off the vine when they are still small, the problem is probably too much water. The solution is to let the soil dry out until the leaves begin to droop a little and then start watering again; but more sparingly.

Many vegetables have a better, more intense, flavor when grown with less water. At this stage of tomato growing, however, do not let the soil dry out too much or you may find the leaves curling and the blossom ends of the fruit turning black and rotting. Also do not prune away protective tomato foliage or your tomatoes may develop green shoulders. For larger tomatoes thin tomatoes growing closely together—the heaviest tomato on record, by the way, was seven pounds and twelve ounces.

In coastal areas, place ripening melons on inverted aluminum pie tins to keep them off the soil. The aluminum reflects the heat which helps the fruit ripen.

Set out winter-garden vegetables during the next months. When space is available, plant broccoli, Brussels sprouts (remember they grow quite tall), cabbage, cauliflower, leeks, lettuce, and peas. Beets, turnips, and other root crops can be grown from seed.

Sow onion seeds or plant onion sets in a sunny spot. Unlike most plants, onions like firm soil, so press down around the seeds or sets. Also sow seeds of chard, lettuce, radishes, and peas. In the hottest areas, wait until next month to sow new crops.

VEGETABLES—HARVESTING

Summer vegetables are at their best now. All vegetables taste better if eaten the day they are picked. For a guide to selecting vegetables at their best see Vegetables—Harvesting; page 189.

WISTERIA

Take a good look at the wisteria vine, which is probably still sending out many more new stems. Cut back to two buds (little knobs felt beneath the skin of the stem) all the stems that are unwanted. This will promote new flower spurs from the two buds left on the stem.

You will need to train the stems that you have left before they twist around one another, which is the habit of wisteria vines. These skinny, sprawling stems will become as thick as ropes. Tie them in place so that they will form a good structure in the future.

Young vines should be watered well and then fertilized. Older vines could use a deep watering this month, although they will survive without summer water once established.

WORMS

Praise be to the humble earthworm. Encourage the earthworm whenever possible by having plenty of organic material on top of or dug into the soil. The earthworm is a machine for creating wonderful soil. Soil with worm castings typically contains five times more nitrogen, seven times more phosphorous, and eleven times more potash than soil without worm castings. A healthy cubic yard of soil can readily contain four hundred earthworms. What does a worm desire most? A warm, moist spot with plenty of organic material to digest. Create such a place, and the worms will come to you.

... September ...

SPREKELIA FORMOSISSIMA

First signs of fall color?

September is often the hottest month of the year in the coastal areas of Northern California. The Central Valley areas are cooling so they no longer draw in the blanket of fog through gaps in the coastal mountains. Without that high, sun-shielding layer of fog, the coastal areas can at last enjoy sunny days. In all areas of Northern California it is a great harvest season. Both fruits and vegetables are plentiful. Gardeners need to think in terms of the coming fall. Bypass the summer vegetables and summer-flowering annuals still available in the nurseries because the coming cool weather will not sustain crops or summer flowers.

It is time to think of permanent landscaping. Trees and shrubs do well when planted in warm autumn soil. The roots are watered by rain and grow strong enough to put out new growth in spring. Native plants do particularly well when planted in fall. They are designed to absorb winter rain and often flounder when confronted with summer water. This is a good month to read up on native plants because native plant societies hold their largest sales in October.

It is also time to begin doing those traditional autumn tasks—fall cleanup and spring-blooming bulb buying. As soon as a spurt of cold weather comes to your area, look at the fall foliage plants in the nursery, because the fall color of seed-grown plants varies greatly even in the same variety.

All Gardeners

For the best selection, purchase spring bulbs as soon as they come on the market. Shop for native plants, trees, and shrubs. Do not buy or plant frost-tender plants such as citrus and bougainvillea (wait until next spring).

❀ Continue to weed. Unfortunately as long as it's the growing season, it is also the weeding season. Add young, seedhead-free weeds and excess summer growth to the compost pile. Remember to keep the pile as damp as a wrung-out sponge for faster composting.

❀ As always, keep after the snails.
Use a strong spray from the hose to wash away aphids.
Ants are likely to become a problem soon. Discourage them by picking up fallen fruit and sealing off cracks that would lead them into the house.

❀ Water plants as needed.

▲ ▼ ▲

Coastal Gardeners

In addition to the tasks listed for all gardeners, hold off fertilizing most plants in preparation for winter. However, fertilize the lawn. Fertilize all flowering plants that are about to bloom. Fertilize roses with a low-nitrogen formula or one that has no nitrogen at all. Do not fertilize most antique roses.

❀ Continue to pinch off dead flowers, particularly off fuchsias. Of course, if you wish to save seeds for planting in the future, you will want to leave the entire flower head, particularly the swollen ovaries where seeds form.

❀ Early this month sow seeds of fall- and winter-flowering plants, such as calendula, Iceland poppy, pansy, primrose, and stock, into the bedding plot. Toward the end of September, set out transplants of cineraria, nemesia, and schizanthus. Stake tall sprawling flowers such as delphiniums and foxgloves.

❀ Harvest vegetables as they ripen. Pick them early in the day. Tie up sprawling tomato vines to supports. Plant the vegetable garden with beets, broccoli, cabbage, carrots, cauliflower, garlics, leeks, onions, and shallots. Thin vegetable seedlings that were sown too close together by snipping them with scissors.

❀ Keep all fruiting trees, particularly citrus, well watered.

▲ ▼ ▲

Central Valley Gardeners

In addition to the tasks listed for all gardeners, hold off fertilizing most plants in preparation for winter, but do fertilize all flowering plants that are about to bloom. Fertilize roses with a low- nitrogen formula or one that has no nitrogen at all. Do not fertilize most antique roses.

❀ Pinch off dead flowers. Of course, if you wish to save seeds for planting in the future, you will want to leave the entire flower head, particularly the swollen ovaries where seeds form.

❀ Postpone transplanting fall- and winter-flowering plants into the bedding plot during a heat wave. Hot weather is hard on newly transplanted plants. If you do transplant, shade them for a few days with the temporary shelter of an umbrella or a wooden shake. Stake tall sprawling flowers.

❀ Harvest vegetables as they ripen. Pick them early in the day. Plant the vegetable garden with beets, broccoli, cabbage, carrots, cauliflower, garlic, leeks, onions, and shallots. In the hottest areas wait until next month to put in new crops.

❀ Keep the garden well watered, particularly citrus trees. Soak all newly transplanted plants.

High Mountain Gardeners

In addition to the tasks listed for all gardeners, continue to dig and divide overgrown perennials. Plant them promptly so that their roots have time to become established before the cold season begins.

◉ As the leaves begin to wither, lift summer-blooming bulbs, such as begonias, dahlias, and gladiolus, and let them dry for a few days before storing them for the winter in a cool, dry place where the temperature does not fall below 32°F.

◉ Set out fall-flowering plants. Fertilize plants that are about to bloom.

◉ Withhold fertilizer from woody plants so that they have time to harden before the cold season begins.

◉ Harvest the vegetable garden, particularly crops with a high water content, such as tomatoes, which are damaged by an early frost.

◉ As soon as they come on the market, plant spring-flowering bulbs such as snowdrops, crocus, and Siberian squill as well as daffodils and tulips.

AZALEAS

Fertilize azaleas with an acid fertilizer. If you are among the azalea growers who believe that twice a year is enough, this second application (the first was after they had finished blooming) is important for brilliant spring displays.

APPLE HARVESTING

Fully mature apples taste the best. To determine whether an apple is truly mature on the tree, simply hold it in the palm of your hand and gently lift up. If the apple is mature, the stem will break free easily. If you have to twist the stem to get it off, wait.

BALCONY AND ENTRYWAY GARDENS

Continue to transplant fall-flowering plants into pots; calendula and chrysanthemums are dazzling bloomers. Established plants should be fertilized with a bloom-promoting formula, such as 0-10-10. Be sure to keep potted plants well watered. For a more dramatic impact consider a shrub in a large pot; Japanese maples and sansanqua camellias are decorative even when not displaying their autumn glories. Several varieties of Japanese maples (*Acer palmatum*) do particularly well in a pot. Look for 'Crimson Queen,' 'Dissectum,' and 'Threadleaf.'

For the best selection, shop for bulbs as soon as they are available in nurseries. Buy spring-blooming bulbs, corms, tubers, and rhizomes such as anemones, crocus, daffodils, hyacinth, Dutch iris, freesias, leucojum, narcissus, ranunculus, scilla, and tulips.

⊛ For carefree, drought-resistant bulbs consider some of the lesser-known species bulbs such as basket-flower or Peruvian daffodil (*Hymenocallis narcissiflora*). Rather than the single-flowered, trumpet-shaped daffodil, chose the cluster-flowering narcissus, which is very persistent in Northern California.

⊛ When selecting bulbs choose the largest ones. The bulb is basically a food storage device, so the larger the bulb, the larger the flower. Look for firm, relatively smooth bulbs that have a healthy appearance. Avoid bulbs with insect damage or soft areas. Diseased bulbs often have blotchy areas of discoloration and damaged scales. Touch the pointed tip of the bulb; it should feel firm, not soft. The papery skin should still be attached to the bulb. It protects the bulb from drying out.

⊛ Bulbs with an offset (another smaller bulb attached to the side) will produce two flowers if the offset is large. If the offset is small, it will not bloom until the following year. You will frequently see twin-nosed or even triple-nosed daffodils. Those will produce two and three flowers respectively in the coming spring. Do not pull twin- or triple-nosed bulbs apart.

⊛ Store hyacinths and tulips in the bottom of the refrigerator for between six and eight weeks. Plant them in November. Hyacinths and tulips will bloom without prechilling, but they will grow taller and bloom earlier if they are prechilled. For growing hyacinths in water see page 262. Store other bulbs in a cool, dry place and plant them at your convenience in September, October, or November.

⊛ Most bulbs prefer a sunny site with well-drained soil. Fast-draining soil is important because many bulbs will rot if forced to remain in a soggy spot during their dormant season. There are several guidelines for planting bulbs. The colder the area, the deeper the bulb is planted. Along the coast bulbs are generally planted twice as deep as they are tall. In the Central Valley, plant bulbs three times as deep as they are tall. In high mountain regions, plant bulbs four or five times as deep as they are tall. Plant bulbs with the pointed end up.

⊛ The addition of fertilizer, bone meal, or manure to the soil beneath the bulb is debatable. Some experts believe that such measures do not help the bulb and are a waste of time. If you do add nutrients, do not let the bulb food touch the bottom of the bulb, or it may burn the vulnerable bulb.

BULBS IN POTS

Bulbs are well suited to pots. Make certain that there is at least one inch of soil beneath each bulb—more soil is much better. Select similar-sized bulbs for uniform bloom. Space the bulbs closely, leaving about a finger's width between them. Here is a neat trick for tulips—place the flat side of the tulip bulb against the side of the pot so that the leaf will curl out over the edge. Gently pack soil between bulbs and barely cover the pointed tops. Water well and place the pots in a cool, dark place, keeping them watered until shoots appear above the soil. Then bring the pots into a warmer, sunny spot. Flowering bulbs in pots will last longer indoors if they are moved to a cool spot each night.

CAMELLIAS

Be sure to keep camellias well watered this month. Some varieties are forming buds now. For large, showy flowers, remove all but one flower bud from every branch tip or branch joint. Gently twist off the unwanted buds. Camellias form two types of buds. The flower buds are fat and round; the growth buds (which form leaves and branches) are thin and pointed. Leave the growth buds alone.

CHRYSANTHEMUMS

Chrysanthemums should be watered, fertilized, and staked this month. The potted gift chrysanthemum (*Chrysanthemum x morifolium*), usually needs three to five more weeks of short days and long nights to flower than do the garden varieties. Outdoors it is best to plant the garden variety.

CYCLAMEN

In mild-winter coastal areas, cyclamen can be grown outdoors. They prefer a cool spot with rich, friable soil. Fertilize cyclamen with an all-purpose fertilizer this month and pick off any snails hiding in the foliage.

CYMBIDIUMS

Fertilize every two weeks with low-nitrogen, high-phosphorus liquid fertilizer formulated for orchids.

DAFFODIL

See Narcissus.

DEER

September is not a kind month for mule deer in chaparral country. On the hill behind my home, the frothy bloom of the chamise (*Adenostoma fasciculatum*), which deer love, dries to a crusty brown. The deer invade gardens in force in September.

Despite the foraging of deer, I have fenced off only a small portion of my garden. I want the wild beasts in my garden. After all, we garden to feel part of the physical world. To garden is to be connected to the living earth. I do not want a garden fit only for *Homo sapiens*.

The deer are the largest wild animals that come into most gardens, but they are hardly the only mammals. There is a gray fox that likes to sneak under the fence into the vegetable garden. There are raccoons that come and press their faces up against the windows at night to see what we are doing. There are two striped skunks that grub in the lawn and then waddle up to the porch where the native grape (*Vitis californica* 'Roger's Red') is trying to take over the house.

A neighbor tells me she has seen a bobcat sunning on her fence. I would like to see this. Once I was strolling among the pines, palms, and eucalyptus of a small garden in St.-Jean-Cap-Ferrat when I heard the unmistakable throaty roar of a lion. I was attempting to scramble up a palm when my host informed me there was a small zoo nearby. There is nothing quite like the roar of lion to put the position of human beings into perspective.

Those who believe that it is impossible to have a flowering garden and wildlife too are mistaken. My garden is in perpetual bloom. True, the lawn is slightly overaerated by little paws that grub for insects, and individual plants now and then look a bit chewed, but that is a small price to pay to coexist with other living mammals.

One glorious fall day, my children and I were eating on the deck when a stag suddenly appeared. He was much too proud to scurry warily as the doe and yearlings do. Balancing his antlers like a crown, he pranced right through the garden. No rhododendron ever gave us such a thrill.

Deer Repellents

Deer repellents really do work if applied after every rain or heavy fog. A report in the *American Rose* magazine indicates that the deer repellent Hinder greatly reduced browsing by deer in the American Rose Center in Shreveport, Louisiana.

A report in the "American Fruit Grower" newsletter indicated that deodorant soap (the brand is unimportant) hung at browsing level in apple trees reduced browsing by seventy percent. The bars of soap still in wrappers were hung every three feet.

I make my own deer repellent by mixing two cups of water with five eggs in the blender and then using the mixture for spraying vulnerable plants. Bob Tanem, a nursery owner in Marin County, added nifty refinements which he described in his field guide "Deer-Resistant Planting," by adding skim milk and a spreader-sticker to the brew. This last ingredient is available at nurseries. The human nose cannot detect the scent of rotten egg that these brews leave on plants; the more sensitive deer nose is repelled. Some people spray every fourteen days; I only respray after rain or a heavy fog.

Deer Protection Plan

There are three steps to living graciously with foraging deer.

1. Plants that deer find irresistible such as vegetables, roses, or apples must either be planted in an area with a deer-resistant fence or, in the case of apple trees, be caged off until they grow tall enough to sustain grazing deer with little damage. Effective fences depend upon the site. Deer are not stupid; a six-foot fence surrounding a small vegetable garden located next to a house will seem like a trap to them. In my experience, they will not jump into such a small enclosure located so close to humans. A large fenced area away from the house may require two parallel fences; deer are better high jumpers than they are broad jumpers. They will see the two parallel fences as a trap and not jump into the fenced area. If you are determined not to have deer in a unfenced garden, a barking dog will keep them away. Be sure to control your dog; some dogs chase deer until they end up killing them.

2. All new plants and plants favored by deer should be protected either by cages or by spraying with a deer deterrent.

3. Gardeners wishing to live in relative harmony with deer should garden with plants known to be deer resistant.

Deer-Resistant Plants

In my experience, deer will eat anything when it is first planted. A tender new nursery plant seems to be like fresh-picked young salad leaves to browsing deer. Then when they are older and presumably less succulent, some of these same plants are avoided by deer. All new plants should be temporarily caged until they are established. The following are plants that the deer eventually declined to eat in my garden; all of them bloom.

⚙ Bulbs: daffodils (*Narcissus*), iris, dahlias, freesia

⚙ Perennials: aster, coreopsis, cyclamen, fleabane (*Erigeron*), foxglove, mimulus, snow-in-summer (*Cerastium tomentosum*), yarrow (*Achillea*)

⚙ Shrubs: butterfly bush (*Buddleia*), small-leafed ceanothus, cotoneaster, golden shrub daisy (*Euryops pectinatus*), lavender (*Lavandula*), *Lychinis coronaria*, oleander, rhododendron

⚙ Vines: bougainvillea, clematis, potato vine (*Solanum jasminoides*), wisteria

DIVIDE

Carefully dig up and divide overgrown agapanthus, bearded iris, daylily, primrose, and Shasta daisy. For instructions and illustrations on dividing bearded iris, see page 183.

For instructions and illustrations on dividing other perennials, see page 239.

FALL CLEANUP

Fall cleanup is an essential part of disease and pest control.

Pick up fallen branches, pots, or other debris from the garden to reduce the number of overwintering sites for snails, slugs, insects, and fungal spores.

Pull up dying annuals and vegetables. Rake up leaves. Add garden debris, except seed-bearing weeds and diseased plants, to the compost pile.

Go through the garden and examine plants for black spots, bright orange rust pustules, white powdery mildew, rotted stems or branches, large, irregularly shaped galls near the soil, or other signs of infection. Pull up the infected plants and rake up infected leaves and dispose of them. Do not put infected material into the compost bin. Bring a trash can with you into the garden so you can immediately dispose of infected material without spreading disease by dragging it through the garden.

Last, rinse gardening tools with a solution of one part bleach to three parts water. Then coat your tools lightly with oil to keep them from rusting.

Even in Northern California we have an impressive display of autumn color from liquidambars, ginkos, and Chinese pistache trees. The sharper the sudden temperature change from summer to fall, the more glorious the display.

As soon as you note the changing of leaf color in the neighborhood trees, it is time to head to the nursery to select trees to plant for fall color. Fall leaf color varies from tree to tree even in exactly the same variety. The best way to choose a young tree is to see its leaf color in the nursery before you buy. Combine trees to get pleasing autumn effects.

My favorite for drought-resistant fall color is a native vine. *Vitis californica* 'Roger's Red' is a native grapevine selected by Roger Raiche, a horticulturist at the University of California, in 1983 at Palmer Creek in Sonoma. It is fast growing and, at least in my garden, disease free. The fall color is glorious; its red leaves are as vivid as a stained-glass window. As the leaves age, they turn a deeper red, like old Moroccan leather.

Liquidambar trees come in fall color shades of red, orange, burgundy, and gold. Liquidambars have maplelike leaves and interesting spiny brown balls (actually fruits) that dangle from the tree before dropping to the ground. The Saratoga Horticultural Foundation, a group of nurserymen who formed a foundation to develop spectacular flora for California, has produced several wonderful liquidambar cultivars ('Burgundy,' 'Festival,' and 'Palo Alto') that are widely sold in Northern California nurseries. These trees provide dependable fall color even in mild coastal climates.

In Central Valley and mountain areas, the Chinese pistache tree (*Pistacia chinensis*) will dazzle you with brilliant red shades. Some people consider the sour gum (*Nyssa silvatica*), to have the finest fall display. It turns a rusty red intermingled with apricot golds, and it has the advantage of growing well even in lean soil.

For the shimmer of yellow, consider the ginkgo tree cultivar *Ginkgo biloba* 'Autumn Gold', or the native bigleaf maple (*Acer macrophyllum*), or a shrub such as the Western serviceberry (*Amelanchier alnifolia*).

Other excellent choices include the flowering trees such as the crape myrtle (*Lagerstroemia indica*); and the flowering plum (*Prunus blireiana*). Among the flowering shrubs with fall color are the snowball bush (*Viburnum opulus* 'Sterile'); the oakleaf hydrangea (*Hydrangea quercifolia*), many varieties of cotoneaster, and deciduous azaleas. Not be overlooked are Japanese maples (*Acer palmatum;* see page 263), heavenly bamboo (*Nandina domestica*), and the Lombardy poplar (*Populus nigra* 'Italica').

Fall Color Techniques

Plant trees and shrubs in full sun so that they will be subject to the sharpest temperature changes. In late summer, reduce or stop watering those plants that provide brilliant fall color. Watering prolongs the summer growing season; you want the plant to assume its autumn habits as soon as the temperature drops.

FALL PLANTING

Fall is the best time to plant trees and shrubs. It is usually better to buy a tree in a smaller container than in a larger container; the root system of the smaller tree will adapt better to new soil than will that of an older tree. After a few years, the smaller tree will have usually grown taller than the originally larger tree. The exceptions will be slow-growing trees.

To Plant a Tree:

1. Gently remove the tree from the container and plant it in a hole at least as big as the container. Leave the soil directly beneath the tree undisturbed. Use soil amendments sparingly or not at all.

2. Stake the tree only in areas of forceful wind.

3. Water well.

Note: Young trees often die from crown rot—a disease caused by planting the tree too low or by allowing soil to mound up around the trunk. The trunk is meant to be exposed to air. When soil piles up around the trunk, it rots the bark in a circle around the trunk, and as the tree is no longer able to conduct moisture and nutrients to the branches and leaves, it soon dies.

FERTILIZE

Fertilize begonias, fuchsias, roses, and all newly planted annuals, vegetables, and perennials after they have been in the ground for two weeks. Citrus plants get their last feeding this month.

s e p t e m b e r

FLOWERS

Plant a few colorful blooming plants to brighten the darkest days of winter. Because most plants do not grow well in cold weather, it is better to set out winter-blooming plants while there is still a month or two of growing weather left for them to reach full size. Toward the end of this month set out transplants of winter-blooming flowers such as dianthus, flowering cabbages, forget-me-nots, Iceland poppies, pansies, primroses, and sweet alyssum.

Remember to fertilize winter-blooming plants with a fertilizer formulated to promote blooming to keep the display coming over the dark months.

FIRE PREVENTION

Long, dry summers promote fire in fall. Fire is a natural phenomenon in California and the gardener can lessen the chances of fire through proper plant control.

FIRE PREVENTION TASKS

1. Begin by reducing or eliminating dry plant fuel that would feed a fire. Typically this means removing plants such as dry grass and weeds, Scotch broom, coyote brush, pampas grass, and poison oak. The first thirty feet surrounding the house are the most critical.

2. Eliminate fire ladders of vegetation and overhanging branches that would lead a fire to your home. You may need a tree arborist to prune large trees.

3. Thin and prune existing shrubs and trees to reduce plant fuel available to a fire. Remove dead branches. Prune lower branches that have leaves near the ground to prevent fire from spreading into trees.

4. Pay attention to the hardscape in your garden such as wooden decks and arbors. Remove or trim vegetation that would likely cause these structures to burn.

FRUIT TREES

Keep the fruit trees watered, particularly citrus, which will bear fruit later. Citrus planted in containers need water almost daily as citrus fruit is mostly water.

FUCHSIAS

Feed with a balanced fertilizer, keep well watered, and remove the old blooms and swollen seed pods to keep the fuchsias blooming.

Alliums such as garlic, shallots, and leeks can be planted at any time from now through November. Garlic is easy to grow. Homegrown garlic often produces bigger, juicier bulbs than those from the supermarket. Fall-planted garlic has the advantage of having longer to ripen the following year. Start with bulbs purchased at the supermarket or nursery. Examine the bulbs carefully for signs of disease, which could contaminate the soil as well as the crop. Gently separate the cloves. Plant the cloves about four inches apart and two inches deep in full sun with the sharp end of the clove pointed up. Water until the rains take over.

Next summer, test for readiness by digging up one of the garlic plants to see whether the cloves are large enough. Carefully remove the plants from the ground, gently wipe off the excess dirt, and suspend them in a cool, dry place for three or four weeks. Then clean the dried husks and store the garlic cloves with or without the stems.

Onions are a particularly useful crop as they can be eaten at all stages of development beginning with the greens known as scallions on through the various sizes of onions that follow. Sow onion seeds in September; start harvesting green onion tops around January. For a continual supply, sow onion seeds every three or four weeks. Unlike most plants, onions like firm soil, so press down around the seeds or sets. After they germinate two weeks later, thin them to between two and three inches apart.

IN BLOOM IN SEPTEMBER

- Annuals: impatiens, lobelia, marigold, and petunia
- Perennials: begonia, campanula, and Shasta daisy
- Shrubs: fuchsia, hydrangea, lavender, and rose
- Bulblike plants: dahlia, gladiolus, and Japanese anemone
- Early blooming chrysanthemums
- Native plants: buckwheats, California fuchsias (*Epilobium*; used to be known as *Zauschneria*), and late penstemons.

IN THE NURSERY IN SEPTEMBER

- Winter-blooming annuals: buy six-packs of calendula and chrysanthemum, Iceland poppy, and pansy
- Spring-blooming bulbs, corms, tubers, and rhizomes
- Container-grown landscaping plants
- California natives

Cool season lawns (bent grass, bluegrass, fescue, and rye) will soon begin a green growth spurt—they need fertilizer and water.

Remember as days cool and grow shorter, lawns will need less water. The California Department of Water Resources has established average ET (evapotranspiration) rates for many Northern California communities. The ET rate is the quantity of water that evaporates from the garden soil plus the quantity of water that transpires from the grass leaves. Based on these ET rates, lawns in different areas need different quantities of water to keep them at their ornamental best without wasting water.

LAWN WATERING GUIDELINES FOR AUTUMN

Adjust your sprinklers to water less now. For autumn the average lawn, watered to a depth of six to eight inches twice a week, will need to have the sprinklers on each time for:

Between four and eighteen minutes in the coastal region
Between ten and twenty-two minutes in the Central Valley
Between six and twenty minutes in the high mountains

The lower figures are for larger pipelines. Your lawn will indicate a need for more water by turning from a bright green to a dull blue green. Also you will see footprints in the lawn because the grass does not spring back up.

NARCISSUS

Bulb vendors are forever admonishing buyers to purchase narcissus in large quantities and plant them in great sweeping drifts. One has to surmise that this advice is intended to increase bulb sales, because the gardener inevitably plants narcissus bulbs a few at a time in pots or in a single row to circle a tree or to line a pathway.

The gardener, I think, has got it right. Narcissus are perfect when planted up close where their small, jaunty blooms and sweet fragrance can be best enjoyed. There is hardly a more cheering sight on a glum spring morning then a row of yellow daffodils lining the path to the front door. The bulb evangelists may have a point; Mother Nature does not plant in straight lines. But humankind does. We make paths, and we enjoy plants that mark our coming and going.

Doubtless, there are places where bulbs grow naturally in great drifts. I see one of those places in my mind's eye whenever I recall lines from Wordsworth's poem "I wandered lonely as a cloud . . ./ When all at once I saw a crowd,/ A host, of golden daffodils; Beside the lake, beneath the trees,/ Fluttering and dancing in the breeze."

Perhaps the poet, given to romanticizing his travels, only stumbled across the ceaselessly multiplying effort of some long-forgotten gardener, just as some of the four hundred thousand bulbs that bloom on Daffodil Hill in the Gold Country are offshoots of bulbs planted many years ago by a gardener lonely for his Dutch homeland.

Narcissus are native to North Africa and Europe, so I imagine that even ancient cave dwellers gathered wild narcissus, and that a few bulbs found their way into those first gardens in Mesopotamia. We know that a cluster-flowered variety (*Narcissus tazetta*) was grown in both ancient Egypt and ancient Greece and through early trade routes made its way to China, where it was known as the Chinese sacred lily or joss lily. The latter name, no doubt, refers to the pervasive fragrance.

Even though they are toxic, narcissus bulbs were standard items in Roman medical bags. Galen, a physician who tended to gladiators, used to glue together wounds and gashes with the juice from a narcissus bulb. The restorative powers of a narcissus extend beyond its medical properties. There was a saying in ancient times, "Let he who has two loaves of bread sell one and buy a daffodil. For bread is but food for the body, while a flower is food for the soul."

Narcissus Growing Simplified

Botanical name: *Narcissus*.

Common name: Daffodil or narcissus. Some still call a narcissus with a long corona (center cup) a daffodil and one with a short corona a narcissus, but the Royal Horticultural Society, which is the International Registration Authority for the genus, does not recognize the distinction.

Site preference: Full sun or part shade. Remember that the flowers will turn to face the sun, so plant accordingly.

Soil conditions: Fast-draining, preferably moist, soil during the growing season.

Planting: Dig a hole one-and-a-half times deeper than the length of the bulb, mix bulb fertilizer into the soil beneath the bulb, and plant it with the pointed end up.

Water: Water after planting. Winter rain should be adequate for growth.

Nutrients: Top-dress with a balanced, slow-release fertilizer every fall.

Problems: Control snails and slugs. Narcissus bulbs are poisonous, so rodents leave them alone, as do deer. Sometimes earwigs attack the new bloom, but narcissus are generally pest free. A light feeding with a general-purpose fertilizer before they bloom or in the fall is about the only additional care they require.

Special care: The only unbreakable rule in growing narcissus is that the foliage must be left to die back naturally before it is removed. The minute I write this I think of a well-known bulb grower who mows down the green tops of his bulbs each spring when they finish blooming; so much for unbreakable rules.

Hints: In truly hot summer areas, plant cluster-flowered varieties such as Tazetta hybrids and jonquils, which hold up and propagate better in the heat.

Borrow a technique used in Monet's garden at Giverny and plant narcissus in the lawn. Every fall, the French gardeners at Giverny cut and roll back the lawn like a carpet, put in the bulbs with a little bone meal, and then roll back the lawn. In the spring, the bulb foliage is allowed to wither to yellow before the lawn is mowed.

NATIVE PLANTS

Because the best time for planting native California plants is just before the fall rains are expected, many native plants societies hold sales in October. You may want to plan ahead now and read up about native plants (see page 243) for a start, as many native plants are not well known. Then visit a nursery or a native plant sale to purchase plants.

ORCHID CACTUS

Continue to fertilize orchid cactus (epiphyllums) with a balanced formula such as 10-10-10. Spray the foliage with a water soluble fertilizer as well as watering the fertilizer into the soil as orchid cactus readily absorb fertilizer through the stems.

ORNAMENTAL GRASSES

There is something about the great grasslands of the Western frontier that beckons the American spirit. Willa Cather in her novel *Death Comes for the Archbishop* referred to it as ". . . that lightness, that dry aromatic odor . . . Something soft and wild and free." Oddly, though we yearn for the wild unhampered ways of grasslands, we have cultivated our gardens into tidy plots of mowed lawn and prim flower beds. Then landscape designers and gardeners discovered ornamental grasses. The whole look of the garden itself is becoming radically altered. This new look, sometimes called the New American Garden, began on the East Coast and is currently infiltrating West Coast sensibilities as well.

By most accounts, the movement toward a natural-looking wild garden based on ornamental grasses started here with two landscape architects, Wolfgang Oehme and James van Sweden. In 1952 Oehme visited a public garden in Hamburg, Germany, called the Planten un Blomen where he saw a wide variety of ornamental grasses and perennials used to create a wild garden design. The German interest in ornamental grasses had been instigated in the 1930s by an exceptional nurseryman named Karl Foerster. When Oehme came to the United States in 1958, he began to champion the new design.

The new look is remarkably well suited to American gardens, suggesting as it does our prairies, meadows, and grasslands. Properly practiced, it emphasizes native plants particular to each region. In the new design, herbaceous perennials and ornamental grasses are planted in large sweeping blocks for a striking visual impact that can, as van Sweden puts it, "be read at thirty miles per hour."

The charm of the new look is based on the constantly changing seasonal effect of grasses, which turn red, brown, and yellow in the fall, and herbaceous perennials, which die back every year. Both plant groups flower and many produce dried seedheads. There is no dull season in the new American garden. The silken flower tassels and feathery seedheads of fall are as evocative as spring's vivid bloom. Grasses also sway gracefully in a breeze and, as they dry, rustle with the wind. And once you have seen a clumpgrass backlit by the setting sun, you will always wish to have ornamental grasses in the garden.

The popularity of the new American garden stems from its ease of maintenance. A key to effective design is the selection of trouble-free, outstanding plants that are vigorous but not invasive and, in our California gardens, plants that are also drought tolerant. The following is a list of outstanding plants suitable for planting in broad sweeps in Northern California gardens.

Ornamental Grass—Types

⚜ Feather reed grass (*Calamagrostis acutifolia* 'Stricta') is a showy, robust grass that grows in a narrow clump to about five feet tall and in late spring forms a fluffy, pink-tinged flowerhead that dries to a wheatlike stalk. This grass is best planted several grasses in a row so the waving effect of the plant in the wind is accentuated as the wind ripples through the row of grasses.

⚜ Silverfeather grass (*Miscanthus sinensis* 'Silberfeder'), is the classic five-foot-tall clumpgrass used back East. A better choice for California is zebra grass (*Miscanthus sinensis* 'Zebrinus'), which grows into a seven-foot clump and becomes fairly drought tolerant when well established.

⚜ Fountain grass (*Pennisetum setaceum*), is a striking clumpgrass known for its graceful green spring form followed by masses of fuzzy, coppery pink flower spikes that dry as the grass turns brown in winter. It grows to three feet and is drought tolerant. 'Cupreum' is a beautiful reddish brown variety with purple spikes.

⚜ California fescue (*Festuca californica*), is a native bunchgrass that forms three-foot clumps. It remains green year round.

⚜ Blue oat grass (*Helictotrichon sempervirens*), is a silvery blue gray bunchgrass with a fine rounded form about two feet tall. It is surprisingly drought tolerant.

⚜ Deer grass (*Muhlenbergia rigens*) eventually forms a three-foot clump of gray-green blades with graceful flower stalks.

Ornamental Grasses and their Friends

⚜ A flowering succulent, *Sedum telephium* 'Autumn Joy', is thought by many gardeners to be a perfect plant. It combines well with ornamental grasses and its pink flowers age to a copper rust color that persists through winter.

⚜ Lamb's ears (*Stachys byzantina*) provides a low-growing silvery ground cover of fuzzy foliage that is easy to care for and drought tolerant. It is particularly striking with purple fountain grass.

⚜ Yarrow (*Achillea*) is a perennial with green fernlike leaves and flat, dense, flowerheads that are still attractive when dry and dead. Different varieties range from six inches to four feet tall. The new hybrid 'Summer Pastels' has vivid pastel blooms rather than the muted yellows and golds traditionally associated with yarrow.

⚜ Coreopsis, which can be an annual or a perennial depending on the climate, forms masses of yellow daisylike blooms. Many varieties are very drought tolerant and will reseed themselves and thrive despite considerable neglect. One of the most outstanding is *Coreopsis verticillata* 'Moonbeam,' which has a long-lived display of pale yellow blooms on two-foot stems.

Daylilies (*Hemerocallis*) form clumps of straplike leaves and showy flowers that reach toward the sun. 'Stella d'Oro' is a two-foot-tall variety with yellow flowers throughout the warm season.

PLANTING

The latter part of September is prime time for planting landscape plants—trees, shrubs, and ground covers—so that they can develop sturdy root systems over the winter rainy period and burst into top growth next spring. See page 221 for the fall planting of trees. Remember that nursery plants may have been nurtured in a protected, lath-covered setting, so shield them after transplanting with temporary shade and temporary protection from drying winds. Shingles, cardboard boxes, and old umbrellas are useful for providing temporary shelter.

POTTED PLANTS

If you are thinking of moving potted plants indoors after a summer vacation or moving them indoors to prevent them from being damaged by the colder weather of oncoming winter, move them with caution. Pests are likely to hitch a ride to the safer interior habitat where birds, frogs, lizards, and other insect-eating predators do not exist. It is a considerable chore to rid indoor plants of pest infestations, so quarantine outdoor plants for several weeks in a room away from other houseplants. During the quarantine period make frequent inspections of both the plants and pots for insects and diseases.

Aphids multiply so rapidly that hitchhikers will soon have enough family members to become obvious during the quarantine. Early signs of aphids are distorted leaves and a sticky substance on the leaves. Aphids are very small (one-eighth of an inch long), soft-bodied insects that suck sap out of leaves and stems. Aphids are easily dealt with by washing the plant with soapy water for several days in a row.

Mealybugs are persistent little rascals so difficult to control that you want to stop them before they spread to other plants. They resemble very small sow bugs (one-fourth of an inch long). They often hang out underneath leaves and along stems. They often leave a white cottony substance like shreds of a cotton ball, and they also leave traces of a sticky substance. Wipe them off with a cotton swab soaked in rubbing alcohol. Keep after them.

Scales are difficult to recognize if you have never seen them before. They certainly do not look like an insect. They look like a flat spot of dirt or a little gray brown bump. After a while you may notice that the bumps are increasing. They tend to hang out around the stem although they can appear anywhere on the plant. They also may leave a sticky substance on the plant. Scrape them off with your fingernail.

Spider mites may also try to hitchhike (see Spider mites, page 230). As a preventative measure, you may want to wash the plants off with soapy water before putting them into quarantine. If, after several weeks, they pass inspection, then they may take up residence with the other houseplants.

PRIMROSES

The common English primrose, *Primula polyantha*, will grow anywhere in Northern California, but it positively thrives along the coast where the weather is cool, mild, and moist. In the coastal area, plants can be left in the ground year after year; in the colder areas of the Central Valley and the high mountains, cover them with several inches of mulch during the coldest weather and pamper them with shade and water during the summer. Because they are sold in six-packs inexpensively, you may just want to treat them as annuals and refuse to fuss over them at all. Once a primrose takes to sulking, yank it out, and add it to the compost bin.

For those gardeners who wish to sustain their primrose population, September is a good month to divide them. Simply dig them up, pull the separate plants apart, and replant them. It is likely that over the years, the primroses have pushed themselves up too high out of the soil. Do not tolerate such bad behavior; put them back in their place by burying the roots deeper, making certain to leave the crowns above ground. Washing them with a botanical soap and water will destroy the mites that often infest primroses. Water well and watch out for invading snails and slugs. After a week of repose (the plant's repose; the gardener is much too busy to rest), feed primroses with a balanced fertilizer. You may want to consider placing a few daffodil bulbs in the primrose bed. Many primroses have, among other bright colors, yellow markings that combine well with yellow daffodils.

PRUNING

Refrain from pruning most plants. Pruning at this time of year stimulates new growth that is vulnerable to winter cold. Do prune back overgrown, scrawny geraniums and pelargoniums. You can propagate them, along with hydrangea, ivy, and fuchsia by pruning a nonblooming tip and planting it in damp sand or vermiculite.

Prune back marguerites, but do not cut back into the woody stems, which will not sprout new shoots; prune only into the green stems.

ROSES

In September the formula for fertilizing modern roses should change to one that encourages flowering but no growth. This feat is managed with a fertilizer that has no nitrogen. A popular formula has the numbers 0-10-10 on the package. The zero means no nitrogen, the numbers 10-10 stand for the percentage of phosphorous and potassium, both of which will promote continued bloom and help to harden the stems for the rigors of winter. Rose fanatics will also feed them again two weeks from now with fish emulsion at the rate of one teaspoon per gallon, using several gallons of this mixture for each bush.

SPIDER MITES

Beware the mighty mite. Spider mites are one-fiftieth of an inch long and barely visible to the eye, but they can suck the chlorophyll out of a leaf and leave behind a toxin that discolors and distorts foliage. They reproduce rapidly in hot, dry weather, which accounts for their predation in September. Wash the little rascals off plants with a forceful spray of water. Do this for at least three days in a row to break their breeding cycle. If that does not work, try an insecticidal soap. Heavily infested sections of plants should be cut away and destroyed.

TOMATOES

It is time for some vegetable gardeners to face the Fall Tomato Challenge. Next month the sunlight hours will be shorter, rains will probably fall, and by November, cool weather, and in the high mountains perhaps even snow, will finish off the crop of tomatoes. How then to maximize the yield?

One trick is to remove all the flower clusters along with the small immature tomatoes, thereby forcing the tomato vine to put its energy into ripening the remaining fruit. The gardener can also stop watering the tomato vine, which makes the stressed plant attempt to ripen all its fruit.

Withholding water makes for a more delicious, intense tomato flavor. The risk of stressing any plant is that it becomes more susceptible to disease, but that is not much of a problem in this case. The tomatoes are almost finished anyway.

Green tomatoes picked before the eventual frost will probably ripen in the house. They will taste more like bland, store-bought tomatoes. One can also follow the example set in *Fried Green Tomatoes* and dredge slices of green tomato in herbed cornmeal and fry until crisp.

VEGETABLES

Plant winter vegetables, such as broccoli, cabbage, lettuce, and turnips this month to take advantage of the warm soil and warm air. Plant also arugula, frisée, escarole, parsley, radish, snap beans, and spinach. Two months from now, the cold nights and short days of November will slow down their growth.

Set out winter-garden vegetables during the next months. There will probably still be seedlings of summer vegetables available in the nursery, but there will not be enough warm weather left to get a crop from them. Buy only cool-season crops now.

When space is available, plant broccoli, Brussels sprouts (remember these grow quite tall), cabbage, cauliflower, leeks, lettuce, and peas. Pea crops are greater when the gardener inoculates the seed with rhizobia. Chinese pea pods and snap peas are particularly fine crops to grow. Beets, turnips, and other root crops can be grown from seed.

Sow onion seeds or plant onion sets in a sunny spot. Unlike most plants, onions like firm soil, so press down around the seeds or sets. Also sow seeds of chard, lettuce, radishes, and peas.

In the hottest areas, wait until next month to sow new crops.

VEGETABLE HARVESTING

September is often the peak harvesting season in vegetable gardens in Northern California. Although we often experience our warmest weather in September, autumn's cool weather will soon be here, signalling an end to summer crops. Harvest soon for the best in Northern California produce. See Vegetable Harvesting, page 189, for guidelines in picking vegetables at their best.

WATERING

September is usually one of the hottest months of the year in Northern California, and gardeners should monitor the water needs of their gardens closely. Watch for yellowing leaves, wilt, or a dull cast to the foliage. The best defense against insects is healthy plant tissue—be particularly vigilant about trees.

OCTOBER
NOVEMBER
DECEMBER

Fig. 1   Fig. 2   Fig.   Fig. 6

...October...

Date of first rain?
What provides fall color?

━◉ *October Features* ◉━

October is a month of surprises in Northern California. Particularly in the coastal areas, October continues to provide some of the warmest weather of the year. Then suddenly it changes. The Pacific High, a mass of cool, heavy air about a thousand miles offshore, which keeps the summer storms from approaching our coast, changes and in sweep the rains, often for the first time since late spring. Gardeners must hurry to finish harvesting their gardens before the weather turns cold or, in some areas, frosty. It is time to pick some of the most stunning flowers and preserve them for dark days of winter. Also be sure and put in winter- and spring-blooming plants now so that their roots can grow in the warm soil and warm daytime temperatures. They will bloom sooner and sometimes even the flowers will be larger on plants that are set in the garden now. Put in later, when the weather turns cold, these same plants will simply sulk instead of grow.

This is the best time of the year to buy and plant native California plants and, accordingly, native plant societies hold their largest plant sales this month. It is also time to continue those traditional autumn tasks—fall cleanup and spring-blooming bulb buying.

KEY GARDEN TASKS

All Gardeners

◉ Purchase spring bulbs for the best selection.

◉ Shop for native plants and set them in the garden.

◉ Purchase fall foliage plants in the nursery; the fall color of seed-grown plants varies greatly even in the same variety.

◉ Continue to weed. Unfortunately as long as it's the growing season, it is also the weeding season.
Add young, seedhead-free weeds and excess summer growth to the compost pile. Remember to keep the pile as damp as a wrung-out sponge for faster composting.

◉ Keep after the snails.

◉ Use a strong spray from the hose to wash away aphids.

◉ Water plants as needed.

▲ ▼ ▲

Coastal Gardeners

In addition to the tasks listed for all gardeners, hold off fertilizing most plants in preparation for winter.

◉ Fertilize cool-season lawns.

◉ Fertilize all flowering plants that are about to bloom.

◉ Water roses but do not fertilize them.

◉ Continue to pinch off dead flowers.

◉ Set out transplants of fall- and winter-flowering plants, such as calendula, Iceland poppy, pansy, primrose and stock, into the bedding plot.

◉ Harvest vegetables as they ripen. Continue to plant the vegetable garden with cool-season crops such as beets, broccoli, cabbage, carrots, cauliflower, onions, parsnips, and turnips. Thin vegetable seedlings that were sown too close together by snipping them with scissors.

▲ ▼ ▲

Central Valley Gardeners

In addition to the tasks listed for all gardeners, hold off fertilizing most plants in preparation for winter.

◉ Stabilize plants that might be harmed by autumn wind.

◉ Water roses but withhold all fertilizer. When the ground freezes in colder areas, mulch the rose bed heavily.

◉ Continue to pinch off dead flowers. When frost comes to the garden, move fuchsias and begonias grown in pots to a sheltered, warmer location.

◉ Finish transplanting fall- and winter-flowering plants into the bedding plot. Soak all newly transplanted plants until the rains come.

◉ Harvest vegetables as they ripen. Plant the vegetable garden with cool-season crops such as beets, broccoli, cabbage, carrots, cauliflower, onions, parsnips, and turnips. If you put your vegetable garden to rest over the winter, cover it with manure so that the manure can decompose and age over the winter.

◉ Flush your watering system to remove mineral deposits.

▲ ▼ ▲

High Mountain Gardeners

In addition to the tasks listed for all gardeners, attend to garden irrigation systems before they freeze. Flush out drip-irrigation lines, then drain well, and turn off the system. Soaker hoses should be put away until next spring.

◎ Finish dividing overgrown perennials and plant them promptly.

◎ Harvest the vegetable garden. When you put the vegetable garden to rest for the winter, cover it with a layer of manure so that the manure can age and decompose over the winter.

◎ Withhold fertilizer from woody plants so that they harden before the cold season begins.

◎ Continue to plant spring-flowering bulbs such as snowdrops, crocus, and Siberian squill as well as daffodils and tulips.

◎ Dig up cannas, dahlias, gladiolus, montbretia, tuberous begonias, and any other bulbs that will not survive deep frosts. Allow them to dry for a few days and then cover them with vermiculite or peat moss before storing them in a sheltered place.

◎ When the soil freezes, apply a thick layer of winter mulch to help protect the garden soil from the heave damage of freezing and thawing.

◎ Carry indoors the vulnerable plants you plan to shelter during the winter.

ANNUALS FROM SEED

Create a vibrant, old-fashioned flower border by sowing seeds now to bloom next spring. Godetia, larkspur, love-in-a-mist, and sweet peas look charming together and are easy to grow.

> ◎ Farewell-to-spring (*Clarkia amoena*) are available in cheerful colors in various strains from low growers of only a few inches high to high thirty-six-inch-tall varieties. Choose a tall variety for long-lasting bouquets. Sow in full sun. In cold areas, wait until spring to sow. Godetia gives many months of graceful bloom if watered when the rains end. This charming flower lasted for five months in my garden and came back for three years in a row from one fall seeding.
>
> ◎ Larkspur (*Consolida ambigua*) blooms with dramatic spikes of the traditional blue shades or in delicate coral or purple shades. In the Central Valley, sow in partial sun, in full sun elsewhere.
>
> ◎ Love-in-a-mist (*Nigella damascena*) is enchanting in spring with its tangled bloom of blue, white, or pink flowers and equally captivating in fall when the seedheads dry to form papery capsules. Sow in either full or partial sun.
>
> ◎ Sweet peas (*Lathyrus odoratus*) offer both vibrant color and fragrance. There is an amazing number of varieties; many need to be tied to some sort of support. Sow in full sun.

ANTS COMING IN FROM THE COLD

As the weather cools and nature's food supply dwindles, ants like nothing better than indoor accommodations with a steady food supply. So in they march—often in large battalions to set up residence in a large potted plant. An entire colony can number up to one hundred thousand ants.

Of the two hundred or so species of ants in California, the most commonly encountered in much of Northern California is the Argentine ant (*Iridomyrmex humilis*). It knew the way to San Jose from its native Argentina by the late 1800s, loves our coastal climate, and plagues both farmers and gardeners.

The first line of defense indoors is to eliminate the food supply. Wash counters with disinfectant to eliminate the scent of their trails. Ants have better noses than they have eyes. Then try tracking the ants to their entry point from outdoors; this often turns out to be along a baseboard. Barricade the troops with a little caulk.

To eliminate them outdoors, track them down to the source. Often they are attracted to fruit trees growing near the house. When the fruit diminishes in late summer or fall, they begin to troop indoors. Look for their subterranean homes and flood them with soapy water—two tablespoons of a garden soap in a gallon of water.

Remember, however, that ants have a handy function to perform in the garden, where they are the most numerous predator. They are good, too good some might say, at patrolling their territory. As long as they are out of the house and not herding aphids and scales in trees and shrubs favored by the gardener, leave them alone.

BALCONY AND ENTRYWAY GARDENS

Continue to transplant fall-flowering plants into pots; calendulas, cyclamen, chrysanthemums, ornamental cabbage, and nemesia are dazzling choices. Established plants should be fertilized with a bloom-promoting formula such as 0-10-10. Be sure to keep potted plants well watered. For a spectacular display, plant spring-blooming bulbs in layers in a large pot, placing the largest bulbs on the bottom. Finish by transplanting sweet alyssum on top.

BULBS

Continue to shop for spring-blooming bulbs, corms, tubers, and rhizomes. Look for plump, top-quality bulbs. Size is important—bulbs are usually graded by their circumference. Bulbs should be firm, heavy for their size, and free from gouges and black marks. Chill tulip and hyacinth bulbs in the refrigerator and wait until November to plant them. To plant the bulbs, first dig the soil to loosen it. Place a pinch of slow-release, low-nitrogen fertilizer into the soil beneath each bulb. Plant large bulbs (daffodil size) six inches deep and six inches apart, with the pointed ends up. Plant small bulbs (crocus or freesia sizes) two inches deep and two inches apart, with the pointed ends up. Cover with soil and water well. For continuous bloom, plant anemones and ranunculus every three weeks until December.

CHRYSANTHEMUMS

When buds begin to bloom, stop fertilizing. Stake the tall varieties.

CYMBIDIUMS

Fertilize every two weeks with a low-nitrogen liquid fertilizer formulated for orchids.

Generally spring- and summer-flowering perennials are divided in the fall. Dig up and divide overgrown perennials such as agapanthus, clivia, daylily, gazania, fortnight lily, primrose, and Shasta daisy.

1. Begin by watering the overgrown plant. Then, preferably on a cool, overcast day, carefully dig up the entire plant including all of the roots.

2. Divide the plant into smaller plants as best you can. Bulblike roots can usually be broken into individual bulbs. Fibrous roots can be cut into sections with a knife—include some green top with each root section. For tough roots, such as those of an agapanthus, you need a sharp shovel and plenty of pressure to work down through the green top to the bottom of the roots. Do not hack; try for one clean cut.

3. Replant at the same depth, water well, and shade from the sun for a few days.

FALL CLEANUP

Fall cleanup is an essential part of disease and pest control. If you have not already undertaken this yearly task, here is a review of the basics I described in September:

◉ Rake up leaves. Continue to pull up dying annuals and vegetables. Add garden debris, except seed-bearing weeds and diseased plants, to the compost pile.

◉ Pick up fallen branches, pots, or other debris from the garden to reduce the number of overwintering sites for snails, slugs, insects, and fungal spores. Continue to go through the garden and examine plants for black spots, bright orange rust pustules, white powdery mildew, rotted stems or branches, large, irregularly shaped galls near the soil, or other signs of infection. Pull up the infected plants and rake up infected leaves and dispose of them. Do not put infected material into the compost bin. Bring a trash can with you into the garden so you can immediately dispose of infected material without spreading disease by dragging it through the garden.

After cleaning up the garden, rinse gardening tools with a solution of one part bleach to three parts water. Then coat your tools lightly with oil to keep them from rusting.

FALL FOLIAGE

October is usually the peak month for brilliant fall foliage in Northern California. Therefore, shop now for fall color while plants in nurseries are at their autumn best. The color of leaves can vary quite a bit from plant to plant. See Fall Color, page 220, for a selection of choice plants.

FERTILIZE

Fertilize azaleas, camellias, and rhododendrons with 0-10-10 fertilizer, which encourages bud formation.

FREESIAS

For fragrant spring bouquets, plant freesia corms. Among the most fragrant freesias are the yellow 'Safari,' the white 'Snowdon,' the yellow and the red-with-yellow-center Tecolotes. Plant freesias two inches deep, with the pointed side of the corms up, in full sun, and in fast-draining soil. In cold-winter areas, grow them indoors in a cool room. They will bloom about fourteen weeks after planting.

FIRE PREVENTION

Long dry summers set the stage for fire in fall. As many residents can painfully recall, the worst fire in California occurred in Northern California on October 22, 1991. The gardener can lessen the chances of fire through proper plant control. Because fire prevention is so important, the list of tasks is repeated from last month to this month.

1. Start by reducing the dry plant fuel that would feed a fire, such as dry grass and weeds, Scotch broom, coyote brush, pampas grass, and poison oak. The first thirty feet surrounding the house are the most critical. The potential of shrubs to fuel fires is amazing. Chamise, an evergreen native shrub, can burn with an energy equivalent to some petrochemicals. With a strong wind behind it, a fire of burning chamise can create a wall of flame eighty feet high hustling up a slope at a mean sixty miles per hour.

2. Next, eliminate fire ladders of vegetation and overhanging branches that would lead a fire to your home. Large trees are best pruned by a tree arborist.

3. It also helps to thin and prune existing shrubs and trees to reduce plant fuel available to a fire. Of course, remove dead branches. Prune lower branches that have leaves near the ground to prevent fire from spreading into trees.

4. The hardscape in your garden, such as wooden decks and arbors, can be dangerous. Remove or trim vegetation that would be likely to cause such structures to burn.

FUCHSIAS

Stop fertilizing fuchsias now, but continue to keep them well watered and remove the old blooms and the swollen seed pods. Gardeners in cold areas who shelter fuchsias over the winter should leave the seed pods on to signal the plant to go dormant.

IN BLOOM IN OCTOBER

⚙ Annuals: impatiens, marigold, lobelia, and petunia
⚙ Perennials: Japanese anemone, begonia, campanula, chrysanthemum, coreopsis, felicia, penstemon, and Shasta daisy
⚙ Shrubs: hydrangea and rose
⚙ Natives: California fuchsia and toyon (which has showy red berries)

IN THE NURSERY IN OCTOBER

⚙ Trees and shrubs from containers, especially ones with fall color
⚙ Sasanqua camellias in bloom
⚙ Spring-blooming bulbs, corms, tubers, and rhizomes
⚙ Winter bedding plants: calendulas, Iceland poppies, pansies, primroses, sweet William, and violas, and in the coastal areas, cineraria, and nemesia.

LAWNS

In the coastal areas, there is still time to start a new lawn. Fertilize bent, bluegrass, fescue, and rye lawns. Water your lawn well and mow it with a lawn mower blade set at one and one-half inches. Reseed bald spots. Do not delay, heavy rains could wash away newly planted seeds.

LIGHT-REFLECTING PLANTS

Plants with silver gray foliage have the ability to reflect light and are decorative even if they are not in bloom. They are particularly useful in areas that will catch light at night such as beside a doorway or where they are lit by floodlights. To highlight an area with silver gray foliage look for the following plants:

⚙ Artemisia: silver spreader (*Artemisia caucasica*) or Silver king (*Artemisia ludoviciana albula*) or Angel's hair (*Artemisia schmidtiana*)

⚙ Blue fescue grass (*Festuca ovina* 'Glauca')
⚙ Globe thistle (*Echinops exaltatus*)
⚙ Dead nettle (*Lamium maculatum* 'Beacon Silver')
⚙ English lavender (*Lavandula angustifolia* 'Hidcote')
⚙ Lavender cotton (*Santolina chamaecyparissus*)

⚙ Snow-in-summer (*Cerastium tomentosum*)
⚙ Yarrow (*Achillea* species)
⚙ Yucca (*Yucca filamentosa* 'Bright Eagle')

October is the month that native plant societies hold their sales. One of the most popular plants at these sales is the mimulus. Like fishermen, gardeners have their tall tales, and one of my favorites concerns a close relative of our native flowering mimulus. As in all good stories, there has to be enough truth in them to make the tales believable. The story is about the *Mimulus moschatus*, also known as the monkey musk flower, an archetypal cottage plant that sat in a pot on many a Victorian window sill. It was collected in the wild by the Scottish plantsman, David Douglas, from somewhere in western North America in 1826. Mimulus were for a time the rage, and this one was valued for its distinctive scent.

The story, simply told, is this. Around 1914 quite unaccountably the scent disappeared completely from the monkey musk flower; not just from potted cottage plants but from every plant in the whole world; including those in the wild. Those who could remember the scent said it was powerful enough to perfume an entire room.

Having never encountered the monkey musk flower, I cannot tell you whether or not it is currently scented. Several hundred sticky monkey flowers (*Mimulus aurantiacus*) bloom on the hillside behind my home, and I do not recall any scent at all from them. I have heard several explanations for the name monkey flower and none of them makes much sense to me. The reason they are called sticky is apparent enough once you touch their leaves.

At first I thought our native mimulus, pale trumpet-shaped orange flowers grasping toward the sun on such spindly branches, was a bit ragged looking. But I have become quite fond of it. Perhaps because it blooms in summer even in drought years. Perhaps because it has its own butterfly, the *Euphydryas chalcedona*, commonly known as the chalcedon checkerspot. Having its own butterfly, of course, means that it also has its own furry caterpillars, but I have even grown fond of those fat black creatures with orange dots, and I seldom bother to pick them off the plants anymore. I regard them the way I might the flowers themselves and bend down to examine them more closely. In any event, plant and butterfly are all part of a scheme grander than any I could devise.

Mimulus has a reputation for being a bog plant and garden books often describe it as suited for wet or damp places. This reputation is derived from several well-known varieties such as the scarlet monkey flower (*Mimulus cardinalis*), which blooms from July to October if given plenty of water. The varieties that grow in our native chaparral hillsides do not, of course, need any water in the summer. Those that have self-seeded into my cultivated garden do bloom longer and have a fuller, lush appearance with water. They also behave like cultivated garden plants and bloom with renewed vigor when pruned rather severely in late fall or early spring.

Many colorful hybrids have been created from a mimulus native to Southern California (*Mimulus longiflorus*) although they are not as hardy or as drought tolerant as native species are. These hybrids come in shades of rose, salmon, copper, yellow, and cream. Another native species, the azalea-flowered monkey flower (*Mimulus bifidus*), with its glossy foliage and myriad azalealike blooms, is considered the most spectacular.

NATIVE PLANTS

October is our best month for setting out native trees, shrubs, and hardy plants. The fall and winter rains will help new plants develop root systems. Native plants put into the ground in spring do not have time to develop much of a root system before they must endure our rainless summer months.

Remember that many native California plants have evolved strategies to survive rainless summers. One way or the other most native plants are designed to do better with no or little summer water. Some curl their leaves inward, some go semidormant. The gardener will need to water newly planted native plants during the first two summers. And those plants that are accustomed to moist river banks and shady woodlands actually do better with summer water.

Sales sponsored by native plant societies, which are usually every October, are the best sources for a wide range of plants. Some nurseries specialize in native plants. And even regular nurseries carry many native plants, usually grouped together in a section called drought-resistant plants.

New cultivars of native plants are always being made available. Plantspeople keep discovering exceptional plants created in nature through cross-fertilization. Walking through Diamond Heights Village in San Francisco, Barry Lehrman of East Bay Nursery noticed an unusual ceanothus sprawling over a hillside. Although not in bloom, this ceanothus charmed Mr. Lehrman with its creamy green, pert leaves dappled here and there with irregular splotches of darker green. Naturally he took a few cuttings and nurtured them along into plants. Eventually he persuaded Skylark Nursery to grow it for the nursery trade. Called *Ceanothus griseus horizontalis* 'Diamond Heights,' it is a well-branched, spreading groundcover-type shrub that will grow between eighteen inches and twenty-four inches high and spread up to eight feet wide. It is covered with pale blue flowers in the spring. To learn more about our native plants, see pages 244-45, 269, and for the address of the California Native Plant Society, see page 313.

NATIVE TREES — TOP CHOICES

◎ California bay (*Umbellularia californica*) has a handsome appearance as it grows slowly to seventy-five feet. The leaves are aromatic and can be used for cooking, although they are stronger than the culinary variety.

◎ Incense cedar (*Calocedrus decurrens*), which also grows slowly at first, will eventually reach a majestic eighty feet with an impressively symmetrical and pyramidal shape. It has lustrous, aromatic green foliage that forms a flat spray of scalelike leaves and cinnamon brown bark that grows in deep furrows. It prefers moist, well-drained soil in full or partial sun. It is particularly useful in high mountain areas where it will tolerate lean rocky soil, the unrelenting glare of the sun and fierce winds. Plant it to stand alone or in groups.

◎ Oaks (*Quercus*) are our majestic signature trees in Northern California. Learn which varieties are native to your area and plant those. See Oaks, page 140, for growing oaks.

◎ Pacific dogwood (*Cornus nuttallii*) is an elegant tree for all seasons. It is best known for its charming white flowerlike bracts in early summer. It also has autumn color and red-orange winter fruit. This woodland tree needs rich soil and occasional summer water.

◎ Pines are numerous in Northern California. Talk to a nursery person before buying one because many are susceptible to insects and diseases, particularly when planted in the wrong location.

◎ Coast redwoods (*Sequoia sempervirens*) are handsome companions for tall city buildings. Look for 'Aptos Blue' for its blue green foliage, 'Los Altos' for its more open branching pattern, and 'Soquel' for its fine, silky foliage and smaller size.

NATIVE SHRUBS — TOP CHOICES

◎ Bush anemone (*Carpenteria californica*) is a gorgeous flowering shrub that has been a favorite of gardeners in Britain for many years. If you saw it in bloom, you would not think that it was a rugged native plant. The anemone-shaped flowers are fragrant and showy. Prune this plant to the best shape; unfortunately the deer prune mine but it grows on despite their foraging. It will take either full sun or part shade. I have grown it in lean rocky soil and in clay soil.

◎ Dwarf coyote brush (*Baccharis pilularis*) is the most widely planted shrub in California. You will often find it alongside freeways. It is popular because it grows in a few years from a tiny sprig to a dense two-foot-high carpet that spreads out to a handsome six feet. Two varieties are often encountered. 'Pigeon Point' has uniformly green leaves all year round; 'Twin Peaks' turns a grayer green during the summer. Both will grow in drought or in flood conditions. One drawback I have encountered in the five hundred coyote brushes I have planted is that they will occasionally die back to an unsightly, barren, twiggy mess. The cure has been to cut the plant off near the base and wait for new growth to fill in as it eventually does. They are also attacked by borers, which are difficult to control.

◎ Flannel bush (*Fremontodendron*) is a show stopper when covered with bright yellow blooms. It is truly drought tolerant and frequently dies when given summer water. Plant it away from paths because the leaves are covered with an annoying fuzz.

◎ Sages are very popular now, and we have several outstanding native varieties that grow about three feet high and bear whorls of blue purple flowers. Best of all is the fragrance of the foliage when crushed. Look for *Salvia clevelandii* and a tall, handsome cultivar, 'Allen Chickering.'

◎ Silktassel bush (*Garrya elliptica* 'James Roof') is at its best in winter when long catkins dangle like white tassels from its dark, leathery green leaves. Eventually it grows to about ten feet.

◎ Spice bush (*Calycanthus occidentalis*) is a handsome slow-growing plant that will eventually became a sizeable shrub with glossy, deep green leaves that could grace an English park and not look out of place. In my experience it has preferred part shade to full sun. The best feature of this attractive nine-foot shrub are the wine-red flowers that resemble miniature water lilies. It may be difficult to find except at native plant sales.

◎ Toyon (*Heteromeles arbutifolia*), also known as California holly or Christmas berry, has a remarkable display of red berries in winter and a handsome spring display of white flowers. The only drawback is that it takes forever to reach its six to eight feet of full growth.

◎ Western azalea (*Rhododendron occidentale*) is a ten-foot shrub with handsome fragrant spring flowers.

◎ Western redbud (*Cercis occidentalis*) is a large, multitrunked shrub resembling a small tree. It is known for its rounded leaves that dangle in wind and for its impressive spring display of small magenta flowers. It is slow growing.

◎ Ceanothus or wild lilacs (*Ceanothus*) are beautiful shrubs that come in many varieties, from low-growing ground-cover types such as 'Anchor Bay' to large tree-sized types such as 'Frosty Blue.' Most have blue to purple blooms, and a few have white blooms. For more about them, see page 85.

NATIVE PERENNIAL FLOWERS—TOP CHOICES

◎ Matilija poppy (*Romneya coulteri*) has amazingly huge white flowers that look as if they are made of crepe paper. Untidy but spectacular, it grows six feet tall and needs to be cut back every year.

◎ Monkey flower (*Mimulus*); see page 242.

◎ Pacific Coast iris (*Iris douglasiana*) have been crossbred to create some stunning cultivars. Look for iris when they are in bloom to get a really choice variety. They are easy to grow along the coast.

◎ *Penstemon heterophyllus purdyi*, also known as 'Blue Bedder' penstemon, sends up showy two-foot stems of tubular flowers.

◎ Common yarrow (*Achillea millefolium*) has the ferny foliage typical of the cultivated yarrows and white, flat flowerheads that persist through the summer and dry to a buff brown in fall. Plant it once and it is yours for life. It is drought tolerant, but will take water and survive. Plant this yarrow at the back of the flower bed or in low-maintenance areas.

ORCHID CACTUS

Fertilize orchid cactus (*epiphyllums*) with a balanced fertilizer such as 10-10-10. Spray the foliage as well as watering the fertilizer into the soil as orchid cactus readily absorb fertilizer through the stems.

PLANTING

October is one of the finest months for planting shrubs, trees, and native plants in the Central Valley and the coastal area. Over our rainy fall and winter seasons, their roots will grow strong to provide a spurt of growth in the spring and help them survive our long rainless summers.

PRESERVING FLOWERS

In autumn the urge to preserve flowers through the winter seizes many gardeners. There are many techniques for preserving flowers. The most obvious is air drying. Some plants such as lavender and most grasses may be simply laid flat on sheets of newsprint or cardboard. Other plants such as statice or hydrangea are dried upright in a vase. Plants with really large or heavy flower heads such as protea or thistle are supported on a wire rack while drying. Most plants can be gathered in bunches and hung upside down in a dry room.

Those who dry flowers in quantity often use desiccants such as silica gel, borax, or sand. These are drying agents that absorb the water content of flowers and leaves. Plants dried with a desiccant have a fresher, truer color and form.

The desiccant is packed completely around the plant (including between unfurling petals). Sand is left uncovered; the silica gel, which absorbs moisture from the air, is tightly sealed. Borax is usually mixed with sand: three parts borax and two parts sand.

Another technique requires the use of glycerine. A few flowers, for example heathers and hydrangeas, are set in a solution of two parts glycerine to three parts very hot water. After a week or two the water evaporates, leaving the plants saturated with glycerine. Evidently leaves soaked in equal parts of water and glycerine and then dried flat have a supple quality much like that of fresh leaves. The color is khaki brown. The glycerine technique is particularly successful with eucalyptus branches.

> ### PRESERVING PLANT FAVORITES
>
> ⚙ Bells-of-Ireland (*Moluccella laevis*)
> ⚙ Chinese lantern (*Physalis alkekengi*)
> ⚙ Cockscomb (*Celosia* 'Cristata')
> ⚙ Delphiniums
> ⚙ Globe thistle (*Echinops exaltatus*)
> ⚙ Lavender
> ⚙ Love-in-a-mist (*Nigella damascena*)
> ⚙ Maple leaves
> ⚙ Money plant or honesty (*Lunaria annua*)
> ⚙ Pearly everlasting (*Anaphalis margaritacea*)
> ⚙ Roses
> ⚙ Sea holly (*Eryngium*)
> ⚙ Statice or sea lavender (*Limonium*)
> ⚙ Strawflower (*Helichrysum bracteatum*)
> ⚙ Yarrow (*Achillea*)

The newest technique is to microwave flowers. In theory, a few flowers can be simply microwaved, allowed to cool, and that is that. First the flower or leaf is wrapped in a paper towel and weighted with a saucer to prevent its curling. Marigolds and chrysanthemums need three minutes of heating and ten minutes of cooling; salvias and tulips need three minutes of heating and twenty-four minutes of cooling. Some authorities recommend placing a glass of water in the microwave oven alongside the flower. The water is said to protect the microwave. Those who dry flowers regularly tell me that it is best to surround each flower to be dried with an inch of silica gel and then microwave it for between two and seven minutes.

I mention these techniques for the benefit of the ambitious gardener. My own technique is simple: I pick flowers that look good when dead, among them statice, yarrow, love-in-a-mist, craspedia (also known as drumstick), and quaking grass.

ROSES

Continue to feed modern roses with a nitrogen-free formula and water them well in the coastal areas. In the Central Valley do not fertilize, but do be sure and water roses. In the high mountains, do not fertilize, do water, and as soon as the ground freezes over cover their roots with a mulch.

October is a good time to review your rose garden. Roses that bloom sparsely or have much mildew might do better if transplanted later this winter to a sunnier location. While roses are still in bloom in botanical gardens, visit one and decide which roses you might want to purchase bare-root this winter. Continue to remove faded blossoms.

SEED COLLECTING

With many vegetables and annuals beginning to wither, gardeners may want to collect seed for planting next spring. It is easy to do. Most flowering plants can be picked when dry, and the seeds shaken into a large paper grocery bag.

For seeds from fleshy fruit, pick a slightly overripe fruit, scrape out the seeds, and put them into a glass of water. After a few days, the heavier and more desirable seeds will sink to the bottom. Save those, dry them on newspapers or paper towels, and then let them air dry for about a week.

Seeds that come in a pod, such as peas or beans, can be removed and allowed to air dry. Place them in an envelope or plastic bag, and then label the seeds before storing them in a cool, dry place.

Do not forget to save some seeds while carving the pumpkin.

SMOG-BELCHING TREES

For your Halloween amusement we have the specter of smog-belching trees. Trees generate a higher percentage of hydrocarbon emissions than do airplanes and trains combined. Nonetheless, the beneficial qualities of trees far outweigh their contribution to pollution.

In Southern California, a study funded by the South Coast Air Quality Management District ranked trees by the quantity of hydrocarbons given off in a twenty-four-hour period. For gardeners concerned about the smog generated in their own gardens, the following is a list of trees ranked by units of hydrocarbon emissions from the least to the most.

- Crape myrtle (0)
- Camphor (1)
- Deodar cedar (10)
- Monterey pine (30)
- Brazilian pepper (43)
- Ginkgo (100)
- Liquidambar (1,233)
- Carrot wood (1,633)

TULIPS

Buy tulip bulbs now while the selection is still good. Local nurseries will have the most popular varieties for sale, and mail-order nurseries will have an astonishing variety. Gardeners have been crazy over tulips for a great many years. I never thought much about tulip varieties until I visited Holland, where I stood beside a small picket fence in Leiden staring at a row of star-shaped, bright yellow tulips (*Tulipa tarda*). They were identical to the bulbs planted by Carolus Clusius in the same place in 1593. The picket fence was an afterthought to keep the bulbs from being stolen. Despite the fence, tulip bulbs were stolen from his garden because they became worth an extraordinary amount of money. Not that the Dutch were the first to grow or to appreciate tulips.

The tulip was beloved by the Turks, who collected them from the wild and honored them with tulip festivals. A certain Sultan Ahmed III was even beheaded, partly because he spent too much money on the annual tulip festival.

An Austrian ambassador to the Ottoman Empire acquired a few tulip bulbs in the mid 1500s and passed them along to his friend, Carolus Clusius, who grew them in a university herb garden. What followed was the worst case of gardening mania known to humankind. The Dutch could not get enough of these small treasures. The price of an entire house was spent on a single bulb. When the tulipmania ended in 1637, many a garden fanatic was financially ruined.

The Dutch are, however, a very practical people and before long bulb growing became a national industry. Many of the bulb-growing farms that I visited in Holland were family concerns that were begun centuries ago. Somehow these growers manage to produce eighty percent of the bulbs on the world market. Twenty percent of their bulbs go to West Germany, sixteen percent to the United States, and thirteen percent to France. Our share, by the way, includes some 270 million tulip bulbs annually.

Why do we buy so many bulbs each year? Aside from their astonishing beauty, it is because we cannot manage to keep tulips blooming year after year and so must replace them annually. The tulip is a perennial and should come back year after year, and so it does on the steppes of eastern Turkey and in the foothills of the Himalayas, where the winters are cold and the summers hot and dry.

Fortunately there is a way for Northern California gardeners to increase their odds of getting tulip bulbs to repeat bloom the following years.

TULIP SELECTIONS

Choose bulbs that are labeled as being good for naturalizing.

Choose species bulbs and their hybridized cultivars such as: *Tulipa tarda* 'Keizerskroon'; lady tulip (*Tulipa clusiana*), and *Tulipa linifolia*.

Choose tulip cultivars that are known to bloom well without having to have a significant chilling period first: 'Bishop' (a rich purple), 'Blushing Lady' (pale yellow blushed with lavender), 'Halcro' (intense red), 'Queen of the Night' (deep purple), and 'Sweet Harmony' (yellow and white).

Tulip Growing Simplified

Botanical name: *Tulipa*.

Common name: Tulip.

Site preference: Plant tulips in full sun, but remember that deciduous trees will not have leafed out yet when tulips bloom, so there is more sun in the spring garden then one might suspect.

Soil conditions: Plant bulbs in a well-drained area. This is essential for naturalizing as wet soil promotes fungus and diseases that can rot the bulbs.

Water: Water bulbs after planting. Water is essential if the plants are to develop a strong root system before going into winter dormancy.

Nutrients: Fertilize with a low-nitrogen fertilizer at planting time and each fall after that. In spring as the shoots break through the soil use a high-nitrogen fertilizer.

Special care: Plant deep. Plant tulip bulbs in the fall about six inches deep, measuring from the base of the bulb. Include the mulch in this measurement.

After the bulbs have bloomed in the spring, cut off the flower heads but allow the green foliage to die back naturally. This lets the plant put its energy into building a strong bulb for next year.

Hints: Always buy the biggest bulbs available, because the bigger the bulb, the bigger the flower. In tulips bigger is relative: The bulbs of a species tulip such as *Tulipa tarda* will be tiny beside those of a huge Darwin hybrid bulb.

Filoli, the magnificent garden and estate in Woodside, California, always has a breathtaking tulip display. One of their favorite combinations is delicate shell-pink 'Angelique' tulips grown with pale blue forget-me-nots.

VEGETABLES

Do not forget to save some seeds while carving the Halloween pumpkin. Place the seeds, and the pulp that clings to them, in water for several days. The heavier seeds will sink to the bottom. Wash and dry those heavier seeds and save them for planting next year.

Winter vegetable gardens are a possibility along the coast and in the warmer sections of the Central Valley. There are many crops that prefer cool weather, and even some crops that get sweeter when the temperature drops. Do not plant too much at one time; spread the planting over the coming weeks to produce a continuing harvest.

The winter vegetable garden grows much more slowly, and the lower winter temperatures also mean fewer pests, less maintenance, and less water.

The site is probably even more important for the winter garden than for gardens producing crops during the rest of the year. Full winter sun is essential. This usually requires a south-facing garden site. If anything, the soil should be even more carefully prepared as many winter crops are root crops that form under the cover of soil.

VEGETABLES FOR WINTER GARDENS

COLE FAMILY CROPS

The champions of the winter garden are vegetables belonging to the cole family such as broccoli, Brussels sprouts, cabbage, cauliflower, and kohlrabi. Not only do they prefer cool weather, but also their flavor is improved by a touch of frost. There is plenty of time to grow these crops from seed, but young seedlings from the nursery are much easier. Planted now, vegetables will be ready for eating in January along the coast and in April in the Central Valley.

Here is a trick for growing seedlings of members of the cabbage family. When setting out seeds, add a small layer of crushed dried eggshells several inches below the seed. Eggshells are high in calcium, which is particularly beneficial to members of the cabbage family.

ROOT CROPS

Also popular for the winter vegetable garden are root crops such as the familiar carrots, beets, and radishes as well as the less familiar rutabagas, parsnips, and turnips. Planted now, these underground vegetables grow over the winter to provide crops in early spring.

Beets should be grown from seed. They sprout in about a week. They should be thinned so that they have several inches of horizontal space to grow in. Carrots are sweeter in winter. Planted now, they will ready about Valentine's Day. Carrot seeds are often soaked for six to twelve hours before planting. They are slow to sprout, so keep the seedbed moist and do not lose patience. Often radishes are tough in hot weather; in winter they will be crisp, tender, and ready to eat in about two-and-a-half months. Sow radish seeds every few weeks to insure a continuous supply.

LEAFY GREENS

Salad greens, such as lettuce and arugula, and leafy vegetables, such as mustard greens, kale, spinach, and Swiss chard, are good in the winter garden. Put in transplanted seedlings this month and you will be peeling off the outer leaves for the holiday season.

You may want to try *mizuna* (*Brassica rapa* var. *nipposinica*) a Japanese leafy green (although it is of ancient Chinese origin). It forms a small, vigorous, rosette-shaped clump that is decorative enough to be included in the flower bed. The easiest way to harvest it is to pull off tender leaves from the outside of the clump, which will force additional leaves to form.

PEAS

Last, but the favorite of many, are peas. Frankly, some homegrown English peas have about as much flavor as a cardboard box, so I recommend snap peas and Chinese peas. Seeds planted now will bring a crop by Saint Patrick's Day.

To get a really good crop, use an inoculant on the seeds. All legumes, such as peas, benefit from an inoculant that supplies rhizobia, a tiny bacterium that enables the nodules on legume roots to take in nitrogen. Inoculants are available from some nurseries and the supply houses listed on page 310. Most peas should have a strong support, such as a trellis, to grow on.

Onions and their fellow alliums, leeks, shallots, and garlic, are also winter crops. See page 223 for details on growing them.

WILDFLOWERS

October is a good month to sow wildflowers. More complete details on wildflower gardening are given in November; see Wildflowers on page 269. Here are the basics: Preparation is essential to a successful sowing of wildflower seeds. Begin by removing all weeds and grasses. Do not add fertilizer to the soil. Mix wildflower seeds with sand so that the seeds can be scattered more evenly. Lightly rake the seeds into the soil. Work the rake back and forth to work the seeds into the soil. Gently tamp the seed to improve the germination. Some gardeners do this by laying pieces of cardboard over the seeds and walking on the cardboard.

Hide the seeds from the birds by broadcasting a light layer of compost over the seeds. Sprinkle the seeds with a fine spray of water. Seed germination depends upon moisture. If the rains do not fall, water weekly with a fine spray to keep the ground moist.

...November...

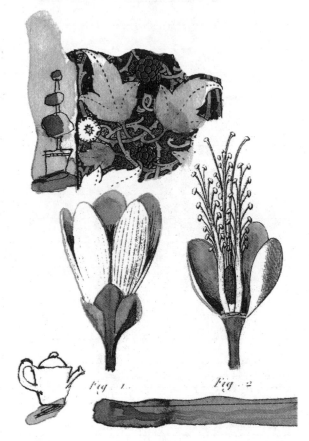

Fig. 1.   Fig. 2.

When do the red-berried plants show color?

November is when the cold usually descends in earnest. There are the annual fall tasks to complete—namely tidying the garden to clear it of debris that would harbor insect pests over the winter. There is still time to set out landscape plants.

It is important to put in spring-blooming annuals now so that they will grow sturdy roots over the winter. Spring-blooming annuals planted in fall significantly outperform spring-blooming annuals planted in the spring. With the fall-planted annuals, you may get five months of bloom; with spring planted annuals, you will probably only get two or three months of bloom.

With the waning of the light, and after a rainstorm or two has soaked the garden, the gardener is soon persuaded to stay indoors. Excursions outdoors are limited to bringing a few red berries, a handful of autumn leaves, and perhaps a few herbs indoors for holiday celebrations. After the feasting on Thanksgiving, the gardener may wish to give back a little to this good earth by sprinkling a few packets of wildflower seeds in the surrounding neighborhood.

KEY GARDEN TASKS

All Gardeners

🌼 Finish planting spring bulbs.

🌼 Shop for native plants and set them in the garden.

🌼 Complete fall cleanup in the garden.

🌼 Despite the drop in the temperature, composting continues. Add disease-free leaves and chopped up, dead annuals to the compost pile. Remember to keep the pile as damp as a wrung-out sponge for faster composting.

🌼 Keep after the snails.

🌼 Watch out for ants invading the house from the garden.

🌼 Wrap vulnerable, young tree trunks, particularly citrus trees, with paper or burlap to protect them from freezing.

🌼 Water plants as needed.

▲ ▼ ▲

Coastal Gardeners

🌼 In addition to the tasks listed for all gardeners, hold off fertilizing most plants in preparation for winter.

🌼 Fertilize cool-season lawns.

🌼 Fertilize all fall- and winter-flowering plants about to bloom.

🌼 Water roses but do not fertilize them.

🌼 Set out transplants of fall- and winter-flowering plants into the bedding plot, using such plants as calendula, Iceland Poppy, pansy, primrose, and stock.

🌼 Harvest what is left of the summer vegetables before the rain and cold destroy them. Plant the winter vegetable garden with cool-season crops

such as beets, broccoli, cabbage, carrots, cauliflower, onions, parsnips, and turnips.

▲ ▼ ▲

Central Valley Gardeners

In addition to the tasks listed for all gardeners, hold off on fertilizing most plants in preparation for winter.

🌼 Stabilize plants that might be harmed by autumn wind.

🌼 Prune wisteria and clematis to control size and encourage new flowering wood in spring. Lightly prune forsythia.

🌼 Water roses but withhold all fertilizer. When the ground freezes, mulch the rose bed heavily.

🌼 Finish transplanting fall-and winter-flowering plants into the bedding plot.

🌼 Harvest what is left of the summer vegetables before the rain and cold destroy them. Continue to plant the winter vegetable garden with cool-season crops such as beets, broccoli, cabbage, carrots, cauliflower, onions, parsnips, and turnips. If you have put the vegetable garden to rest over the winter, cover it with manure so that the manure will age properly over the winter.

🌼 Flush your watering system to remove mineral deposits. Soak all newly transplanted plants until the rains come.

▲ ▼ ▲

High Mountain Gardeners

🌼 In addition to the tasks listed for all gardeners, protect vulnerable plants from the coming winter. The idea of protection is to insulate plants from the heave damage of freezing and thawing by providing a constant temperature.

🌼 As soon as the ground has frozen, protect woody shrubs such as roses by mounding soil up around the crown to cover the graft union.

(Of course, use soil from another part of the garden, not soil near the rose roots.) Also protect perennials that go dormant by covering the roots with at least two inches of mulch. Be sure to cover the roots of both shrubs and perennials. Keep the mulch in place by covering with evergreen prunings. In very cold areas, cover the mulch over perennials and the soil mounds over woody shrubs with a layer of straw.

◉ Protect trees from winter scavengers who gnaw on bark, by wrapping trunks with burlap or surrounding them with a leaf-filled wire barrier.

◉ Store clay and ceramic pots in a heated garage or basement to protect them from breaking in freezing weather.

◉ Attend to garden irrigation systems before they freeze. Flush out drip irrigation lines, then drain them well, and turn off the system. Ooze hoses should be put away until next spring.

◉ Attend to the winter protection of specialized plants (see Coping with Snow, page 16) and carry indoors the vulnerable plants you plan to shelter during the winter.

BALCONY AND ENTRYWAY GARDENS

Continue to transplant winter-flowering plants into pots. Calendulas, cyclamen, and primroses are good choices. Established plants should be fertilized with a bloom-promoting formula such as 0-10-10. Be sure to keep potted plants well watered. For dramatic impact consider a shrub in a large pot such as a sansaqua camellia; try one of the spectacular varieties described on page 258.

BARE-ROOT PLANTING

Prepare the soil—before it becomes too rain soaked—for the planting of bare-root plants (such as roses, fruit trees, and berries) several months from now. Dig, weed, and amend the soil if needed. See page 45 for information on buying and planting bare-root plants, which are usually available from January through March.

BLUEBERRIES

In the coastal areas and in partial shade in Central Valley areas, blueberries are a handsome addition to the garden. They are often sold bare-root in the winter, so the gardener should be making a planting area for them now. Be sure to dig in lots of peat moss as blueberries thrive on rich acid soil. There are blueberry farms in the Sacramento Valley and elsewhere in Northern California. Based on their success, gardeners should try the following varieties: 'Berkeley,' 'Bluecrop,' 'Blueray,' 'Bluetta,' 'Cape Fear,' 'Earliblue,' 'Georgia,' and 'O'Neal.'

BULBS

November is a good month to plant tulips, hyacinths, and other spring-blooming bulbs such as anemone, crocus, daffodil, Dutch iris, freesia, leucojum, ranunculus and scilla.

BULB FORCING

It is relatively easy to force certain bulbs, usually daffodils and hyacinths, by putting them through a cycle of cold and dark followed by a period of heat and light in order to get them to bloom indoors. It is definitely a fall and winter pleasure. Forcing daffodils to bloom indoors is described on page 260 and forcing hyacinths to bloom indoors is described on page 262.

CAMELLIA SASANQUA

The sansanquas bloom in fall and early winter with a profusion of showy flowers. They are hardier and more drought tolerant than the more familiar *Camellia japonica*. They are also much better suited to sunny locations. Now, when they are in bloom, is a good time to purchase and plant them. Several cultivars are considered exceptional.

- 'Setsugekka' has large, white flowers with fluted petals that make good, long-lasting cut flowers.
- 'Yuletide' produces an abundance of bright red blooms with yellow stamens on a dense compact plant that will grow up to eight feet tall.
- 'Rainbow' has charming white petals edged in deep pink with bright yellow stamens.

CHRYSANTHEMUMS

Stake chrysanthemums so that they do not bend and break under heavy rain. When chrysanthemums finish blooming, cut them back to between four and six inches above ground level so that they will make new growth for cuttings that may be taken in the spring to provide flowers in the fall.

COTONEASTER

All is flux, nothing stays still, wrote Heraclitus some twenty-five hundred years ago. He probably got it right. Even members of the plant kingdom, rooted solidly to the earth, manage to get around. Take cotoneasters, those red-berried shrubs so beloved by native birds and so well adapted to foreign soil that most gardeners mistake them for natives.

Most cotoneasters come from the Himalayas, China, and Tibet, and there they remained until the director of the Botanic Gardens at Calcutta introduced them to Western gardens almost two centuries ago. The most familiar cotoneaster, the rockspray or rock cotoneaster (*Cotoneaster horizontalis*) named in honor of its striking branching habits, was collected in China and sent to botanical gardens only a little over one hundred years ago.

Somehow, in the way plants have of taking root, the cotoneaster has managed to become a staple in many American gardens. Once established, it continues on despite neglect. Typically it survives the demise of the gardener who planted it. Anyone wishing to decorate a winter hearth could drive down almost any back alley and find an old cotoneaster arching out over a fence.

That the birds have taken to cotoneasters is not surprising. When other berries are withering in the gloom of fall, bright red cotoneaster berries must appear as enticing as if they had been gift wrapped. Birds, particularly bluebirds, mockingbirds, robins, sparrows, and thrushes, flock to them. All cotoneaster berries appeal to birds except for the berries of *Cotoneaster glaucophyllu*s and *Cotoneaster conspicuus*, which are rarely eaten.

The cotoneaster is typically a sprawling shrub with leaves that have smooth edges. The pyracantha (to which it is closely related and with which it is often confused) has thorns, toothed leaves, and usually brighter, shinier red berries. Pyracanthas, too, are loved by birds.

When selecting a cotoneaster remember that it is as vigorous as a weed, so take into account its eventual size before planting. Two varieties known for producing abundant, long-lasting fruit are *Cotoneaster lacteus*, which will grow into a gracefully arching eight-foot tree, and *Cotoneaster microphyllus*, which forms a two-foot-high shrub spreading to about six feet. All the birds in the neighborhood will thank you.

Cotoneaster Growing Simplified

Botanical name: *Cotoneaster*.

Common name: Cotoneaster.

Site preference: Full sun is best, but it will tolerate some shade.

Soil conditions: It prefers well-drained soil, thrives in what is thought of as poor soil, but will grow in any soil except a bog.

Water: After it is established, it will tolerate drought; some authorities believe that cotoneaster actually look and fruit better on limited water.

Nutrients: Low-nitrogen fertilizer applied annually helps but is not necessary.

Problems: Watch out for spider mites in dry, hot climates. Fireblight (*Erwinia amylovora*), which is a disease that causes tender shoots to die back as if scorched, should be cut away immediately and the pruning tools sanitized.

CYCLAMEN

With Thanksgiving rapidly approaching, the gardener may want to brighten the indoors with cyclamen. Nurseries offer a dazzling variety of brightly colored cyclamen.

The trick to keeping cyclamens indoors is to put them in a self-watering pot, as they quickly wilt if allowed to go dry. You can also mist them daily. They came originally from the cool climate of Persia, and the warm, dry air of indoor living exhausts them. The miniature cyclamen is not so fussy about heat, and it is often fragrant.

In coastal areas, when you are finished with the cyclamen indoors (or what is more likely the case, it is finished with you), plant it outdoors in a shady, moist spot and it will continue to grow and bloom for years.

CYMBIDIUMS

Fertilize every two weeks with a low-nitrogen liquid fertilizer formulated for orchids. In areas where frost is expected this month move cymbidiums to a warmer, sheltered spot.

DAFFODILS FORCED IN WATER

Forcing daffodil bulbs to bloom indoors is easy. Start by buying a variety of *Narcissus tazetta* that is known to do well when forced, either 'Paper White,' 'Soleil d'Or,' or 'Grand Soleil d'Or.' Other varieties can also be forced but most require about twelve weeks in a dark, cool place before being brought into sunlight.

> *1.* Place daffodil bulbs (pointed side up) on top of gravel or small rocks set in a shallow bowl. Add water to reach the bottom of the bulbs and place the container in a cool, dark place for about three weeks.
>
> *2.* As soon as the roots sprout (if you wait too long the tops stretch out too long and topple over), move the container to a cool, sunny spot and about three weeks later the bulbs will bloom.
>
> *3.* After the daffodil buds show color, move them into indirect light to help the flowers last as long as possible. Throw the used bulbs away; they have exhausted themselves by trying to survive without soil.

DAHLIAS

Stop watering dahlias, so that they will go dormant. Along the coast and the warmer areas of the Central Valley, dahlias can be left in the ground over the winter. In areas where the ground freezes deeply, carefully dig up the tubers, preferably with a spading fork, brush off the soil, and trim away the brown stalks, leaving a piece of stem attached to each tuber. Discard any diseased tubers. Divide the healthy tubers into sections and store them in a cool, dry place, preferably in vermiculite or sand.

DIVIDE PERENNIALS

There is still time to divide perennials such as agapanthus, daylily, primrose, and Shasta daisy. See page 239 for step-by-step instructions.

FLOWERS

Do not delay in putting spring-flowering bedding plants (such as transplants of alyssum, columbine, coral bells, cyclamen, dianthus, Iceland poppy, nemesia, primroses, schizanthus, snapdragon, and sweet William) into the garden. Except in areas subject to snow and hard, long frosts, transplants of spring-flowering plants put in during November will outflower transplants of the same plants put in next spring. The difference in intensity and length of display is significant.

Begin by preparing the planting area by incorporating soil amendments into the soil. Dig in the transplants and water them well. Over the winter the plants will develop a root system capable of sending them into a burst of bloom next spring.

You may want to add large-sized transplants of winter-flowering plants to the same bedding area for instant color now. Purple ornamental cabbage, also known as flowering kale, planted with golden yellow calendulas provide a cheerful combination for dark days.

FROST

Protect tender garden plants from winter's cold. Withhold fertilizer and cut back on the amount of water used in the garden. Both these measures will help harden plants to the cold and will reduce the amount of tender new growth, which is particularly susceptible to frost damage.

Although the coldest months of the year are usually January and February, gardeners should watch for signs of approaching frost, because it is the early or late frosts that cause the most plant damage. See page 14 for information about signs of impending frost and methods of protecting plants.

FRUIT TREES

In areas subject to frost, wrap the trunks of young citrus, kiwi, and avocado trees with heavy paper to protect them from frost damage. Be sure to remove the paper next spring. You may also spray the leaves with an antitranspirant for frost protection. Available at nurseries, antitranspirants are commonly used on indoor Christmas trees and greens to form a protective coating on foliage to hold in moisture. This is probably the easiest method of frost protection in mild winter areas, as the gardener does not need to monitor the weather each night. The antitranspirant should be applied again in January.

FUCHSIAS

Hold the fertilizer but continue to water fuchsias. Do not cut off the seed pods in November; allow them to form so as to signal the plant to go into dormancy.

n o v e m b e r

The Victorians were so enamored of the fragrant bloom of the Dutch hyacinth that they invented a special glass container to support the bulb over a reservoir of water. These glasses are still popular today and are sold as hyacinth glasses in import shops and nurseries in November. They range in design from sleek modern cobalt blue glasses from Yugoslavia to delicate Italian pastel glasses. Although I have read that one can hold the bulb in the refrigerator until ready, I have found that if I wait too long, the bulb will go ahead and grow roots and a green top right in the refrigerator. So mark the date on your calendar and remove the bulbs from the refrigerator before they sprout.

1. Store hyacinth bulbs in a brown bag in the refrigerator for between six and eight weeks.

2. Place the chilled bulb in a hyacinth glass with the water just barely touching the base of the bulb.

3. Place the glasses with their bulbs in a cool, dark place for three weeks. The bulbs should form long, thick, white roots.

4. After three weeks, move the glasses to bright, direct sunshine. Rotate the glasses every few days.

5. You can change the water if it becomes dirty or smelly. Feed with diluted liquid plant food if desired.

6. Healthy plump bulbs can be planted in the garden after blooming.

In Bloom in November

- Annuals: calendula, sweet alyssum, and pansy
- Perennials: begonia, chrysanthemum, and Japanese anemone
- Sasanqua camellias
- New Zealand tea tree
- Autumn foliage and red-berried shrubs
- Natives: Fall color is provided by the berries of madrone and toyon, leaves of cottonwoods, deciduous oaks, dogwoods, hawthorn, willows, and the vine maple

In the Nursery in November

- Annuals: calendula, Iceland poppy, and pansy
- Perennials: cineraria, chrysanthemum, cyclamen, primrose, and violet
- Sasanqua camellias
- Spring-blooming bulbs, corms, tubers, and rhizomes

Many trees are praised by gardeners but few as highly as the Japanese maple. It is prized, as a great flowering shrub is valued, and is given an honored place in the garden. Its glory is the uncommon grace of its leaves and their startling colors, particularly in autumn.

Gardeners enjoying the majesty of Japanese maples now cloaked in dazzling red leaves will be amazed to learn that Japanese maples were probably first acquired through the persistence of American warships. Had it not been for the American insistence that Japan open up its borders to foreign trade, the red Japanese maple might have continued to grow in isolation on the island of Honshu. Certainly it seems the Japanese would have wanted it that way.

Shortly after the Pilgrims settled at Plymouth, the Japanese constructed a tiny manmade island called Deshima. It might as well have been called Alcatraz, for all foreigners were required to reside in its prisonlike confines. Naturally, this severely limited trade, not to mention botanical exchange.

For the next two hundred years, the only contact with Japan came through the Dutch East India Company, which used Deshima as a base for its long and lucrative spice voyages. Our limited knowledge of Japanese plants came from botanical enthusiasts, usually physicians, stationed by the Dutch on Deshima. Everything changed in 1854 with Commodore Perry and his gunboat diplomacy, which persuaded the Japanese to sign a trade treaty.

Botanists set out on notably successful plant excursions. One of the most prominent plant hunters was E. H. Wilson, who collected for the Arnold Arboretum in Boston. Wilson made a special trip to Sakamoto off the coast of Honshu where he took several saplings of a Japanese red maple (*Acer pycnanthum*). This maple is closely related to the abundantly distributed American red maple (*Acer rubrum*), but the Japanese red maple was then a rare species restricted to a small region of central Honshu.

Now, of course, there is a wide variety of Japanese maples for the American gardener to chose from, including some formerly rare varieties. More than eighty varieties of Japanese maples are grown in American nurseries and arboretums. Many of them are choice indeed.

Some authorities recommend buying only grafted, named varieties of Japanese maples because they should come true to the characteristics of the named variety. Other authorities recommend seedlings because they are hardier, faster growing, and more drought tolerant.

Japanese Maple Growing Simplified

Botanical name: *Acer palmatum.*

Common name: Japanese maple.

Site preference: Debatable. Probably filtered light has the edge. However, red-leaved or green-leaved varieties color best in full sun. Variegated and finely cut–leaved varieties will suffer from sunburn unless planted in filtered sunlight. Because they can be damaged by a late frost, avoid planting Japanese maples where the late winter sun would cause them to leaf out early.

Soil conditions: Best in rich, well-drained soil, so add humus and compost.

Water: Flood them occasionally to leach out salts, which cause curling brown leaf edges.

Nutrients: Nitrogen fertilizer should be applied after the leaves appear in the spring and again in early fall. A slow-release fertilizer is good for container plants.

Problems: Verticillium wilt (also known as dieback) is a serious problem. This soil-borne fungus wilts and discolors leaves, turning them yellow, and can kill maples. Prune away dead branches and clean the pruning shears afterward to prevent spreading the disease.

Special care: Prune to shape.

Japanese Maple Recommendations

The names are confusing because growers use different common names and often do not label them with botanical names. My personal favorite is often labeled as a 'Threadleaf' Japanese maple. Its botanical name is probably *Acer palmatum* 'Dissectum'. It may also be called 'Ever Red' (*Acer palmatum* 'Dissectum Atropurpureum'). It has wonderful, delicate, lacy foliage colored a deep purple red in spring and taking on a slight green tinge during the summer. Left unpruned, it will develop slowly into a small, graceful dome-shaped shrub. At five years, it is only about three feet tall. At twenty years, it is only about six feet tall, so it is an excellent container plant.

> ◎ Laceleaf maple ('Dissectum Viridis') has a charming dome shape and bright green summer leaves.
>
> ◎ 'Bloodgood' is red in the spring and turns bright crimson in the fall. I have noticed a number of landscape architects using it in estate gardens in the Napa valley.
>
> ◎ 'Maiku Jaku' has spectacular burgundy fall foliage.
>
> ◎ The coral bark maple 'Sango Kaku' (also known as 'Senkaki') has coral colored bark with pale yellow spring leaves that turn green and then gold in fall.

LAWNS

Along the coast there is probably still time to put in a cool-season lawn such as bent, bluegrass, fescue or rye. Do not delay. Heavy rains could wash away carefully planted seeds.

Feed cool-season lawns. Warm-season lawns are going into dormancy (turning brown); do not feed them.

ORCHID CACTUS

Fertilize orchid cactus (*epiphyllums*) with a bloom-promoting fertilizer such as 0-10-10. This is the last time the orchid cactus needs to be fed until shortly before it blooms next year. It can withstand temperatures below 32°F for only a limited period, so move an orchid cactus to a sheltered spot before the first frost and continue to water it over the winter.

PLANTING

Along the coast and in the warmer areas of the Central Valley, November is probably still a good month for setting out basic landscape plants such as trees, shrubs, and ground covers. Over the winter, the roots will become well established and able to support spring growth. Plants that display fall color, such as Japanese maples, liquidambars, and smoke trees, should be purchased from the nursery now when you can see their fall color as the color often varies from plant to plant.

POINSETTIAS

When buying poinsettias, look for plants with green foliage all the way down to the soil line, which indicates active, healthy roots. The beautifully colored petals are actually bracts and the true flower is that little yellow smudge of berries in the middle. Avoid plants with too much green around the edges of the bracts because that is an indication that the plants are underdeveloped. The smaller bracts near the center should be entirely colored or the plant will be likely to fade when you bring it home.

Fertilize the poinsettias with a general-purpose houseplant fertilizer once you have them home. Never let them sit in water, and water them only when the soil is dry to the touch. Poinsettias should be placed in bright indirect light (enough light to read by). Keep them away from drafts—either cold gusts from outside or warm blasts from furnace vents. Also avoid temperatures below 50° F even while transporting them home. A healthy, well-cared-for poinsettia will keep its good looks for several months indoors.

RAIN DAMAGE

Rain as a natural phenomenon in Northern California should not be underestimated. In 1862, one-fourth of the state's taxable wealth was eliminated by a flood that turned the Central Valley into a four-hundred-mile-long inland sea. In 1986, one eleven-day storm unloaded forty-nine inches of rain north of Sacramento and caused fifty thousand people to be evacuated from their homes. As Marc Reisner, a frequent commentator on Northern California water policy, has noted, California's climate has two speeds: "off and fast-forward." Heavy rain can create havoc in the garden. Examine the garden to determine where drainage needs to be improved. You may want to dig a few trenches to divert heavy runoff, add heavy rocks to the base of a raised garden bed to help stabilize it, or sow bald spots with wildflower seeds or hardy annual seeds such as sweet alyssum.

SARRACENIA

These carnivorous pitcher plants need a chilly dormant period, so in coastal areas set their container outdoors from Thanksgiving to Valentine's Day; in cooler mountain and valley areas, place in an unheated room.

STRAWBERRIES

November may seem a strange month to be thinking of strawberries, but it is the best month for coastal gardeners to plant strawberries. (Central Valley and high mountain gardeners plant strawberries in early spring; see the February section on Strawberries, page 75.) Since cold increases a plant's ability to bear heavily, plants sold in November are often raised in areas with cold autumn months. The commercial strawberry growers in our coastal areas actually buy chilled strawberries this time of year much the same way we put hyacinth bulbs in the refrigerator to chill. Strawberries are regional plants and local nurseries carry appropriate varieties. Count on one plant producing about one quart of strawberries each year. Figure on ten plants per person. A favorite is the 'Sequoia,' an ever-bearing variety with sweet strawberries in spring, summer, and fall. 'Sequoia' was developed especially for coastal California. Also look for the great-tasting, everbearing 'Fort Laramie' and 'Quinault.'

Many gardeners plant strawberries on eight-inch-high mounds and spread the roots out before filling in around the hill. *It is important to place the crown (the center where the roots meet the stem) just above the soil level: lower and the crown will rot; higher and the roots will dry out. Use a fertilizer high in nitrogen one inch beneath the roots.* A slow release fertilizer is ideal. Clear plastic (not black, which snails like to hide under) helps warm the soil in coastal gardens and should be laid on either side of a row of strawberries. Do watch out for strawberry-loving snails.

THANKSGIVING

Would it be preposterous to add at the end of the shopping list, after the turkey and the sweet potatoes, a packet of California poppy seeds? Compared with the rest of the country, California is newly settled. Here in the northern part, it is still possible to know those oak-studded valleys described by Captain George Vancouver when he explored Northern California in 1796: "We entered a country I little expected . . . it could only be compared to a park."

A short journey will take any Northern Californian into the gently rolling valleys where the stately valley oaks (*Quercus lobata*) congregate, as communal yet independent trees that hold one another at arm's length and shelter wildlife in pools of dappled shade. Vancouver has been dead some hundred years and the sapling oaks he saw have passed through much of their three-hundred-year cycle from cylindrical youth to stately maturity to magnificent old age, when the huge trees brush the earth with weeping branches of languid grace. Some of the trees he saw must be dead or dying now—fallen snags still harboring wildlife in the recesses of their decaying wood.

Who will preserve this beauty? Who will make sure that there are young oaks to grow old with grace? We gardeners will, of course. Why not?

Why not use Thanksgiving as a time for giving back to this good earth? Why not finish off the Thanksgiving meal with a stroll through the neighborhood? With packets of California poppy seeds in hand and few acorns plucked from local oak trees, why not look for a desolate spot that could use a little help?

Collecting acorns is easy enough. There are nineteen species of native California oaks, and nine of them grow to tree size. No matter where you live, there are probably native oaks within walking distance. The acorn crop peaks from September through October. The acorns resemble pointed cartridge shells and have the power to transform the landscape. After removing the shallow cup attached to the end, inspect the acorns and discard those with insect holes.

There are various ways of planting acorns. The simplest is accomplished regularly by the scrub jay who pokes about seven thousand acorns a year into the ground. Most are devoured, of course, before they sprout. You may follow the example of the scrub jay: plant an acorn just below the soil surface, and then protect it with a lightweight screen, such as a few dried leaves or a small leafy branch. An alternative method is first to sprout the acorn by wrapping it in damp peat moss until roots appear several weeks later. If you water the seedlings during the first year, the odds that they will become saplings improve.

Sowing seeds of the California poppy (*Eschscholzia californica*) is even easier. Find an area that could use a little beauty—a vacant lot or a parking strip—and pull up the weeds to disturb the soil and lessen the competition. Sprinkle the seeds over the ground and scuff your shoe over the spot to work them in a little. It is a good idea to cover the seeds with a few leaves to discourage the birds from eating them. The fall and winter rain should sprout the seeds.

I imagine the Pilgrims would approve.

TREES

Particularly in areas with fierce winter winds, it is a good idea to prune dense trees to open gaps for the wind to pass through. Otherwise dense trees may act like sails in the wind and keel over. In damp soil, heavy winds can even uproot a tree. Staking trees, by the way, is a matter of controversy. A tree should be able to move in the wind without breaking.

This is a good month to transplant young deciduous trees that are growing in the wrong location. Wait until all the leaves fall off. Be sure to dig deeply beyond the natural drip line and then underneath the tree. Cover the roots and the earth clinging to the roots with a heavy tarp or burlap before moving the tree to its new location. Plant the tree at the same depth that it was growing before it was moved. Water it well.

One last note on trees in November as the season of hibernation approaches—those cozy hollows in trees, where squirrels curl up for a winter's sleep, are made by microbes rotting out an injured limb. The tree protects itself by walling off the wounded area. Some trees, however, are not good rotters. Among those are alder, bigleaf maple, elm, poplar, and willow. Gardeners may want to help those trees by cutting out the dead wood. Be very careful not to cut into the trunk wood and avoid cutting into the branch collar or callus roll that joins the branch to the trunk.

TULIPS

Tulips make a spellbinding display and are particularly well suited to pots in Northern California. Gardeners, however, should probably think of tulips as an annual. Many tulips will not bloom again in Northern California. For a discussion of tulip growing and persuading at least some varieties to behave like perennials, see page 248.

VEGETABLES

Cold weather will limit growth in the vegetable garden. Coastal gardeners can grow and harvest certain types of crops through the winter. Most gardeners simply put the vegetable patch to rest for the winter as few of us enjoy gardening in the rain. Enthusiasts may, however, want to continue the vegetable garden with winter crops. Plant seeds of arugula, bok choy, fava beans, lettuce, *mizuna*, radish, and spinach. Also plant garlic, onions, and shallots. From flats, plant out cold-tolerant lettuces, cabbage, cauliflower, celery, broccoli, parsley, and Swiss chard. See page 250 for more information on winter vegetable gardens.

WATERING

Gardeners need to monitor the amount of rain reaching the garden. Until the ground is truly soaked with rain, you may need to water. Cooler weather and waning daylight hours make fewer demands on plants, so water less heavily. Newly planted annuals and winter vegetables will still need to be soaked thoroughly.

Wildflowers will often grow in difficult areas where other plants fail. However, this does not mean that the gardener can toss wildflower seeds out before a rain storm and expect to have a gorgeous garden the following spring. Mother Nature sows thousands of seeds to get a few to grow. The gardener cannot afford this technique and must improve the odds by proper preparation.

To create a meadow of wildflowers it is essential to remove the weeds and grasses. Small areas can be spaded or raked; large areas are usually rototilled, plowed, or harrowed. First, remove the grasses and weeds that are already growing there and then wet down the area and wait for grass and weed seeds to sprout. Remove the new weeds and grasses, wet down the area again, and wait for the remaining seeds to sprout. Some gardeners repeat this process yet again for a third time. It may seem to be a lot of work, but it is really much easier to remove the weeds and grasses before the wildflowers have sprouted. Most wildflowers prefer lean soil, so do not add fertilizer. Fertilizers encourage weeds and grasses, which have stronger root systems than most wildflowers and will quickly crowd them out.

To sow wildflower seeds, mix wildflower seeds with a bucketful of sand or fine compost so that the seed can be scattered more evenly. Lightly rake the seed into the soil. Work the rake back and forth in a scuffing motion to push the seeds into small crevices. Do not bury the seed. Many gardeners believe that a light tamping of the seed improves germination. One way to do this is to lay pieces of cardboard over the seeds and then walk on the cardboard.

The birds are now a major threat to the creation of the garden because they are sharp-eyed consumers of wildflower seeds. Hide the seeds by broadcasting a light layer of compost over them, or cover them lightly with leaves, hay, straw, or any lightweight twiggy growth.

Then sprinkle the seeds with a fine spray of water. Seed germination depends upon moisture. If the rains do not fall, water weekly with a fine spray to keep the ground moist.

WILDFLOWER SEEDS

Be wary when buying wildflower seeds: Many of them are mixed with large quantities of filler. The idea behind the fillers is to allow the gardener to see where the seeds fall, but one popular brand is a whopping eighty-five percent filler. Wildflower seeds can be purchased without filler in single or mixed varieties.

Sow orange California poppy (*Eschscholzia californica*) with baby blue eyes (*Nemophila menzeisii*) and pink and lavender farewell-to-spring (*Clarkia amoena*). They will bloom in the order listed and provide easy-to-care-for flowers from spring to midsummer. My favorite is the white blushed with pink mountain phlox (*Liananthus grandiflora*), which seems to bloom for months.

...december...

fig - fig 6

Camellias in bloom?

━●◄◎ *December Features* ◎►●━

December is a month of rest for the Northern Californian gardener. Generally the gardener's attention is turned toward indoor plants as guests arrive for the holiday season. Depending upon the climate, many of these same indoor flowering plants such as azaleas and cyclamen can be planted outdoors after the holidays are over.

If rain does not fall, as it sometimes does not in December, the gardener must attend to watering chores. The colder temperatures and shorter daylight hours, however, mean that less water is required in the garden than at other times of the year. Be sure to water plants that are protected from rain by overhanging eaves. Also watch the sky for the possibility of frost, which does serious damage early in winter when plants are less hardened against the cold. Susceptible plants include bougainvillea, citrus, fuchsia, and succulents. Container plants should be moved under the eaves of an overhanging roof or beneath a leafy tree. Plants that cannot be moved should be covered.

December is also the month to begin the dormant spraying of leafless trees and shrubs to destroy overwintering insects and diseases. It is the month when garden catalogs begin to arrive with their alluring descriptions and glossy photographs to tempt the gardener. Many a fine evening is spent in a cozy armchair dreaming of the resurrection of spring.

All Gardeners

❋ Water plants as needed.

❋ Watch out for frost.

❋ Direct water from downspouts to avoid damage to the garden.

❋ Save wood ashes from the fireplace as a source of potash for the compost pile.

❋ Request seed and nursery catalogs from mail-order companies. See page 300.

▲ ▼ ▲

Coastal Gardeners

❋ In addition to the tasks listed for all gardeners, survey the garden to determine what needs to be done to protect it against winter storm damage.

❋ Set out large-sized transplants of winter-flowering plants into the bedding plot, using such plants as calendula, Iceland poppy, pansy, primrose, and stock.

❋ Apply dormant spray to deciduous flowering plants and fruit trees.

❋ Protect vulnerable plants from frost by spraying them with an antitranspirant; see page 261.

❋ Prune pines, magnolias, junipers, and red-berried plants for holiday greens.

❋ Cut back chrysanthemums as they finish blooming.

❋ Harvest winter vegetables as they ripen.

▲ ▼ ▲

Central Valley Gardeners

❋ In addition to the tasks listed for all gardeners, survey the garden to determine what needs to be done to protect it against winter storm damage.

❋ Set out large-sized transplants of winter-flowering plants into the bedding plot, using such plants as calendula, Iceland poppy, primrose, and stock.

❋ Apply dormant spray to deciduous flowering plants and fruit trees.

❋ In areas with only a light frost annually, protect vulnerable plants from frost by spraying them with an antitranspirant; see page 261.

❋ Prune pines, magnolias, junipers, and red-berried plants for holiday greens.

❋ Cut back chrysanthemums as they finish blooming.

❋ Hold off fertilizing most plants in preparation for winter.

❋ Stabilize plants that might be harmed by wind.

❋ Harvest winter vegetables as they ripen.

▲ ▼ ▲

High Mountain Gardeners

❋ In addition to the tasks listed for all gardeners, protect vulnerable plants from the coming winter. The idea of protection is to insulate plants from the heave damage of alternate freezing and thawing by providing a constant temperature.

❋ As soon as the ground has frozen, protect woody shrubs such as roses by mounding soil up around the crown to cover the graft union. (Of course, use soil from another part of the garden, not soil near the rose roots.) Also protect perennials that go dormant by covering the roots with at least two inches of mulch. Be sure to cover the roots of both shrubs and perennials.

Keep the mulch in place by covering with evergreen prunings. In very cold areas, cover the mulch over perennials and the soil mounds over woody shrubs with a layer of straw.

⊙ Protect trees from winter scavengers who gnaw on bark, by wrapping trunks with burlap or surrounding them with a leaf-filled wire barrier.

⊙ Prune pines, junipers and red-berried plants for holiday greens.

BALCONY AND ENTRYWAY GARDENS

Continue to transplant winter-flowering plants into pots. Azaleas, calendulas, chrysanthemums, cyclamen, and primroses are good choices. Be sure to keep potted plants that are sheltered from rain well watered. For dramatic impact consider a shrub in a large pot. Dwarf pines, the twisted, contorted branches of a *Corokia cotoneaster* or the bizarre hazelnut, Harry Lauder's walking stick (*Corylus avellana* 'Contorta') are all dramatic plants in winter and will grow well in a large pot.

BIRDS

Many birds migrate south before the weather turns cold, but for those that do not, winter is difficult. A winter treat that offers birds a source of quick, high energy is suet (a form of fat available from a butcher) held in a nylon mesh bag (of the type often used to sell bulk produce) or stuffed into a pine cone. Winter's cooler temperatures keep suet from turning rancid. Commercially packaged combinations of suet and bird seed are available. Their favorite foods include black-striped sunflower seeds, oil-type sunflower seeds, sunflower kernels, red and white proso millet, and peanut kernels. Place the bird foods where feeding birds will not become cat food.

BULBS

Be sure to get in the last of the spring-blooming bulbs this month. Remember that wet soil is difficult to dig properly. Be careful not to plant the bulbs too deeply.

CHRISTMAS CACTUS

This entry should be subtitled Confessions of a Plant Slayer, because that is how I came to appreciate the widely grown houseplant known as the Christmas cactus.

Murder was not exactly on my mind when I moved the ungainly Christmas cactus outside. Not that I would have objected to its sudden demise. It is just that gardeners are more inclined to nurture than to destroy. I merely wanted it out of my way in the house. Out of bloom, a Christmas cactus has limited appeal. Worse, it requires too much space.

I put it under the miserable female kiwi vine that clutches the fence in the garden. In this loser's corner, as I have come to think of it, the Christmas cactus sulked. Whenever I came out to check on the espaliered apples, which are planted in front of the kiwi vines, I would splash some water on the Christmas cactus.

Little by little, the Christmas cactus slipped out of my mind, if not out of my view. Surely I must have noticed that I was not watering it anymore. The puffy leaves shrank and became mottled. Soon it would die, and I could toss it out.

One day, when I was out poking around the apples, I noticed a splash of pink among the kiwi vines. The Christmas cactus, which I had not watered for at least two months, was blooming. I am not speaking of minor bloom. I mean the full-fledged show, the cast of thirty spectacular cancan dancers, that only a Christmas cactus can produce.

It seemed to cry out at me in reproach. How could I have disregarded a plant capable of such a display? Of course, I carried it indoors promptly, where it will remain.

Since this incident I have learned more about these curious cacti. In nature they grow in moist jungle settings in the crevices of tree branches. Although it is not very often mentioned in gardening books, one method of forcing them to bloom is to withhold water until buds form. The Christmas cactus is a long-lived plant, so it is worth the gardener's efforts to cultivate a nice specimen. If you manage to hang on to one, it could even become an heirloom.

Christmas Cactus Growing Simplified

Botanical name: *Schlumbergera bridgesii*.

Common name: Christmas cactus.

Site preference: Grow indoors in bright light but not direct sun. It may be placed outdoors in the shade in the summer.

Soil conditions: Prefers rich, well-draining soil. Add leaf-mold and sand to create a perfect mix.

Water: Water regularly. Some growers withhold water for a few weeks after the plants have finished blooming, but of course, you would not withhold water both before and after the plants bloom.

Nutrients: Professional growers use a fertilizer formula such as 20-10-20 every two weeks. Stop feeding six weeks before you want buds to form.

Problems: Do not let the name cactus fool you. The leaves will burn in hot sun.

Special care: It will bloom naturally in mid-December so do not go to ridiculous lengths to shorten its days and reduce the night temperatures. Nor, of course, should you artificially prolong summer by putting it under night lights or over a heater.

Hints: Start new plants by breaking off between one and three phylloclades (sections) at the leaf joints and rooting them in vermiculite or potting soil. Two similar plants are the Thanksgiving cactus (*Schlumbergera truncata*), also called the crab cactus, which has sharp points on the leaves, whereas the leaves of the Christmas cactus have smooth, rounded margins, and the Easter cactus (*Rhipsalidopsis gaertneri*), which has smooth, elongated leaves. All bloom naturally around the related holiday.

CHRISTMAS GREENERY

See Greenery on page 280.

CHRISTMAS TREES—THE DOUGLAS FIR

In 1824, David Douglas sailed around Cape Horn to the primeval forests of the Pacific Northwest. Here he would collect the beautiful Christmas tree that would be forever known by his name—the Douglas fir (*Pseudotsuga menziesii*). It would be a difficult journey. But right from the start, he was strong willed and incorrigible.

As a boy little Douglas behaved so contumaciously that his despairing mother sent him away to school. As a student he continued his ill-tempered, stubborn ways, until he was hired to assist the head gardener of the Earl of Mansfield, who decided to rebuild the ancient palace of Scone—all one hundred and twenty-five rooms.

As with many gardeners, it was love at first sight. During his seven years of apprenticeship, the pig-headed boy became a proficient gardener and an amateur botanist. Soon his passion for collecting plants led to friendships with influential members of the Horticultural Society of London. Before long, the Society appointed Douglas to collect fruiting plants in the eastern United States.

Douglas's first journey was such a success that the Society sent him on a second, much grander adventure—one that would test the Scot's tenacity. The trek through uncharted forests would have finished off anyone less stubborn. The land was so hazardous—his journal tells of river snags, avalanches, rapids, snowdrifts, and slime pits—that he lost his entire botanical collection. Twice he became so unbearably hungry that he ate one of his horses. Rats gnawed through his packs to devour seeds and specimens. Indians confronted him. Insects attacked him. Rainy weather left him soaked for days. He suffered injury and illness. In 1826 he wrote in his journal " . . . if a change does not take place, I will shortly be consigned to a tomb."

There were also days of joy as Douglas trekked through the giant Christmas trees, and he counted it worth the hardships. Few trees are as sweetly fragrant as branches of the Douglas fir when crushed underfoot. The trees live for up to a thousand years and soar higher than any other trees save the sequoias. Their deeply furrowed dark bark can surround a specimen forty-eight feet in circumference. The ground around them is soft with mosses and fallen needles.

Douglas recognized the value of the tree that was to bear his name. When he had collected seeds from the giant trees, he raced them to the coast and packed them aboard the ship *Dryad* that was setting sail for London.

He was not the only one to value the fir tree. Less than two years after Douglas collected the seed, the first sawmill in the Northwest began cutting the firs down. The lumber became a favorite of carpenters and architects because the wood does not warp. Many thousands of miles of railroad tracks are laid on Douglas fir ties. The tree provided telegraph and telephone poles as well as ships' masts. Today the Douglas fir is widely planted by gardeners and commonly used for Christmas trees.

d e c e m b e r

David Douglas collected so many other conifers that he wrote to his sponsor, "You will begin to think I manufacture Pines at my pleasure." When he returned to London, it became evident that his grouchy, Scrooge-like nature was better suited to tramping through the wilds than to elegant drawing rooms.

In 1830 he set off for a Mexican colony called California, where he spent nineteen months and sent back seeds of hundreds of species including the California poppy and the Monterey pine. While collecting in the Hawaiian Islands he fell into a pit trap that unfortunately contained a wild bull. That was the end of the prolific collector who introduced more than two hundred species of plants into cultivation, including the one many people know as the Christmas tree.

Christmas Tree—Care

Several techniques help living Christmas trees survive indoor stays. Before bringing one indoors, water well and spray with an antitranspirant, which will preserve moisture in the needles. Add water to the container every two or three days while it is inside. Keep the tree indoors for the shortest time possible; two weeks is usually tops. Deep soak the tree when you bring it outdoors again.

Christmas Tree Caution

Unfortunately, a disease called pitch cancer is spreading from the Monterey pine (which, in addition to the Douglas fir, is also used frequently as a Christmas tree in Northern California) to other pines and across species to the Douglas fir. A beetle is suspected of carrying the disease from tree to tree, and the disease has been found in Christmas tree nurseries in the Bay Area. The disease begins at the trunk and causes the tree to exude excess resin. If you should buy a Christmas tree with the disease, bag it up after the holiday and dispose of it in a land fill. See page 177 for more information on pitch cancer.

CYMBIDIUMS

Cymbidiums will begin blooming soon. Watch out for snails around the spikes. Once the buds have reached full size, the gardener can bring the cymbidium indoors where the warm temperatures will open the blooms. Continue to fertilize every two weeks with a low-nitrogen liquid fertilizer formulated for orchids.

DORMANT SPRAYING

Dormant spraying with horticultural oils kills overwintering insect eggs, mites, softbodied insects, and some scales by blocking the supply of oxygen and suffocating the pests. Applied in winter, the dormant spray does not reach fruits or harm beneficial insects.

Dormant spraying is done in two or three doses, and the first application is made in December or January. Deciduous fruit trees, some deciduous shrubs, and rose bushes should be sprayed after they have lost their leaves. Horticultural oils (also called dormant oils) are highly refined petroleum oils that are manufactured specifically for use on plants. Follow the directions on the horticultural oil, use a good sprayer, and aim the fine spray onto the bare branches and limbs. Spray only when the temperature is above 45°F. Dormant spraying is usually limited to fruit trees and roses.

Note: Do not spray Japanese maples or blue spruce with horticultural oil.

Mineral solutions of lime sulfur or hydrated lime and copper sulfate are also sometimes used for dormant spraying to control specific pests on specific trees. Mineral solutions can be combined with horticultural oil for broader coverage. Some of these sprays are caustic, so be sure to wear protective clothing, goggles, and rubber gloves.

Lime sulfur controls anthracnose, apple scab, brown rot, peach leaf curl, and powdery mildew. It is frequently used on peach trees and on other fruit trees as well. Peach leaf curl, a water-activated fungus, attacks during the blossoming stage; it is important to spray peach trees with lime sulfur and oil just before the pink buds open when they resemble popcorn about to pop. Note that lime and sulfur are very caustic, so protect yourself.

Bordeaux mixture (hydrated lime and copper sulfate) controls brown rot, peach leaf curl, some grape diseases, some apple diseases, downy mildew, and many fungal diseases.

Sulfur controls fungal spores, brown rot, peach scab, apple scab, and powdery mildew.

FROST

Protect tender garden plants from winter's cold. Withhold fertilizer and cut back on the amount of water used in the garden. Both these measures will help harden plants to the cold and will reduce the amount of tender new growth, which is particularly susceptible to frost damage.

Although the coldest months of the year are usually January and February, gardeners should watch for signs of approaching frost: a cloudless sky, still air (no wind), cold (less than 45°F by 10 P.M.), and dry (no moisture condensing on windshields).

Plants that need to be protected from frost include bougainvillea, citrus, fuchsia, and succulents. Susceptible plants in containers should be moved under the eaves of an overhanging roof or beneath a leafy tree. Plants that cannot be moved should be covered with burlap, plastic, old drapes, or newspaper arranged over the stakes set in the ground. The covering, particularly if it is plastic, should not touch the plants. Remove the covering the next morning when the temperature rises.

In most of coastal Northern California, where the temperature does not go much below freezing and the frost is short-lived, you can also protect vulnerable plants by spraying them with an antitranspirant. Available at nurseries, antitranspirants are commonly used on indoor Christmas trees and greens to form a protective coating on foliage to hold in moisture. This is probably the easiest method of frost protection, as the gardener does not need to monitor the weather each night. Each application lasts several months, so antitranspirants are usually sprayed on twice during the cold season.

When a plant is injured by frost, it is best to leave the damaged portions on the plant to protect the portion below the damage until the cold season has passed.

FRUIT TREES

To destroy overwintering pests and diseases, spray fruit trees with horticultural oil during the winter. See page 279.

FUCHSIAS

Keep fuchsias watered but let them go dormant by leaving the seed pods on. Move fuchsias to a spot that is protected from frost and mulch them heavily.

GREENERY—TOP CHOICES

When buying cut greenery to bring indoors for the holidays, test for freshness by feeling the foliage. It should be supple and not shedding excessively.

- Noble fir is at the top of the list. It is considered to be very long lasting.
- Douglas fir does not hold up very well as cut greenery indoors. When selecting Douglas fir, remember that, contrary to expectations, its needles will snap, not bend, when they are fresh.
- Cedar is an excellent cut green. It even holds its shape when it dries.
- Eucalyptus leaves are very useful and long lasting.
- Ivies, particularly the variegated varieties, are excellent when mixed with other greens. Submerge the entire length of ivy in a conditioning mix (see below) before using it.
- Loquat greenery is long lasting.
- Magnolia boughs are excellent because they are showy, tough, and long lasting.
- Heavenly bamboo, which looks like a bamboo but is not, is good as cut greenery.
- Pine greenery is not universally useful; it depends on the variety. Fresh pine needles will bend, not snap.

GREENERY—CONDITIONING

Bringing fresh cut greenery into the house is more successful when care is taken to preserve the rich scent and freshness of the boughs.

- Whether you cut the greenery yourself or buy it, recut the stems and then split them for an inch or two. Christmas trees; too, should be resawed at home.
- Plunge the recut stems into a bucket of water mixed, if possible, with a conditioning preservative. My favorite recipe follows.
- Let the greenery soak for several days before using it. The greenery conditioner can also be used in a Christmas tree stand.
- Spray greenery with an antitranspirant, which helps prevent the loss of moisture.

Greenery Conditioner

Mix together:
- ◉ 4 gallons warm water
- ◉ 2 aspirins (325 milligrams each)
- ◉ 1 cup white corn syrup
- ◉ 1 tablespoon liquid household bleach
- ◉ 1 tablespoon chelated iron powder

Caution: Do not use this conditioner with fir boughs because aspirin and bleach cause severe needle drop.

HOLIDAY PLANTS

Just because the temperature is dropping toward freezing does not mean that the gardener's green thumb has turned blue. On the contrary, with the home filling up with holiday guests, the gardener needs both the solace of greenery and, truth be told, an opportunity to show off a splendid plant specimen or two.

It helps if the gardener has a choice selection of container plants ready to be placed by the front door; perhaps a December-blooming camellia that has been pruned over the years to perfect form. Top choices include two fiery red camellias with brilliant orange stamens that resemble tassels in the middle of each perfect flower: *Camellia sasanqua* 'Yuletide' and *Camellia japonica* 'Wildfire,' which has larger flowers with a double layer of petals.

Not that the gardener need be reduced to indoor poinsettias and amaryllis if no such perfect container plants are at hand. Instead, treat yourself to one of the new, fragrant miniature cymbidiums that grow no more than eighteen to twenty-four inches high. They are in full bloom this month and are usually carried by neighborhood nurseries. Although full-sized cymbidiums need to grow outdoors most of the year, some of the new miniatures will grow indoors in an unheated sun-room. Cymbidiums are surprisingly easy to grow outdoors along the coast where temperatures do not fall below 30°F. For orchids, they are very forgiving of the gardener's faults and are much to be recommended.

Not to be overlooked is the spectacular azalea. Azaleas are outdoor plants despite the rows of them inside the local supermarket. They despise being trapped inside a hot, dry house, but they endure it; much like the gardener on that account. Misting azaleas keeps them happier indoors and moving them each night to a room where the temperature does not exceed 60°F will prolong their perkiness indoors. Unlike chrysanthemums, azaleas sold for indoor use do just fine when transplanted outdoors. Before transplanting them outdoors, prepare the soil by digging in lots of peat moss and organic compost. Azaleas like well-drained, light, acid soil.

When planting the azalea, remember to plant it with the root ball an inch or two above soil level. Then mulch well with an acid mulch such as pine needles or oak leaves. Keep the mulch away from the stems of the plants.

Cyclamen are another good choice for showing off a green thumb; keeping one in bloom indoors is a bit tricky. An occasional misting and moving the cyclamen to a cool spot each evening will help prevent the buds from falling off before they open. There is even a fragrant cultivar of cyclamen called 'Laser'.

An unusual plant to brighten the holidays indoors is the Jerusalem cherry *(Solanum pseudocapsicum)*. This striking bush comes self-decorated with large, bright red balls resembling shiny Christmas ornaments. The fruit may be toxic to children so be sure to warn them not to sample it. Place the plant in filtered indoor light and keep the soil moist. After the holidays you may move the plant outdoors, but like the poinsettia, it is usually grown as an annual and discarded when it begins to look shabby.

Then of course there are the poinsettias themselves, which are discussed on page 283. Bred to become truly long-lasting indoor holiday plants, they now come in shades of yellow or salmon mottled with cream to give them a fresh look for the coming new year. Any of these bloomers will revive the gardener's spirits over the holidays.

IN BLOOM IN DECEMBER

- Annuals: calendula, Iceland poppy, pansy, stock, and sweet alyssum
- Perennials: Christmas rose, chrysanthemum, clivia, cyclamen, primrose, salvia, and violet
- Shrubs: camellia and heather
- Natives: early blooming manzanita, silktassel bushes, and red-twigged shrubs add color
- Trees: New Zealand tea tree
- Early blooming bulbs: freesia
- Poinsettia

IN THE NURSERY IN DECEMBER

- Annuals: calendula, Iceland poppy, stock, and pansy
- Perennials: cineraria, cyclamen, primrose, and violet
- Shrubs: azalea and camellia
- Spring-blooming bulbs, corms, tubers, and rhizomes
- Bare-root plants at the end of December

KIWI VINES

Kiwis are pruned during their dormant season. On mature vines that have already produced fruit, prune the arms (the main canes that carry the canes that bear fruit) back to about seven feet in length; remove the canes that have borne fruit for three years, and prune back the side shoots on the remaining canes to about eight buds. If this sounds too complicated, do not worry about it; kiwis will go ahead and bear fruit for those gardeners who do nothing more than prune back the overly long arms each summer.

MAINTENANCE

Continue with routine maintenance chores such as weeding, raking, and general garden cleanup, which will discourage garden pests from wintering in your garden.

NATIVE PLANTS

Two native California shrubs, the toyon (*Heteromeles arbutifolia*) with its bright red berries, and the silktassel bush (*Garrya elliptica*) with its long silky catkins hanging like tinsel, are at their best in winter. You may have to phone several nurseries before finding them to plant in your own garden, but it is worth the effort. Both of these outstanding plants require good drainage.

Also look for many fine new cultivars of our native Pacific Coast iris. The array of exquisite colors now available is bound to bring cheer to both the garden and gardener. Generally native irises prefer light shade and soil that drains well. They are fairly drought tolerant once established and will often naturalize to create a striking, easy-to-care-for ground cover. The most widely available and hardiest are selections of *Iris douglasiana*, which is native to the coast.

POINSETTIAS

The traditional Christmas flower has come a long way in a mere twenty-five years. Early varieties were both fragile and short lived. They tended to drop their green foliage and red bracts soon after Christmas. But new poinsettia cultivars have stronger stems, larger bracts, and are longer lasting.

Select poinsettias with green foliage all the way down to the soil line, which indicate active, healthy roots. Those brightly colored petals are actually bracts, and the flower is that little yellow smudge of berries in the middle. Too much green around the bract edges indicate that the plant is underdeveloped; do not choose that plant. Select a plant with the smaller bracts near the center that are entirely colored or the plant will be likely to fade when you bring it home.

Poinsettia Growing Simplified

Botanical name: *Euphorbia pulcherrima*.

Common name: Poinsettia.

Site preference indoors: Bright, sunny natural daylight; at least six hours daily is recommended. Place the plant near a sunny window, but avoid letting the hot afternoon sun shine directly on the colorful bracts. The sun sometimes fades the bracts. To prolong the bright red of the bracts, temperatures should not exceed 70°F during the day or fall below 65°F at night. Avoid placing the plants near drafts or dry heat from ventilating ducts.

Site preference outdoors: Potted plants are not recommended for outdoor use as poinsettias that were raised in hothouses dislike winds, cold, frost, and rain. Damage occurs when the temperature dips below 50°F, causing the plants to drop their leaves as if dead. Even exposure to a short frost usually kills a poinsettia plant.

In the frost-free areas of Northern California, transplant a potted poinsettia in the spring to a fast-draining, prepared garden bed rich in organic matter. A protected area along a south-facing garden wall is best.

Water: Moist soil, neither too wet nor too dry, is ideal. Water when the soil surface feels dry. Water just enough for water to drip out of the bottom of the pot and discard excess water to avoid root rot.

Nutrients: Store-bought potted poinsettias should not need fertilizer, but a well-balanced, all-purpose houseplant fertilizer could help maintain the foliage color and promote new growth after the holidays. Poinsettias have an amazing ability to remain in bloom until March or even April.

Hints: Avoid temperatures below 50°F even while transporting them home.

According to poinsettia growers, the popular notion that poinsettias are poisonous is a myth. The Society of American Florists and Ohio State University are said to have effectively disproved the charge that the poinsettia is harmful to human and animal health. The Poisindex Information Service, the primary information resource used by most poison control centers, states that a fifty pound child would have to ingest over five hundred bracts to surpass experimental doses, and there was no toxicity at that level. When I confirmed this information with a physician on the Poison Control Center Hotline, I was told that the only way a child would die of eating parts of the poinsettia is by choking on it.

Poinsettias for Bloom Next Year

I strongly recommend that you discard potted poinsettias and buy new indoor plants next year. However, for the indoor gardening enthusiast with lots of time and patience, following are the directions for getting one to bloom again next year.

1. In March or April, when the bracts begin to turn a muddy green, cut the plant back to about eight inches high. Admittedly the plant will now resemble a few sticks poked in the ground. With luck, by the end of May vigorous new growth will develop. Keep the plants near a sunny window.

2. During the summer, place the plant outdoors. Water the plant regularly and fertilize it twice a month until December with a balanced complete fertilizer.

3. Around June 1, transplant the poinsettia to a slightly larger pot using a rich, fast-draining potting soil.

4. The poinsettia begins to set buds and produce flowers as the winter nights become longer, which is why it naturally blooms during November or December. Any stray artificial light such as that from a street light or table lamp indoors could delay or halt the reflowering. Therefore, beginning about the first of October, keep the plants in complete darkness for fourteen continuous hours each night, either by moving the plant to a closet or by placing a box over it. Either way the gardener is kept busy seeing that the poinsettia receives the required six to eight hours of bright sunlight during the day and fourteen hours of darkness each night. Also keep in mind that the poinsettia requires a constant temperature between 60° and 70°F or it may not set flower buds. After two-and-a-half months of this regimen, the poinsettia should be in full bloom.

POMEGRANATES

One of winter's most beguiling fruits is the pomegranate. Traditionally, Eve tempted Adam with an apple. More likely it was a pomegranate (*Punica granatum*). "Thou art fair, my love," murmured Solomon, and with an image that seems less than flattering, continued, "Thy temples are like a piece of pomegranate within thy locks." The pomegranate had been cultivated in the Biblical world long before King Solomon. Given its luscious, red-speckled skin, Eve could have easily tempted Adam with a pomegranate.

The gardener does not need to be a temptress to grow pomegranates. What is required is sustained summer heat and nothing cooler than light, short-lived frosts in the winter. Once the pomegranate finds its niche, it is likely to continue without aid from the gardener. Pomegranates have been grown in California since they were first imported by Spanish mission priests.

In the Middle East, where it is still prized, the best varieties are sweet and have small seeds. There are varieties with no seeds, but in the areas where pomegranates are popular, so are the seeds. The seeds, as many a child can tell you, are sucked and then chewed. Like sunflower seeds, pomegranate seeds require a leisurely attitude toward eating.

Regrettably, pomegranates usually fail to set fruit in the cooler sections of our coastal climate. However, they still make handsome, decorative shrubs and trees. The new growth is bronzy and in fall the bright green, narrow leaves of summer turn yellow. The flowers are quite showy and, depending on the variety, range in color from pink to bright orange red to a striped creamy coral.

Several varieties are commonly sold in Northern California.

‘Wonderful’ grows about ten feet tall and can be pruned into a small tree, left as a multi-stemmed shrub, or trained into an espalier. Where the weather is warm and dry it produces a vigorous crop of juicy fruit. In cool, damp climates it may not set any fruit.

‘Nana’ is a dwarf pomegranate that grows to about three feet and produces small fruit.

‘Chico’ is another dwarf with showy flowers but no fruit.

Pomegranate Growing Simplified

Botanical name: *Punica granatum.*

Common name: Pomegranate.

Site preference: For best bloom and fruit grow in full sun. It will tolerate a light frost and considerable heat. Many varieties will flower but not set fruit in cool coastal climates.

Soil conditions: Good garden soil is preferred, but it will grow even in alkaline soil.

Water: For best fruit, be sure to water during dry periods. It will tolerate drought when established.

Nutrients: Fertilize lightly, if at all.

Problems: If fruit has formed during a dry period, deep watering will probably cause the fruit to split.

Special care: Prune in late summer or early spring. The flowers and fruit form at the tips of the current year's growth.

Hints: Pick the fruit when it turns red. If you leave it on the tree, it may split open. Ornamental varieties such as ‘Mme. Legrelle’ and ‘Chico’ produce flowers but no fruit.

PRUNING

When deciduous fruit trees have dropped all their leaves and gone dormant, the gardener can begin pruning. The trees can be pruned at any time up until new buds swell in spring. Because the type of pruning depends upon the type of fruit tree, gardeners are well advised to consult a pruning book before whacking away at the hapless tree. Apple trees, for example, set fruit on the same spurs year after year. If the zealous gardener mistakenly prunes off the spurs, that's the end of the fruit. Better not to prune than to do real damage. Pruning is not difficult—learning where to prune is the tricky part. Many Northern California nurseries give classes in pruning. See page 30 for a basic, illustrated review.

ROSES

The bare-root rose season begins at the end of December. These are plants that are dug up while dormant and sold without soil clinging to their roots, which makes them easier to handle and hence less expensive to buy than container-grown plants. Bare-root roses are typically about one-half the price of container plants. In addition to saving money, bare-root roses tend to adjust quickly to a new location because they do not have to make a transition from nursery container soil to your garden soil. For instructions on how to select and plant a bare-root rose, see page 45. For a list of roses, both modern and antique varieties, recommended for Northern California, see page 55. Gardeners who have the space may also want to consider shrub roses.

SHRUB ROSES—TOP CHOICES

Shrub roses are roses that admirably fill the role of a landscaping plant in addition to offering wonderful cut flowers. As landscaping plants they are known for hardiness and ease of care. They require little pruning or spraying to keep them in good form, and they flower over a long season.

‘Bonica’ is smothered with clusters of pink roses throughout the summer. In fall and winter it has bright red hips that are decorative. It grows between four and five feet high with upright arching branches. It was the first shrub rose ever to win the All-American Rose title.

‘Iceberg’ is another terrific bloomer with clusters of large white roses that are also fragrant. It grows between five and six feet tall and equally wide. Its shiny, light green leaves are unusually attractive.

‘Sally Holmes’ is at last available here in the United States. This marvelous shrub rose was hybridized by an Englishman and not generally available here until recently. Sometimes sold as a climbing rose, it will reach ten feet high when attached to a trellis. It can also be grown as a five-foot mounding shrub. The flowers are carried in pronounced clusters of pale peach fading to creamy white.

VEGETABLES

Cold weather will limit growth in the vegetable garden, and most gardeners shut the garden gate to the vegetable patch for the winter. Gardeners with the milder weather (and an inclination to garden in the rain) can grow and harvest through the winter, planting seeds of arugula, bok choy, fava beans, lettuce, *mizuna*, radish, and spinach; setting out garlic, onions, and shallots, and transplanting seedlings of cold-tolerant lettuces and cabbage.

WILDFLOWERS

Sowing wildflower seeds is one of December's more pleasant tasks. For instructions on sowing and recommendations, see Wildflowers, page 269.

WISTERIA

Shorten the flower-bearing spurs to two or three buds; the buds that form flowers are nice and plump.

‖‖‖‖ 287 ‖‖‖‖

d e c e m b e r

PART THREE

GLOSSARY

MAIL-ORDER PLANTS, SEEDS, AND SUPPLIES

RESOURCES

WORKS CONSULTED

INDEX

Gardeners, like other specialized groups of people, have their lingo. These specialized words are a sort of shorthand to spare lengthy and repetitious explanations. The following glossary is an explanation of the gardening terms pertinent to this book. Some are familar words that take on a special meaning in the world of gardening. Words that, in the definitions, are set in SMALL CAPITALS are themselves defined in this glossary.

Acid (alkaline) soil. Acidity and alkalinity are used to describe a range of one aspect of soil chemistry, the concentration of hydrogen ions, which ranges between zero and fourteen. An ion is an electrically charged molecule. This concentration is represented by the abbreviation pH followed by a number. Neutral soil has a pH of 7, which means that it is neither acid nor alkaline. A pH above 7 indicates alkalinity; a pH below 7 indicates acidity. Plants differ in the type of soil they prefer. This is of much greater concern to the commercial gardener than to the home gardener.

Actual nitrogen. *See* Nitrogen.

Air layering. Air layering is a technique used to propagate plants. One method of air layering is to find a node (a bump beneath the skin of a stem or branch), make a small slit with a knife beneath the node and pack the cut and the stem with wet sphagnum moss. Then wrap the moss with plastic and tie off at both ends of the plastic. Roots will then form in the wet moss. This will take at least one growing season. Once the roots have formed, you cut off the section and pot it up. *See also* Layering.

Alkaline soil. *See* Acid soil.

Amendment. *See* soil amendment.

Annual. An annual is a plant that completes its life cycle in a year or less. Many annuals are sown from seed, marigolds and zinnias for example. Some PERENNIAL plants, such as petunias, are often grown as annuals. When gardeners refer to annuals they often merely mean flowering plants that are used for a showy, seasonal display.

Anther. The part of the flower that produces the pollen is called an anther. Some anthers, lily anthers for instance, carry such powerful pollen that it is capable of staining clothes, so they are cut off when the flowers are used in a bouquet.

Antitranspirant. Antiranspirants are commercial products that are sprayed on plants, leaving a film that slows the transpiration of moisture out of the plant and therefore migates damage from wind, heat, and cold. Often used on Christmas trees, they are used by gardeners to help prevent frost damage and TRANSPLANT SHOCK.

Axillary bud. An axillary bud occurs in the leaf axil, the angle at the point where the leaf joins the stem. Gardeners sometime pinch off axillary buds to make stronger plants.

Balanced fertilizer. A balanced fertilizer contains equal qualities of the three major elements (nitrogen, phosphorus, and potassium) that plants need.

Bare-root. A bare-root is one that is offered for sale with the soil removed from around its roots. In winter and early spring, nurseries offer certain deciduous shrubs and trees, and a few perennials, for sale as bare-root plants. They are cheaper when sold this way.

Bark. The outer covering of a tree or a shrub branch. It can be as thin and as pliant as the skin of a tomato or as thick and as rough as a slab of pavement. *See also* Ground bark.

Beneficials. These are the much favored insects, arachnids, NEMATODES, and other organisms that eat or parasitize harmful insects and mites. Many beneficials already exist in our gardens; others can be purchased from nurseries or mail–order houses.

Biennial. This is a plant, such as a foxglove, that completes its life cycle in two years.

Bolt. This term is often used of vegetables that rush into the flowering stage at the expense of producing edible parts. It occurs in plants set out too late in the year or when hot weather accelerates growth. Lettuce often bolts in hot weather.

Bonsai. A Japanese word used to describe carefully trained, dwarfed plants grown in small shallow containers. To achieve an ancient look in a young plant, the gardener wires and prunes branches and trims roots.

Botrytis. This is a fungus characterized by fuzzy, wet filaments and blackened and swollen plants. Lengthy spells of wet weather or frequent overhead watering will often trigger it.

Bract. A bract is a modified leaf often growing just below a flower or flower cluster. Not all flowers have bracts. In bougainvillea and poinsettia the bracts are more colorful than the petals and are often confused for flower petals.

Branch collar; callus roll. This is the swollen ridge of bark surrounding a tree branch where it meets the trunk or a bigger branch. When trees are pruned, the branch collar of the limb to be removed should be preserved.

Broadcast. To scatter seed by hand over the soil to be planted.

BT. The abbreviation BT stand for *Bacillus thuringiensis*, a bacterial disease that kills caterpillars. Preparations containg BT are sold under several trade names such as Attack, Dipel, and Thuricide. It is sprayed or dusted on plants, and is popular with organic gardeners.

Bud. This word has several definitions. Most people already know that a flower bud develops into a blossom. For gardeners, it is important to know that buds are also little swollen areas along a stem, branch, or trunk where new growth may occur. Cutting above one of those dormant buds stimulates it into growing. *See also* Axillary bud

Bud union; graft union. This applies only to a grafted plant (most roses and fruit trees are grafted). It is a swollen area just above the soil level where one variety has been grafted onto the root-stock of another variety. The bud union is not always swollen, and on some older plants it can be difficult to find. On lemon trees there may be simply a change in the size of the trunk. On young bare-root trees the bud union may look like only a slight bend. On roses the bud union is usually obvious.

Bulb. Commonly, gardeners refer to any thickened underground storage structure that sprouts a plant as a bulb. But technically a bulb is rounded and composed of scales (actually modified leaves) that store food and protect the embryo plant inside. Other underground plant structures have technical names such as CORM, RHIZOME, TUBER, and TUBEROUS ROOT.

Cane. A cane refers to the woody stem of a rose or a berry plant such as a raspberry or a blackberry. It also refers to the jointed and often hollow or pith-filled stem of bamboo or sugar cane.

Catkin. A catkin is a flower cluster. Catkins are either male or female.

Chaparral. Chaparral is a type of dense, dry growth native to some of the foothills in Northern California. Chaparral growth is designed by nature to burn to the ground periodically. Gardeners living in chaparral should be very vigilant with their fire-prevention measures.

Chelate. Chelate is a soluble form of trace elements (iron, manganese, and zinc) that plants can use.

Chilling requirement. This term is used most often of fruit trees that need a certain amount of cold weather in winter in order to bloom and bear fruit well the following year. The chilling requirement is measured in a required number of hours at temperatures below 45° F. Gardeners in milder winter areas should choose varieties with low chilling requirements.

Chlorosis. Chlorosis is a condition indicating a lack of chlorophyll (a green pigment in plant cells). It is often brought about by insufficient soluble iron in the soil. Gardeners suspect chlorosis when a leaf looks yellower than it should (especially when the leaves are yellow and the veins are dark green). Iron CHELATE can be used to correct chlorosis. In lemon and orange trees, yellow leaves can also indicate that the soil is waterlogged.

Clay. When you can grip a handful of damp soil and it holds together, the soil is said to be clay soil.

Complete fertilizer. A plant fertilizer that contains all three of the primary nutrient elements (nitrogen, phosphorus, potassium) is a complete fertilizer. *See also* Fertilizer.

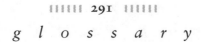

Compost. Organic materials piled up and kept damp until they rot form compost, which is the very best SOIL AMENDMENT.

Conifer. Conifers are trees such as cedars, cypresses, junipers, and pines, most of which have narrow, needlelike leaves or tiny scalelike leaves. All conifers have cones or conelike seed structures.

Cool-season lawn. A variety of grass well adapted to a cool climate produces a cool-season lawn. It grows fastest during late fall, winter, and early spring.

Cool-season vegetable. A vegetable that grows best at cool temperatures is a cool-season vegetable.

Corm. A corm is a thickened underground stem that produces a plant from buds on top. Crocus, gladiolus, and freesia grow from corms.

Crop rotation. A system to preserve the soil fertility and to minimize pests and diseases, crops that are subject to similar soil-borne pests and diseases are grown on a particular plot of ground no more frequently than once every three years.

Crown rot. A number of fungus diseases that can attack the crown of a plant at the point at which it emerges from the roots through the soil produce crown rot. Water or mud collecting around the plant's trunk contribute to crown rot.

Cultivar. A cultivar is a VARIETY of a plant that has been created by horticulturalists rather than one found in nature. The term is a condensation of "cultivated variety" and is abbreviated as cv.

Cutting. A section of a plant that is cut off and ROOTED to create a new plant is called a cutting.

Damping off. This is a plant disease caused by fungi in the soil. It makes seedlings rot.

Deadhead. The clipping off of faded flower heads before they can set seed is called deadheading. This encourages the plant to continue to flower.

Deciduous. Deciduous plants drop all their leaves once a year.

Diatomaceous earth. Diatomaceous earth is an organic pesticide powder made of the crushed, sharp skeletons of tiny diatoms. It pierces the bodies of pests like broken glass.

Divide; Dividing. This is an easy way to increase certain perennials, bulbs, and shrubs by breaking apart the clumps of stems with their roots still attached. The divisions created by dividing are then replanted.

Dormant. The term dormant describes the inactive or sleeping state in which a plant stops growing but is still alive.

Dormant spray. A solution of horticultural oil and water (sometimes including lime or sulfur) sprayed in winter on deciduous plants that have gone DORMANT and dropped their leaves. It kills overwintering pests and some fungi.

Drainage. The word *drainage* is used to describe how rapidly or how slowly water moves through the soil in a plant's root area. When water percolates through quickly, the drainage is good. When it percolates slowly, the drainage is bad. Plant roots need oxygen as well as water, so soggy soil deprives roots of oxygen. Drainage is considered fast when the water drains out of a planting hole within ten minutes, and slow when water remains in a planting hole after an hour has passed. HARDPAN can create drainage problems.

Drift. When used as a garden design term, *drift* simply indicates a graceful shape with rounded edges in a flower bed or open field; usually used to describe plants set out in swathes rather than rigid rows.

Drip line. The rough circle that may be drawn on the ground around a tree where rain would drip off the outermost leaves is called the drip line. The most active roots are often located along this line.

Drip system. A drip system is a method of watering by which water is fed at a controlled low pressure through a very small plastic hose that in turn feeds small tubes that terminate in emitters from which water drips out to irrigate individual plants.

Drought. A drought is a lack of adequate rainfall or less than normal rainfall lasting for a prolonged period: several months, a season, or several years. "Summer drought" describes the customarily dry summers of Northern California.

Drought resistant. A plant that requires less irrigation, once established, than other plants do to survive a drought is considered to be drought resistant.

Drought tolerant. A plant that, once established after a year or two, will survive on our annual rainfall with little or no irrigation is considered to be drought tolerant.

Espalier. To espalier a shrub or a tree is to train it into a flat, ornamental shape against a wall or along wires or a fence.

Evergreen. A plant that never loses all its leaves at one time is an evergreen plant.

Eye. An eye is an undeveloped growth bud that will produce a new plant. Potatoes, for instance, have eyes.

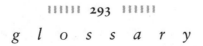

Family. A group of plants sharing certain broad characteristics are part of a family. Sometimes, as in daisy plants, the relationship among them is obvious; at other times the relation is obscure to most gardeners. The rose family, for example, includes both the apple tree and the rose bush. The family name is not part of an individual plant's scientific name, but knowing the family does help one to guess about a plant's needs.

Fertilize. To fertilize a plant is to provide it with nutrients.

Fertilizer. The material, organic or inorganic, applied to feed a plant nutrients is called fertilizer. The proportions may vary widely. Fertilizers high in nitrogen result in rapid plant growth; fertilizers high in phosphorus and potassium will promote fruiting and flowering.

Fireblight. Fireblight is a bacterial disease that causes the branches and fruit on apple trees, evergreen pear, pyracantha, and members of the rose family to turn black and die. An apt name, the plant looks as if it had been scorched.

Force. To force a plant is to make it bloom ahead of its natural schedule.

Foundation plant. A plant used to hide the house foundation, or any shrub planted near the house walls, is a foundation plant.

Frond. Fronds are the foliage of ferns; also used commonly to describe palm leaves.

Furrow. A furrow is a groove or trench in which seeds are planted or down which water runs to irrigate the garden.

Genus. The first word in a plant's scientific name is its genus. To gardeners the term is useful because it designates a group of closely related plants, e.g., angel's trumpet (*Brugmansia candida*). *See also* species.

Glyphosate. A glyphosate is a type of weed killer made from a biodegradable salt that is absorbed through the leaves and will kill the roots.

Grafting. Grafting is a way to propagate a plant by inserting a section of one plant (the scion) into another plant (the stock).

Ground bark. The bark of trees broken up into chunks to use as a mulch or as a soil amendment is called ground bark.

Gypsum. Calcium sulfate ($CaSO_{42}H_2O$), commonly known as gypsum, is a natural rock product used as a SOIL AMENDMENT to loosen clay soils and make them drain better.

Harden off. This is a process by which a shelted plant is exposed, over a week or more, to increasing time outdoors. This prepares the plant to be transplanted out in the garden with the minimum shock.

Hardpan. Hardpan is bad news for the gardener because this layer of hard, compacted soil is very difficult or even impossible for roots to penetrate. Some gardeners drill through this layer to let water and roots through; some gardeners build containers above ground for the plants to grow in.

Hardscape. No green thumb is needed to add hardscape to the garden—elements that have been constructed, not cultivated, including decks, gazebos, hot tubs, patios, pergolas, planter boxes, stairs, steps, walkways, and walls.

Hardy. This term describes a plant's success at surviving frost or freezing temperatures. The older the plant, the more likely it is to survive, and cold early in the season is harder on plants than it would be later in the season. In descriptions of plants, the quality is usually expressed as "hardy to −30°F".

Heading back. This is a type of pruning cut by which the end of a branch is removed to stimulate branching farther back on the branch or trunk.

Heavy soil. A soil, such as clay, that is made up of extremely fine particles packed closely together is considered heavy soil; it is the antithesis of FRIABLE SOIL.

Heel in. To heel in means to cover the roots with soil or other damp material until the gardener can attend to planting the shrub or young tree.

Herbaceous. The term describes a plant that dies down to the ground each year and then regrows from the roots up during the following growing season.

Honeydew. This is a sticky substance secreted by aphids and several other sucking insects. Ants feast on honeydew and often herd aphids to obtain it.

Humus. The organic constituent of soil, made up largely of decomposed animal and vegetable matter and usually light or dark brown in color, is called humus. Sawdust, leaf mold, peat moss, and manure are organic SOIL AMENDMENTS that eventually break down to become humus in the earth, but they are not the same as humus until they break down.

Hybrid. When two plants that are not exactly the same cross, their offspring are called hybrids. Seeds from hybrid plants often produce plants that are throwbacks to the grandparents. Some hybrids cannot reproduce.

Insecticidal soaps. These soaps are biodegradable fatty acids (considered to be environmentally safe) that kill soft-bodied pests such as aphids by clogging their pores.

Integrated pest management (IPM). This is an environmentally sensitive system of pest control in which beneficial insects are used and little or no chemical spraying is needed. When insecticides are used, they are not the BROAD-SPECTRUM products that may also kill beneficial insects, but are targeted at a specific pest.

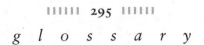

Iron chelate. This is a chemical that makes iron readily available to roots. *See also* Chelate.

Layering. A technique used to propagate plants. A live branch, while still attached, is pinned down to the ground until it roots. In air layering the nicked branch is packed in PEAT MOSS until it roots. *See also* Air layering.

June drop. This is an imprecise term used to describes the normal dropping of immature fruits that often occurs in June.

Mildew. There are several fungus diseases (brown, powdery, and downy) that are called mildew. They appear on leaf surfaces and stems and if severe, can harm the plant.

Mulch. A layer of organic matter, such as GROUND BARK, sawdust, straw, or leaves, applied to the surface of the soil is called mulch. Mulches are valuable because they reduce the evaporation of moisture from soil, limit weed growth, and insulate the soil.

Mushroom compost. Mushrooms are grown in a HUMUS of manure and straw. The used growing medium, called mushroom compost, is often sold cheaply to gardeners.

Naturalize. Plants that multiply without any help from the gardener are said to naturalize.

Nitrogen. Nitrogen is a chemical element, known by the symbol N, that is used by plant tissues for growth. The first number (of the three listed on a fertilizer package as, for example, 10-5-12) tells the percentage of nitrogen in the fertilizer. The actual nitrogen is the amount of pure nitrogen in a fertilizer. To calculate the amount of actual nitrogen, multiply the total weight of the fertilizer by the percentage of nitrogen it contains. This calculation helps the gardener determine the nutritive value of a particular fertilizer.

Peat moss; sphagnum moss. Peat moss comes from naturally occurring peat bogs in which dead moss has decomposed over hundreds or thousands of years. Because the moss comes from an irreplaceable habitat, gardeners should be aware that they are depleting a natural resource when using it. It is quite feasible to limit the use of peat moss as other more replaceable, organic materials will also add acid HUMUS to the soil. Oak leaves and pine needles can be composted to create an acid SOIL AMENDMENT for azaleas, camellias, and rhododendron.

Perennial. This somewhat confusing term commonly means a flowering, nonwoody plant that lives for more than two years. Some perennials, such as pansies and petunias, are often grown only as ANNUALS.

Phosphorus. This is a chemical element, known by the symbol P, that helps plants to grow strong roots to produce flowers. The second number of the three on a fertilizer package as, for example, 10-5-12, tells the percentage of phosphorus in the FERTILIZER.

Pinch back. This is a very handy technique employing the thumb and the forefinger to nip off the end of a young branch, thereby forcing side growth and creating a more compact plant.

Pollination. Pollination is the transfer of pollen from the the male part of flowers (the anthers) to the female part (a stigma). The transfer is accomplished by insects, particularly bees and, for some plants, the wind. This is one reason for the importance of insects in the garden and a reason that gardeners should be wary of insecticides.

Potash. The term *potash* is a common name for POTASSIUM, a chemical element and also one of the three basic ingredients of FERTILIZERS.

Potassium. Potassium is a chemical element and one of the three basic ingredients of fertilizer. The third number of the three listed on a package of fertilizer as, for example, 10-10-5, tells the percentage of potassium in the product. Potassium helps a plant to flower and also helps in the overall health of the plant.

Pseudobulb. The term *pseudobulb* usually refers to a fat stem on certain orchids, such as cymbidiums. Although it often does not look very elegant, it is left on the plant because it stores food for the plant.

Rhizome. A rhizome is a thickened, modified stem found in certain plants such as bearded irises and calla lilies, that grows horizontally underground or on the surface of the ground. It is to an iris as a BULB is to a daffodil.

Rootbound. When its roots become tangled, matted, and grow in circles, a plant is said to be rootbound. Always untangle rootbound plants when replanting them in larger containers or in the ground.

Rust. Rust is a fungus disease that attacks many plants in Northern California. It is often recognized by the yellowish spots that show through on the top side of a leaf. Turn the leaf over and there will be rusty pustules of powder directly under the yellow spots.

Soil amendment. Anything, but particularly organic material, added to soil to improve its texture, structure, or pH is called a soil amendment.

Soil test. The term *soil test* refers to a chemical test to determine the pH (acidity or alkalinity) of soils and soil mixes. Home tests are sold in kits and soil-testing labratories will accept samples of soil from home gardens for testing.

Species. Every plant has a scientific name consisting of two words. The first word is the name of the GENUS the plant belongs to (similar to a family last name), and the second word identifies the species. The combination of these two words refers to only one specific plant, which is recognized by those two words all over the world. This is the reason it is best to refer to a plant by its scientific

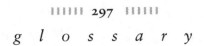

two-word name rather than by a common name, which might be one of several common names used for the same plant. Species in a genus share many common characteristics but are different in at least one characteristic, e.g., Angel's trumpet, *Brugmansia candida* and *Brugmansia versicolor*. A plant described as a "species plant" closely resembles the form orginally found growing in nature. *See also* Genus.

Sphagnum moss. *See* Peat moss.

Spreader-sticker. *See* surfactant.

Spur. Some fruit trees, particularly apple trees, bear their fruit on a short twig called a spur.

Succulent. Succulent refers to a type of plant that stores water in thick leaves or stems. Examples of succulents are jade plants, aloes, cacti, and most euphorbias.

Sucker. On a rose, a CANE that emerges from below the BUD UNION, and therefore comes from the rootstock rather than from the variety grafted onto it, is called a sucker. On other plants, a sucker is any, usually unwanted, fast-growing, upright growth from roots, trunk, crown, or main branches.

Surfactant. A surfactant is a chemical product that breaks down the surface tension of water and makes it wetter. Some surfactants are also called wetting agents because they help water to penetrate soil. Others surfactants are referred to as spreader-stickers and are mixed into sprays so that the solution is sprayed out in a smooth film rather than in droplets.

Tender. Tender is a term describing the vulnerability of a plant to cold. A plant that cannot survive freezing is tender.

Thatch. A tough layer of partially decomposed leaves and stems between the ground and the blades of grass in a lawn is called thatch. It should be broken up or removed.

Topsoil. The top layer of HUMUS-rich soil suitable for growing plants is called topsoil. Occasionally a builder scrapes this topsoil off a building site and then more topsoil must be brought in to use for gardening.

Tuber. A tuber is a short, fat stem that stores food for the plant, serving the same purpose as a BULB or a RHIZOME. The best-known tuber is the potato.

Tuberous root. A tuberous root, such as a dahlia, is a thickened underground root, which stores nutrients for the plant.

Vermiculite. Vermiculite is a mineral, mica, that is heated and puffed up to form lightweight granules that are added to soil mixes to hold water and air.

Warm-season lawn. A lawn planted with grass that does best in warm, subtropical weather and grows fastest in spring and fall is said to be a warm season lawn. Both St. Augustine grass and Bermuda grass are used for warm-season lawns.

Wetting agent. *See* Surfactant.

Alas, a gardener's love is blind. Many a gardener has been wooed by the trumped-up descriptions and glossy photographs in a mail-order catalog. Many unsuitable matches have been made for the Northern Californian garden.

The best plants are obtained through those knowledgeable matchmakers who work in the neighborhood nursery. They know the gardener's growing conditions well because the conditions are the very ones they themselves garden under. Every plant needs to suit the site, the weather, and the skill of the gardener. Whenever possible buy plants from a nursery where you can examine what you are buying and discuss the plant with experienced personnel.

This is not to say that nursery mail-order catalogs are useless inventions. Many rare and unusual plants can be purchased only through catalogs. Many mail-order catalogs are produced to sell specialized plants.

But before you become spellbound by a particular variety in a garden catalog, look first at the fine print to determine if it can be shipped to California. Our horticultural paradise is also an agricultural paradise and the mail-order trade is governed by many rules to protect California from agricultural diseases and pests. The regulations are confusing because they vary depending on where the nursery plants were grown. Stark Brothers in Missouri may ship stone fruit; Southmeadow Fruit Gardens in Michigan may not. Many mail-order catalogs indicate which plants cannot be shipped to California. Some catalogs only let you know when you actually order the plants. To avoid frustration, I've tried to eliminate those catalogs from the following list. Of course, by ordering from a company in California, you will eliminate the problem.

In general, deciduous trees are shipped in the spring before they break dormancy and leaf out. Evergreens may be shipped at any time but many nurseries avoid shipping plants when temperatures reach extremes such as midsummer or midwinter. Many shippers remove all the soil from the roots and wrap them in wet sphagnum and paper to insure the health of traveling plants. March is often the beginning of the shipping season.

Some catalogs are produced with such lush photographs and such rapt descriptions that they ought to be served with whipped cream. Plants produce "clouds of bloom" at White Flower Farm and "team up to work their summer magic. In the still of the evening, you may hear the soft notes of Mendelssohn." Such language is part of the joy of perusing garden catalogs.

Incidently, White Flower Farm sometimes offers tuberous-rooted begonias, many of which, according to one issue of the catalog, come from a fine grower in California. It seems a bit absurd to order tubers grown in California from a mail-order catalog in Connecticut. If you desire rare varieties of tuberous begonias, visit the growers in Capitola (next to Santa Cruz), which considers itself to be the tuberous begonia capital of the world.

It makes more sense to order clematis, which are usually grown back East and shipped to nurseries in California. White Flower Farm carries thirteen varieties of clematis including several varieties that are difficult if not impossible to obtain locally. Another large, colorful mail-order plant catalog is that of Wayside Gardens in South Carolina. Wayside Gardens offers twenty-eight varieties of clematis, evidence that mail-order catalogs can sometimes offer a wider selection than is available locally.

One of the most amazing catalogs is that from Mellinger's Garden, which appears to sell everything you could possible desire for the garden including fourteen varieties of clematis, as well as carnivorous plants, bamboos, Hawaiian plants, and orchids, not to mention herbs, shrubs, perennials, and trees. Half of the 120-page catalog is devoted to products such as bonsai supplies, plastic pink flamingos, pinwheel flying ducks, and Dutch wooden clogs (for gardening naturally—just send in a tracing of your foot). I do not know anywhere else to buy five brands of rooting compounds, in six strengths, or four different systems of heated propagation mats.

A marked contrast to the slick full-color catalogs from the East and Midwest are the plainer newsprint-paper catalogs offered by several nurseries in Oregon and Washington. In these catalogs, which concentrate on fruits and trees, you will find a lot of earnest growing instructions as well as a concern for the environment. Among these nurseries are Bear Creek Nursery, Forest Farm, and Raintree Nursery. California has its share of environmentally oriented nurseries. The Natural Gardening Company in San Anselmo sells organically grown plants by mail-order.

Note: Most nurseries will deduct the cost of the catalog from your first order.

General Suppliers of Plants

MELLINGER'S
2310 W. South Range Road
North Lima, OH 44452
Telephone (216) 549-9861
Fax (216) 549-3716
This company offers the Sears catalog of mail-order nurseries. If for some reason you are unable to get to a nursery, this is the catalog for you. Mellenger's sells everything needed for the garden. The catalog is free.

THE NATURAL GARDENING COMPANY
217 San Anselmo Avenue
San Anselmo, CA 94960
Telephone (707) 766-9303
Fax (707) 766-9747
The company offers a small but choice selection of organically grown plants from its own nursery. The catalog is free.

WAYSIDE GARDENS
P.O. Box 1
Hodges, SC 29695
Telephone (800) 845-1124
Wayside Gardens has several catalogs each year and an extensive list, with glorious photographs, of shrubs and flowering perennials. The catalog costs $1.

WHITE FLOWER FARM
Route 63
Litchfield, CT 06759
Telephone (203) 496-9600
Fax (203) 496-1418
This company is a classy operation complete with a fictional Yankee gardener known as Amos Pettingill, who writes a foreword in the beautiful catalog, which costs $5.

Primarily Fruits, Nuts, Berries, and Trees

ARBOR & ESPALIER CO.
201 Buena Vista East
San Francisco, CA 94117
Telephone (415) 626-8880
The company works with Sonoma Antique Apple Nursery to train and grow espaliered fruit trees. It offers a number of low-chill apple varieties, trained in several styles, as well as pears and figs. The catalog is $2.

BEAR CREEK NURSERY
Box 411
Northport, WA 99157
The nursery has an educational, free catalog that offers a very large selection of apples and other fruits, nuts, and berries. It prefers not to do business by phone.

FOREST FARM
990 Tetherow Road
Williams, OR 97544-9599
Telephone (503) 846-7269
Forest Farm is one of my favorite mail-order nurseries because it offers more than two thousand plants, including some rare collector's plants, at reasonable prices. The catalog costs $3.

GREENMANTLE NURSERY
3010 Ettersburg Road
Gaberville, CA 95440
Telephone (707) 986-7504
The well-informed owners of Greenmantle Nursery specialize in antique apples, particularly varieties associated with the plant breeder, Albert Etter, who created the wonderful 'Pink Pearl' apple. They also offer roses and other fruit trees. The catalog costs $3.

RAINTREE NURSERY
391 Butts Road
Morton, WA 98356
Telephone (206) 496-6400
Fax (206) 496-6465

The nursery has an informative and free catalog that includes growing instructions and landscaping advice.

SONOMA ANTIQUE APPLE NURSERY
4395 Westside Road
Healdsburg, CA 95448
Telephone (707) 433-6420

The nursery offers a superb selection of apples and other fruits for Northern California including many antique and low-chill varieties. Tastings of antique apples are held every fall. The catalog is $2.

SOUTHMEADOW FRUIT GARDENS
Box SM
Lakeside, MI 49116
Telephone (616) 469-2865

The owner of this nursery, Theo Grootendorst, is the genealogist of the fruit tree industry and he sells a huge selection of antique fruit trees and berries. The bad news is that his stone fruits and grapes cannot be shipped to Northern California. The illustrated catalog is $9; the price list is free.

STARK BROTHERS NURSERIES
P.O. Box 10
Louisiana, MS 63353
Telephone (314) 754-5511
Fax (314) 754-5290

Started in 1816, Stark Brothers is one of the largest mail-order fruit-tree nurseries. The catalog is free.

Specialists on Ornamental Plants

Bamboo

BAMBOO SORCERY NURSERY
666 Wagnon Road
Sebastopol, CA 95472
Telephone (707) 823-5024

Over a hundred varieties of bamboo are available at this nursery. The catalog costs $2.

Begonias

ANTONELLI BROTHERS BEGONIA GARDENS
2545 Capitola Road
Santa Cruz, CA 95062
Telephone (408) 475-5222; 475-9928

The Antonellis are famous for colorful tuberous begonias, and the nursery is a wonderful place to visit when the plants are in full bloom in summer. The catalog costs $1.

Carnivores

CALIFORNIA CARNIVORES
7020 Trenton-Healdsburg Road
Forestville, CA 95436
Telephone (707) 838-1630
This is a truly amazing nursery with beautiful plants. It is best to select the plants in person, but the nursery will ship plants. A growing guide costs $2; the price list is free.

Daylilies

AMERICAN DAYLILY & PERENNIALS
P.O. Box 210
Grain Valley, MO 64029
Telephone (816) 224-2852
Fax (816) 443-2849
The company has a nice, full-color catalog with a large selection of daylilies and lantanas. The catalog costs $3.

BLOOMINGFIELDS FARM
Route 55
Gaylordsville, CT 06755
Telephone (203) 354-6951
The farm offers only daylilies but plenty of those. The catalog is free.

Geraniums

SHADY HILL GARDENS
Geranium Specialists
821 Walnut Street
Batavia, IL 60510
No telephone listed
Fax (708) 879-5679
The nursery offers more than a thousand varieties of geraniums and pelargoniums. The catalog costs $2.

Iris

BAY VIEW GARDENS
1201 Bay Street
Santa Cruz, CA 95060
No telephone listed
The owner, Joseph Ghio, is probably the best-known hybridizer of Pacific Coast iris, and this nursery has beautiful varieties of our native iris as well as a good selection of other iris. The catalog costs $2.

COOLEY'S GARDENS
11553 Silverton Road, NE
P.O. Box 126
Silverton, OR 97381
Telephone (503) 873-5463
Fax (503) 873-5812
The nursery offers a large selection of bearded iris, and they describe themselves as the world's largest iris grower. The full-color catalog costs $4.

MARYOTT'S GARDENS
1073 Bird Avenue
San Jose, CA 95125
Telephone (408) 971-0444
The nursery offers a good selection of bearded iris. To receive the catalog, send a long envelope with two first-class stamps.

RORIS GARDENS
8195 Bradshaw Road
Sacramento, CA 95829
Telephone (916) 689-7460
Fax (916) 689-5516
The nursery has a large, colorful catalog with a large selection of iris. The catalog costs $5.

SCHREINER'S IRIS GARDENS
3629 Quinaby Road
Salem, OR 97303
Telephone (800) 525-2367 or (503) 393-3232
Fax (503) 393-5590
The large, colorful catalog has often tempted me to buy by iris by the dozens. The catalog costs $4.

Grasses

GREENLEE NURSERY
301 East Franklin Avenue
Pomona, CA 91766
No telephone listed
Fax (909) 620-6482
The owner, John Greenlee, travels to Northern California to lecture and promote the use of ornamental grasses. This is the source for many fine, unusual grasses. The descriptive catalog costs $5; the plant list is free.

Orchids

Rod McLellan Co.
1450 El Camino Real
South San Francisco, CA 94080
Telephone (415) 871-5655; (800) 237-4089
Fax (415) 583-6543
The company will ship a large variety of orchids. The nursery offers a daily tour of their large facility. The catalog costs $2.

Orchid Cactus (epiphyllums)

Epi World
1067 Glenview Avenue
Cupertino, CA 95014
Telephone (408) 865-0566
The knowledgeable owner has a good selection of cactus orchids. The catalog costs $2.

Palms

Neon Palm Nursery
3525 Stony Point Road
Santa Rosa, CA 95407
Telephone (707) 585-8100
Many subtropical plants are sold by this nursery including palms, cycads, and ferns. The catalog costs $1.

Roses

Garden Valley Ranch
498 Pepper Road
Petaluma, CA 94952
Telephone (707) 795-0919
The owner, Ray Reddell, knows everything about roses both modern and antique. His bare-root plants are sold only during January; container-grown plants are sold the rest of the year. The catalog costs $1.

Jackson & Perkins
P.O. Box 1028
Medford, OR 97501
Telephone (800) 292-4769
Fax (800) 242-0329
One of the best-known rose companies offers a free, glossy, full-color catalog that will tempt the hapless reader with every lush photograph.

ROSES OF YESTERDAY & TODAY
803 Brown's Valley Road
Watsonville, CA 95076-0398
Telephone (408) 724-3537
Fax (408) 724-1408
The nursery has a delightful catalog offering many antique roses and some modern ones too. The catalog costs $3.

Waterplants

LILYPONDS WATER GARDENS
P.O. Box 10
6885 Lilyponds Road
Buckeystown, MD 21717
Telephone (800) 723-7667; (301) 874-5133
Fax (301) 874-2959
If you do not want to have a water garden now, you will after you look at the lush catalog, which costs $5.

VAN NESS WATER GARDENS
2460 North Euclid
Upland, CA 91768
Telephone (909) 982-2424
Fax (909) 949-7217
The company considers its catalog to be a complete guide to water gardening and that it is. The catalog costs $6.

Mail-Order Seeds

W. ATLEE BURPEE CO.
300 Park Avenue
Warminster, PA 18991
Telephone (800) 888-1447
One of the largest seed companies, Burpee offers many varieties of vegetables and flowers and a few trees and shrubs. Many of the vegetable varieties are heirloom types without being listed as such. The well-illustrated catalog is free.

THE COOK'S GARDEN
P. O. Box 65
Londonderry, VT 05148
Telephone (802) 824-3400
The owner, Shepherd Ogden, has long been an advocate of tasty varieties of vegetables for the home garden. His company is particularly strong in salad greens, including unusual salad crops. The catalog, which includes recipes, costs $1.

LE JARDIN DU GOURMET
P. O. Box 75
St. Johnsbury Center, VT 05863
Telephone (802) 748-1446
Many French and American varieties of herbs and vegetables are offered by this company. The really great news is that the company offers an inexpensive seed packet with only a few seeds. The catalog costs 50 cents.

JOHNNY'S SELECTED SEEDS
Foss Hill Road
Albion, ME 04910
Telephone (207) 437-9294
Because Maine gardeners must deal with a very short growing season, the company offers extra-early varieties of vegetables. This is an advantage to Northern California coastal gardeners and to high mountain gardeners. The company is used by many organic truck gardeners and the catalog offers supplies in addition to seeds. The catalog is free.

KITAZAWA SEED CO.
1111 Chapman Street
San Jose, CA 95126
No telephone listed
The seed company has a small but select range of Asian vegetables, including eleven Japanese radishes. The small catalog is free.

LARNER SEEDS
P. O. Box 407
Bolinas, CA 94924
Telephone (415) 868-9407
Larner Seeds is the best source that I know of for seeds of plants that are native to Northern California. Not only will you find a large variety of wildflowers but also seeds for grasses, shrubs, vines, and trees. The catalog costs $3.

NICHOLS GARDEN NURSERY INC.
1190 North Pacific Highway
Albany, OR 93721
Telephone (503) 928-9280
Nichols Garden Nursery has an interesting catalog with unusual varieties of herbs and vegetables well described; also garlic, particularly elephant garlic, onions, and a selection of unusual items such as wine-making supplies. The catalog is free.

PARK SEED CO.
P. O. Box 46
Greenwood, SC 29648-0046
Telephone (803) 223-7333
Park is often compared to Burpee because it is one of the biggest seed companies in the United States. The well-illustrated catalog, offering a bit of everything, is free.

REDWOOD CITY SEED COMPANY
P.O. Box 361
Redwood City, CA 94064
Telephone (415) 325-SEED
I have always enjoyed looking through this unusual catalog, which offers seeds for many plants, including native American beans, corn, peppers, and squash, some of which would be difficult to find elsewhere. The catalog costs $1.

CLYDE ROBIN SEED CO.
3670 Enterprise Avenue
Hayward, CA 94545
Telephone (510) 785-0425
This company specializes in wildflower seeds. The catalog costs $2.

RONNINGER'S SEED POTATOES
Star Route, Road 73
Moyie Springs, ID 83845
No telephone listed
Fax (208) 267-3265
Potatoes, potatoes, and more potatoes. The catalog costs $1.

SEEDS BLUM
Heirloom Seeds
Idaho City Stage
Boise, ID 83706
No telephone listed
Fax (208) 338-5658
The heirloom vegetable varieties, including blue, yellow, and fingerling potatoes, offered by Seeds Blum are so popular that the company insists that you order almost a year in advance of planting. If you are interested, send for the catalog promptly; it costs $3.

SEEDS OF CHANGE
621 Old Santa Fe Trail, #10
Santa Fe, NM 87501
Telephone (505) 438-8080
This company is in a class by itself. It sponsors conferences in the hope of changing the world

and is very enthusiastic about encouraging gardeners to care for the earth. A variety of seeds, particularly grains, is sold. The catalog includes many interesting essays written for the conferences. It costs $3.

SHEPHERD'S GARDEN SEEDS
6116 Highway 9
Felton, CA 95018
Telephone (408) 335-6910
Rene Shepherd's company has a lovely catalog, which will soon have you coveting the vegetables, herbs, and a few flowers. Most of the seeds are imported from Europe. The catalog costs $1.

TERRITORIAL SEED COMPANY
P.O. Box 157
Cottage Grove, OR 97424
Telephone (503) 942-9547
The Territorial Seed catalog is excellent for much of Northern California because the company specializes in seeds for the Northwest. Plenty of great advice is included. The catalog is free.

THOMPSON & MORGAN
P.O. Box 1308
Jackson, NJ 08527
Telephone (800) 274-7333
Thompson & Morgan is the American branch of a British company. The free, color catalog usually goes out of stock quickly because it is a favorite of many. The selections are often choice and the gardener soon wants one of everything.

TOMATO GROWERS SUPPLY COMPANY
P.O. Box 2237
Fort Myers, FL 33902
Telephone (813) 768-1119
Tomatoes, tomatoes, and more tomatoes in this catalog, which is free.

VERMONT BEAN SEED COMPANY
Garden Lane
Fair Haven, VT 05743
Telephone (802) 273-3400
The company specializes in, you guessed it, beans. The catalog is free.

Mail-Order Garden Supply

HARMONY FARM SUPPLY
Warehouse Store
3244 Gravenstein Highway North

Sebastopol, CA 95472
Telephone (707) 823-9125
Fax (707) 823-1734
Mailing address: P.O. Box 460, Graton, CA 95444

An informative catalog offers sprinkler and drip-irrigation systems, organic fertilizers, organic soil amendments, natural fertilizers, ecological pest controls, gopher wire and root cages, beneficial insects, bare-root fruit trees, gardening books, cover-crop seeds, and even canning supplies. The catalog costs $2.

MELLINGER'S
2310 W. South Range Road
North Lima, OH 44452
Telephone (216) 549-9861
Fax (216) 549-3716

If for some reason you are unable to get to a nursery, the Mellinger catalog is the catalog for you. The company sells everything needed for the garden. The catalog is free.

THE NATURAL GARDENING COMPANY
217 San Anselmo Avenue
San Anselmo, CA 94960
Telephone (707) 766-9303
Fax (707) 766-9747

The company offers a small, choice selection of organic amendments, fertilizers, pest controls, and high-quality tools. The catalog is free.

PEACEFUL VALLEY FARM SUPPLY
P.O. Box 2209
Grass Valley, CA 94945
Telephone (916) 272-4769
Fax (916) 272-4794

The company offers a large selection of supplies for organic growers including fertilizers, soil amendments, pest controls (including gopher-proof root cages), cover-crop seeds, high-quality tools, floating row covers, and books. The catalog costs $2.

THE URBAN FARM STORE
2833 Vicente Street
San Francisco, CA 94116
Telephone (415) 661-2204
Fax (415) 661-7826

The Urban Farm store specializes in drip- and automated irrigation systems and supplies. The catalog costs $1.

Major Northern California Gardening Publications

Pacific Horticulture is a handsome quarterly journal characterized by fine writing and good photography and botanical drawings. The editor, George Waters, publishes a wide range of articles of interest to Pacific Coast gardeners including articles on plants, landscape design, and botanical gardens; it is a truly wonderful journal. Subscriptions cost $20 annually. The address is Pacific Horticulture, P.O. Box 680, Berkeley, CA 94701.

The Growing Native Research Institute produces an excellent newsletter on native plants of California. The editor, Louise Lacy, publishes articles on native plants and of interest to gardeners growing native plants. "Native American Use of Californian Plants" or "California Birds Attracted to Berries" are two examples. I always find it interesting. Membership, which includes the newsletter, costs $30 a year. The address is P.O. Box 489, Berkeley, CA 94701.

Gardening Organizations

There are many garden associations devoted to one type of plant such as irises, roses, or herbs. For more information on various groups, consult *Gardening By Mail: A Source Book* by Barbara Barton (published by Houghton Mifflin) in which hundreds of national horticultural organizations are listed. One of the major benefits of joining a local plant society is that the members exchange plants or cuttings from plants. This enables gardeners to enjoy a varied collection of their favorite plants quickly and inexpensively.

Fuchsia

The American Fuchsia Society has many chapters in Northern California. The society produces a bimonthly bulletin and sponsors plant trips and exhibits. The address is care of the County Fair Building, 9th Avenue at Lincoln Way, San Francisco, CA 94122.

Fruit

The California Rare Fruit Growers Association has several local chapters that meet five times a year and hold scion exchanges, field trips, and plant sales. The fruits, by the way, are not necessarily rare. This is definitely the group to join to find out what fruit thrives in your area. Write California Rare Fruit Growers, care of Kathleen P. Smith, P.O. Box W, El Cajon, CA 92022; telephone (916) 441-7395. Dues are $16 and include a bimonthly newsletter "The Fruit Gardener."

There is also the Rare Fruit Council International, care of Carolyn Betts, 12255 S.W. 73rd Avenue, Miami, FL 33156; telephone (305) 378-4457. Dues are $35 and include a monthly newsletter.

And also consider joining North American Fruit Explorers, Route 1, Box 94, Chapin, IL 62628; telephone (217) 245-7589. This group is for home fruit growers. The annual dues are $8.

Herbs

Each month the Northern California Unit of the Herb Society of America schedules several activities centered around culinary, horticultural, craft, and plant study. Membership includes the national newsletter three times a year and the local calendar. For information write the Herb Society of America, 9019 Kirtland Chardon Road, Mentor, OH 44060; telephone (212) 256-0514.

Iris

The American Iris Society is very active locally, partly because there are more iris hybridizers here than there are in any other region of the world. The society is interested not only in the tall bearded irises, but also in other species such as Pacific Coast native irises and Japanese irises. Each group has its own bulletin. To join, write the American Iris Society, Marilyn Harlow, Membership Secretary, P. O. Box 8455, San Jose, CA 95155; telephone (408) 971-0444. Membership includes the national quarterly bulletin (100 pages of iris news) and the quarterly regional bulletin. There is a small additional fee for the species sections. New members also receive an attractive, informative booklet on growing irises. Each year the society holds several sales in Northern California.

One section of the American Iris Society is the Society for Pacific Coast Iris, 4333 Oak Hill Road, Oakland, CA 94605; telephone (510) 638-0658.

Narcissus and Daffodils

The Northern California Daffodil Society meets four times a year to exchange information. The annual daffodil show includes an artistic arrangement class, which has a theme such as "Daffodil Melodies" and entries with titles such as "The Breeze and I." Write the American Daffodil Society Inc., 1686 Grey Fox Trails, Milford, OH 45150-1521; telephone (513) 248-9137.

Native Plants

The California Native Plant Society has many local chapters in Northern California. Native plants are popular right now, and this is a very active organization. Most of the action is at the local level; the many chapters offer monthly meetings, native plant sales, and wildflower shows. They also chase after "escaped exotics" such as pampas grass and Scotch broom, which are invading native plant territory. To locate the nearest local chapter and join the CNPS, write the state headquarters: California Native Plant Society, 1722 J Street, Suite 17, Sacramento, CA 95814; telephone (916) 447-2677. Membership includes the quarterly journal *Fremontia* (a rather technical publication), the CNPS Bulletin (events and issues), and the local chapter's newsletter. Native plant societies hold plant sales in fall, usually in October, which is the best time to plant natives.

Roses

The American Rose Society has groups throughout Northern California that hold monthly meetings, social events, and rose shows. To find a local group, contact the national headquarters, P.O. Box 30000, Shreveport, LA 71130. Membership includes the monthly *American Rose* magazine. Also ask for a list of consulting rosarians in your area who will answer your rose-growing questions for free, whether or not you are a member. The San Francisco Chapter has produced a terrific 126-page book titled *Growing Roses in the San Francisco Bay Area*. You may order a copy from the San Francisco chapter or buy one at the chapter's annual rose-pruning demonstration held every year in Golden Gate Park in January.

There are several local chapters of the Heritage Rose Group, which specializes in what I call antique roses. Annual dues are $5. To receive a copy of the "Heritage Rose Letter" send a self-addressed envelope with two first class-stamps to Miriam Wilkins, 925 Galvin Drive, El Cerrito, CA 94530.

Rock Gardens

The Western Chapter of the American Rock Garden Society meets approximately once a month at a member's home or a public garden to hear lectures or hold workshops. The group also schedules field study trips. Write the national secretary at P. O. Box 67, Millwood, NY 10546; telephone (914) 762-2948.

Bernhardt, Peter. *Wily Violets and Underground Orchids*. New York: William Morrow, 1989.

Bodanis, David. *The Secret Garden*. New York: Simon and Schuster, 1992.

Brennan, Georgeanne, and Mimi Luebbermann. *The Little Herb Gardens*. San Francisco: Chronicle Books, 1993.

_____. *Beautiful Bulbs*. San Francisco: Chronicle Books, 1993.

Brooks, John. *Gardens of Paradise*. New York: New Amsterdam Books, 1987.

Brown, Lauren. *Grasses, An Identification Guide*. New York: Houghton Mifflin, 1979.

"Carnivous Plant Growing Guide." Forestville, CA: California Carnivores, 1993.

Chatfield-Taylor, Joan. *Visiting Eden: the Public Gardens of Northern California*. San Francisco: Chronicle Books, 1993.

Davis, Brian. *Trees and Shrubs*. Emmaus, PA: Rodale Press, 1987.

Ferreniea, Viki. *Wildflowers in Your Garden*. New York: Random House, 1993.

Fisher, M. F. K. *The Art of Eating*. New York: World Publishing, 1954.

_____. *Here Let Us Feast*. San Francisco: North Point Press, 1986.

Flint, Mary Louise. *Pests of the Garden and Small Farm*. Davis, CA: Division of Agriculture and Natural Resources, University of California, 1990.

Griffiths, Trevor. *The Book of Classic Old Roses*. London: Michael Joseph, 1987.

Hickman, James C., ed. *The Jepson Manual: Higher Plants of California*. Berkeley, CA: University of California Press, 1993.

Hiss, Tony. *The Experience of Place*. New York: Knopf, 1990.

Hobhouse, Henry. *Seeds of Change*. New York: Harper & Row, 1986.

Imes, Rick. *Wildflowers: How to Identify Flowers in the Wild and How to Grow Them in Your Garden*. Emmaus, PA: Rodale Press, 1992.

Jeavons, John. *How to Grow More Vegetables*. Berkeley, CA: Ten Speed Press, 1995.

Johnson, Hugh. *The Principles of Gardening*. New York: Simon and Schuster, 1979.

Keator, Glenn. *The Complete Garden Guide to the Native Shrubs of California*. San Francisco: Chronicle Books, 1994.

Royal Botanic Gardens, *Kew* (Autumn 1992).

Lacy, Allen. *The Garden in Autumn*. New York: Simon and Schuster, 1990.

_____, ed. *The American Gardener*. New York: Farrar, Straus and Giroux, 1988.

Lloyd, Christopher, and Tom Bennett. *Clematis*. Deer Park, WI: Capability's Books, 1989.

Marranca, Bonnie. *American Garden Writing: Gleanings from Garden Lives Then and Now*. New York: PAJ Publications, 1988.

Martin, Laura C. *Wildflower Folklore*. Chester, CT: Globe Pequot Press, 1984.

Moerman, Daniel E. *Geraniums for the Iroquois*. Algonac, MI: Reference Publications, 1982.

Page, Russell. *The Education of a Gardener*. New York: Random House, 1983.

Peattie, Donald Culross. *A Natural History of Trees of Eastern and Central North America*. Boston: Houghton Mifflin, 1991.

_____. *A Natural History of Western Trees*. Boston: Houghton Mifflin, 1991.

Peirce, Pam. *Golden Gate Gardening*. Davis, CA: agAccess, 1993.

Phillips, Roger, and Martyn Rix. *The Random House Book of Bulbs*. New York: Random House, 1989.

_____. *Roses*. New York: Random House, 1988.

Reddell, Rayford Clayton. *The Rose Bible*. New York: Harmony Books, 1994.

_____. *Growing Good Roses*. New York: Harper & Row, 1988.

Reddell, Rayford Clayton, and Robert Galyean. *Growing Fragrant Plants*. New York: Harper & Row, 1989.

Root, Waverly. *Food*. New York: Simon and Schuster, 1980.

Royal Horticultural Society. *The New Royal Horticultural Society Dictionary of Gardening*, 4 vol. London: Macmillan; New York: Stockton Press, 1992.

San Francisco Landscape Garden Show. *Where on Earth! A Gardener's Guide to Growers and Sellers of Specialty Plants*. Davis, CA: agAccess, 1993.

Spongberg, Stephen A. *A Reunion of Trees: The Discovery of Exotic Plants and Their Introduction into North American and European Landscapes*. Cambridge, MA: Harvard University Press, 1990.

Stein, Sara. *Noah's Garden: Restoring the Ecology of Our Own Back Yards*. New York: Houghton Mifflin, 1993.

Stuart, David, and James Sutherland. *Plants from the Past*. New York: Viking, 1987.

Taylor's Guide to Bulbs. Boston: Houghton Mifflin, 1986.

Taylor's Guide to Trees. Boston: Houghton Mifflin, 1988.

Tanem, Bob. "Deer-Resistant Planting." Marin County, CA: self published, 1993.

Tyler-Whittle, Michael S. *The Plant Hunters*. New York: PAJ Publications, 1988.

Whiteside, Katherine. *Classic Bulbs: Hidden Treasures for the Modern Garden*. New York: Villard Books, 1991.

Wilder, Louise Beebe. *The Fragrant Path*. New York: Macmillan, 1932.

Wilson, Jim. *Landscaping with Wildflowers: An Environmental Approach to Gardening*. New York: Houghton Mifflin, 1992.

Wyman, Donald. *Trees for American Gardens*, 3d ed. New York: Macmillan, 1990.

Xerces Society and Smithsonian Institution. *Butterfly Gardening*. San Francisco: Sierra Club Books, 1990.

Yang, Linda. *The City Gardener's Handbook: From Balcony to Backyard*. New York: Random House, 1990.

feeding, 46, 275
Blackberries, 175, 197
Bleeding heart, 161
Blooms, forcing, 65–66
Blueberries, 84, 108, 131, 257
Blue gum eucalyptus, 7–9
Blue oat grass, 227
Borage, 163
Bordeaux mixture, 279
Boston ivy, 165
Bougainvillea, 84, 108
Boysenberries, 175, 197
Brown rot, 279
Brugmansia. *See* Angel's trumpet
BT. *See Bacillus thuringiensis*
Bulbs
    autumn-blooming, 175, 196
    forcing, 258, 260, 262
    planting, 216, 238
    in pots, 216
    selecting, 216, 238
    spring-blooming, 64, 85, 108, 216,
      238, 257, 275
    summer-blooming, 99, 119
Bush anemone, 244
Butterflies, 35, 175, 197–98, 242

C
Cabbage family, 75, 250
California fan palms, 204–5
California fescue, 227
California Native Plant Society, 313
California poppies, 269
California Rare Fruit Growers Association, 312
Calycanthus occidentalis. See Spice bush
Camellias
    buying, 64
    fertilizing, 85, 131, 152, 175, 199, 240
    as holiday plants, 281
    petal blight, 64, 85
    pruning, 131–32, 152
    sasanqua, 258
    varieties, 64
    watering, 187, 217

Campsis radicans. See Trumpet vine
Canary Island date palm, 204
Canna lily, 154
Cape primrose. *See* Streptocarpus
Cape weed, 183
Carnations, 109
Carnivorous plants, 152, 304
Carpenteria californica. See Bush anemone
Carpobrotus edulis. See Ice plant
Carrots, 164, 189, 250
Catalogs, selecting from, 300–301
Cauliflower, 75
Ceanothus, 85–86, 151, 245
Centaurea solstitialis. See Yellow star thistle
Cercis occidentalis. See Western redbud
Cestrum nocturnum. See Jessamine
Chamomile, 201
Cherry trees, 50, 65
Children's gardens, 159, 163–64
Chilies, 176
Chinese pistache trees, 220
Chitalpa, 108–9
Chlorosis, 30, 54, 198–99
Christmas cactus, 275–76
Christmas trees, 48, 277–78. *See also* Greenery
Chrysanthemums
    cut flowers, 134
    cutting back, 258
    cuttings from, 109
    edible, 163
    fertilizing, 199, 217, 238
    staking, 199, 217, 238, 258
    watering, 217
Citronella, 140
Citrus trees
    fertilizing, 89, 221
    pruning, 50, 153
    watering, 222
Clarkia amoena. See Farewell-to-spring
Clematis
    about, 132
    growing, 132
    mail-order source, 300
    varieties, 132, 165

GARDENING NOTES

GARDENING NOTES

GARDENING NOTES